Routledge Revivals

The Contentious Tithe

First published in 1976, this book studies the impact of a uniquely unpopular tax on English rural communities. It examines the tithe system during a period when it was subject to mounting attack from political economists, agricultural improvers and radicals alike. Professor Evans has made extensive use of ecclesiastical and estate records to explain why the tithe issue became so unpopular at this time. He also studies in detail the work of the tithe commission, offering new evidence on the important question of how much the tithe system hindered agricultural improvement. This was in a period of considerable strain for the old village community, when tithe disputes significantly added to existing tensions and, particularly in the south of England, helped bring relations to crisis point.

The Contentious Tithe
The Tithe Problem and
English Agriculture 1750-1850

Eric J. Evans

First published in 1976
by Routledge and Kegan Paul

This edition first published in 2018 by Routledge
2 Park Square, Milton Park, Abingdon, Oxon, OX14 4RN
and by Routledge
711 Third Avenue, New York, NY 10017

Routledge is an imprint of the Taylor & Francis Group, an informa business

© 1976 Eric J. Evans

All rights reserved. No part of this book may be reprinted or reproduced or utilised in any form or by any electronic, mechanical, or other means, now known or hereafter invented, including photocopying and recording, or in any information storage or retrieval system, without permission in writing from the publishers.

Publisher's Note
The publisher has gone to great lengths to ensure the quality of this reprint but points out that some imperfections in the original copies may be apparent.

Disclaimer
The publisher has made every effort to trace copyright holders and welcomes correspondence from those they have been unable to contact.
A Library of Congress record exists under ISBN: 76371490

ISBN 13: 978-1-138-55478-8 (hbk)
ISBN 13: 978-1-315-14924-0 (ebk)
ISBN 13: 978-1-138-55491-7 (pbk)

THE CONTENTIOUS TITHE
The tithe problem and
English agriculture, 1750-1850

ERIC J. EVANS

Department of History
University of Lancaster

ROUTLEDGE & KEGAN PAUL
London, Henley and Boston

First published in 1976
by Routledge & Kegan Paul Ltd
39 Store Street,
London WC1E 2DD,
Broadway House,
Newtown Road,
Henley-on-Thames,
Oxon RG9 1EN and
9 Park Street,
Boston, Mass. 02108, USA
Manuscript typed by Brenda Hutt

© Eric J. Evans 1976
No part of this book may be reproduced in
any form without permission from the
publisher, except for the quotation of brief
passages in criticism

ISBN 0 7100 8324 6

For my mother

CONTENTS

	PREFACE	ix
	ABBREVIATIONS AND NOTE ON SPELLING AND PUNCTUATION	xiii
1	THE ECONOMIC AND SOCIAL STATUS OF THE EIGHTEENTH-CENTURY CLERGY	1
2	THE NATURE OF THE TITHE PROBLEM	16
3	TITHE DISPUTES AND LITIGATION	42
4	THE MOUNTING PRESSURE FOR REFORM	67
5	TITHES AND THE ENCLOSURE MOVEMENT	94
6	THE TITHE COMMUTATION ACT AND ITS ANTECEDENTS	115
7	TITHE COMMUTATION AND THE AGRICULTURAL INTEREST	136
8	EPILOGUE: FROM COMMUTATION TO EXONERATION, 1850–1936	161
	APPENDIX	170
	BIBLIOGRAPHY	171
	INDEX	181

PREFACE

The tithe problem was very much a live issue in the late eighteenth and early nineteenth centuries. Discussions of it filled the pages of the agricultural and political magazines. In itself an inefficient and anachronistic impost, tithe symbolized far more. The agricultural improvers saw it as the major obstacle to increased cultivation and higher profits, arguing that it operated as a tax on yield and penalized the more adventurous farmer to the unfair advantage of the more cautious. Many concerned for the welfare of the Church of England pointed to the huge number of disputes the system produced and argued that, while it lucratively lined the pockets of the lawyers, it set parson against parishioner and poisoned relations in a village community already subjected to great strain because of population pressures and growing poverty. The political economists attacked the irrationality of tithe, and some were prepared to suggest that it contributed to the massive problem of rural poverty by hindering projects for labour-intensive improvements. The radicals and political reformers saw in tithe the weakest link in the armour of the state church, through which an overall assault, aimed at disestablishment, could be mounted. The church's supporters were forced back on trusty eighteenth-century notions of property right and were given, by the early abolition of tithes by the French revolutionaries, an appropriate example to set before the legislature of what happened to both church and state when an essential plank supporting the former was removed.

Tithe, therefore, was an important part of the broader issues of the day. It is perhaps surprising that, although most textbooks acknowledge its importance, so little direct attention has been given to it. Twenty years ago, Christopher Hill provided a useful and succinct account of the problem in the sixteenth and seventeenth centuries in his masterly 'Economic Problems of the Church'. The issues, however, were broader and still more contentious between 1750 and 1850 and here, apart from a few articles on specific aspects of the subject, there has been silence. This book is the first attempt to throw light on the subject as a whole. It draws on pamphlet and periodical literature, of course, but tests the arguments and presuppositions by a scrutiny of estate records, solicitors' papers, account books and diaries now collected in large numbers in county record offices throughout the country. A study has also been made of relevant enclosure records, since tithe was frequently exchanged for land at enclosure, and of the tithe commutation records which survive in the Public Record Office, but which are still under-used by historians.

The preparation of this work has been greatly facilitated at every stage by many kindnesses which I am happy to acknowledge. It seems appropriate, given my odyssey around the various repositories, to acknowledge a heavy indebtedness to the many archivists who have answered so many questions, corrected so many misapprehensions and saved me so much time by displaying an amazing facility to extend the information contained in their catalogues from the voluminous mental card-index which seems to be a prerequisite of their profession. I cannot name them all, but would like to give particular thanks to Mr F.B. Stitt and his staff at Stafford, Dr D.B. Robinson, now Surrey county archivist, who guided me expertly through the ecclesiastical records at Lichfield during his time as assistant-archivist there, Mr Sharpe-France and his staff at Preston, Mr Bruce Jones at Carlisle, Miss Sheila MacPherson at Kendal and Mr Edward Milligan, Librarian of Friends House. I have pestered these more than most, but everywhere I have met with unfailing courtesy, prompt production of documents, and great help, some of it beyond the strict call of duty.

I have benefited likewise from discussions with friends and colleagues at the Universities of Warwick, Stirling and Lancaster. I have also learned much from criticism and ideas generated by the presentation of my often half-baked notions at seminars and in talks given in each of these places and in Birmingham, Carlisle and Newcastle-upon-Tyne. I owe especial gratitude to Professor Eric Richards, now of Flinders University, South Australia, Dr John Rule of the University of Southampton and Mr M.J. Thomas, now working at Friends House, each of whom made the fruits of their own researchers freely available to me.

Every author will know that the production of a book entails the kind of domestic dislocation which no spouse should be expected to bear, but which a surprisingly large proportion do. Christine has permitted far more of our house to become a study than either she or I anticipated, as books, notes and drafts proliferated. I owe much to her forbearance and never-failing cheerfulness in the face of still higher mounds of paper, as also to her ability to keep two small children away from essential material.

This work began life as a doctoral thesis longer in period but narrower in concept. I should like to acknowledge an enormous debt to the supervisor of that thesis, Mr E.P. Thompson. He first suggested the general area from which the project developed. He was no less stinting of his time at the end of the thesis, by which time it had taken some different turns from those originally envisaged, than he was at the beginning. Relatively little remains here of that original thesis, as four more years of work have broadened its scope and changed the structure of the argument considerably. It may well be that this process has moved the work even further from Mr Thompson's idea than it was in 1970. Nevertheless, had it not been for his amazing availability in such a busy man, the scope and range of his historical imagination and the friendly yet incisive criticism he advanced, the project would have foundered on the rocks of aridity long before this. If that hazard has been successfully navigated, Mr Thompson is responsible to a larger extent than I suspect he realizes. I can only, and inadequately, say that I am deeply grateful.

All of these, and many more, have helped me along the way. They have prevented many errors of fact and interpretation. For those which remain, I am entirely responsible.

Hornby
October 1975

E.J.E.

ABBREVIATIONS AND NOTE ON SPELLING AND PUNCTUATION

The following abbreviations are used:

'Agric. Hist. Rev.'	'Agricultural History Review'
BM	British Museum
BRL	Birmingham Reference Library
CCF	Church Commissioners' File (Millbank, London SW1)
DNB	'Dictionary of National Biography'
'Econ. Hist. Rev.'	'Economic History Review'
HCJ	House of Commons Journals
LCA	Leeds City Archives, Sheepscar Library
LJRO	Lichfield Joint Records Office
MMS	Minutes of the Meetings for Sufferings (Friends' House, London NW1)
MYM	Minutes of the Friends' Yearly Meeting (Friends' House)
PMG	'Poor Man's Guardian'
PP(HC)	Parliamentary Papers (House of Commons)
PRO	Public Record Office
RO	Record Office - usually prefaced by the name of a county to indicate its county record office
WSL	William Salt Library, Stafford

The spelling of extracts from source material has been retained in the original form, with elucidation in parentheses where necessary. Punctuation has been simplified and modernized where the sense might otherwise be obscured.

The Priest he merry is and blithe
    Three Quarters of the Year
But Oh! it cuts him like a scythe
    When tithing time draws near

For then the farmers come, jog, jog
    Along the miry road
Each heart as heavy as a log
    To make their Payments good

Now all unwelcome, at his gates
    The clumsy swains alight
With rueful faces and bald pates
    He trembles at the sight

And well he may, for well he knows
    Each bumpkin of the clan
Instead of paying what he owes
    Will cheat him if he can

                    Cowper

Verses from 'The Yearly Distress, or Tithing Time at Stock in Essex' (1779), H.S. Milford, ed., 'The Poetical Works of William Cowper', 4th ed. (1934).

CHAPTER 1
THE ECONOMIC AND SOCIAL STATUS OF THE EIGHTEENTH-CENTURY CLERGY

I

The eighteenth-century Church of England was a huge but ramshackle organization. Its influence was undoubtedly great, despite disfiguring cracks in the edifice. It bulked large in the lives of most Englishmen. The vast majority of the adult population were confirmed members of the Church. Conscientious bishops found that confirmations of many thousands of parishioners took up a large part of their time during Visitations around their dioceses. (1) Much of what educational opportunity there was in eighteenth-century England for the village poor was provided by, and to propagate the ideals of, the established church. (2) Sanctions against non-attendance at the local church could still bite, and the ecclesiastical courts continued to hear personal morality cases into the second half of the eighteenth century. (3) Excommunication for non-cognizance of church courts remained a penalty which could be enforced by the state in the form of imprisonment upon the issuing of the writ 'De Excommunicato Capiendo' until 1813. (4) Though not the fearsome weapon of the sixteenth century, excommunication was still a potent threat for the poorest members of society who could not buy their peace with the church.

The state continued to discriminate against those who rejected the doctrines of the state church. Roman Catholics were liable to hefty recusancy fines. They and protestant nonconformists were effectively excluded from posts of civic responsibility by the Corporation and Test Acts of 1661 and 1673. All attempts to remove these from the statute book were easily defeated in Parliament by those who argued, and probably continued to believe, that church and state must be mutually self-supporting if either were to survive. William Pitt echoed the collective wisdom of the political establishment throughout the century when he asserted in 1790 that Parliament 'ought not to relinquish ... those acts which had been adopted by the wisdom of our ancestors to serve as a bulwark to the church, whose constitution was so intimately connected with that of the state, that the safety of the one was always liable to be affected by any danger which might threaten the other'. (5)

It is arguable that the state church was more obviously 'established' in the eighteenth century than at any other period. Certainly at no other time was the influence of state over church so great. Robert Walpole, ever mindful of the need to extirpate the threat of Jacobitism, ensured that the episcopal bench was filled with faithful Whigs. First through his 'Pope', Edmund Gibson, Bishop of London, and after 1736 through the Duke of Newcastle, Walpole and the Pelhams ensured that all leading clerics should be political animals, trained to march into the appropriate lobby at need. (6) So reliant was Walpole on episcopal votes in the Lords, and so anxious were many of the bishops to enjoy the social life of London which the regular provision of those votes necessitated, that many of his creations were seen only rarely in their dioceses. The privileged clergy were an integral part of the extravagant patronage network which dictated how England was governed, and high office in the church was determined by political considerations. Movement from one diocese to another was rapid as prelates jockeyed for political advantage. Preferment was seen by the ubiquitous Newcastle in terms of political encouragement, reward or admonition. A bishop might be placed in Bristol or one of the Welsh sees, realizing less than £500 a year in mid-century, as the first rung on a ladder of episcopal preferment which reached up to Canterbury (£7,000), Durham (£6,000), Winchester (£5,000) or York (£4,500). Or he might be stuck there for years as were Secker at Bristol and Richard Watson at Llandaff for impolitic and injudicious speeches or writings. (7) Interests had to be nicely balanced. When the Bishop of Oxford was translated to Salisbury in 1766 Newcastle found it expedient to compensate Frederick Cornwallis, Bishop of Lichfield and Coventry, for disappointed expectations with the lucrative Deanery of St Paul's which he held 'in commendam'. (8)

Though episcopal incomes varied very greatly there was no correlation between income and the difficulties in running a diocese. Norwich and Lincoln both had over 1,000 benefices in their care, but the income of both sees combined was only about one-third of Durham's which, with fewer than 150 benefices, was one of the smallest in the country. (10) Rationalization of ecclesiastical administration had not advanced far by the end of the century.

The gross disparity in the value of episcopal livings was only the best publicized of the enormous variations in clerical incomes. The impecunious bishop straining to keep up appearances and administration in Bristol, Rochester or Llandaff usually found financial solace in the deaneries or rich rectories which he held in plurality. By no stretch of the imagination could a poor bishop be called a poor man. By contrast, many curates were very poor indeed, and quite unable to enjoy the comfortable personal circumstances which were deemed necessary for the effective discharge of parochial responsibilities. Well-endowed rectors and poor perpetual or stipendiary curates were worlds apart and the great gulf between them was a source of embarrassment to the evangelical clergy and of glee to the growing number of radical critics of the church establishment at the end of the century. T.B. Macaulay, writing in the 1840s, drew attention to the disparity in rank between most contemporary clergymen and their predecessors 150 years previously. The clergy 'were regarded as, on the whole, a plebeian class. And, indeed, for one who made the figure of a gentleman, ten were menial servants". He pictured the English clergyman 'toiling on his glebe ... feeding swine ... and loading dungcarts' to keep himself from poverty. (11) Macaulay is above the need to quantify, and he provides precious few examples. But despite a Whig aristocrat's natural distaste for Tory menials, his portrait of the English clergy as labourers in the vineyard is for the most part accurate. Few clerics in 1700 could comfortably attend to the cure of souls without working also for the provision of their daily bread.

A handful of the 11,000 or so parochial benefices in the middle of the eighteenth century realized £500 a year or even more, making their holders men of substance. The patronage system ensured that only the very well connected were presented to such livings. More than half of all benefices were worth less than £50. These qualified for the somewhat haphazard supplementations provided by Queen Anne's Bounty after 1704. (12) In the diocese of Carlisle 60 of the 100 benefices were worth £50 a year or less, and only 8 realized more than £100. (13) In Oxfordshire in the last quarter of the century, when clerical incomes generally were benefiting from the increased profitability of agriculture, 45 per cent of livings were still worth less than £50. (14) The poverty line, below which discharge of pastoral duties became difficult or embarrassing, was £50 at the beginning of the century and about £150 by the early nineteenth century. Roughly the same proportion of livings were poor by this standard at both periods.

The poorest clergy, most of them curates, were forced either to seek extra work outside the church or to become pluralists turning two or three inadequate stipends into a barely adequate living. Many curates received additional remuneration as teachers in the local school or, if they were fortunate, as private tutors to the sons of the gentry. Some became practising farmers. Others took on a variety of clerical tasks, such as the administration of local charities, which might carry a small stipend. William Wilberforce told the Commons in 1806 of a curate who was also a practising weaver. (15) A few with an appropriate entrepreneurial flair and an eye for the main chance were able to make a comfortable living from these ancillary activities. Rev. John Willan, curate of St Peter-at-the-Arches from 1752 to 1773, was a successful gambler and money lender in addition to discharging numerous preaching and prison chaplaincy engagements. (16)

For most curates, pluralism was an economic necessity. Many livings were still worth less than £20 in the second half of the century. Bishop Horsley even found curacies worth £10 and less during his visitation of St David's in 1778. (17) It is not surprising that it was normal practice to hold two, three or even four such livings in plurality. By the end of the century, indeed, many livings worth less than £100 were held in plurality by curates who could not make ends meet. Rev. James Hakewell held the livings of Fritwell, North Aston, Weston-on-the-Green and Tusmore (all Oxfordshire) together from 1767 to 1799. The richest of these provided an income of only £40 and the total value of all four in 1786 was £117. (18)

Plurality, leading to non-residence and non-performance or desultory performance of clerical duties, was forced on incumbents by the low level of stipends. It has been calculated by Mary Ransome in Wiltshire that 124 of the 262 clergymen officiating in 1783 were pluralists, and that no fewer than 89 of these were pluralists of necessity. (19) Plurality and non-residence went hand in hand. Staunch Tories such as Dr Johnson were convinced that widespread non-residence conduced to savagery and immorality in the deprived parish, thereby weakening the entire fabric of the establishment. (20) In 1808 it was revealed that almost 60 per cent of English and Welsh livings were served by non-resident incumbents and that of the 3,998 livings worth less than £150 only 1,560 had resident incumbents. (21)

Despite the fears of Dr Johnson, it should not be assumed that non-residence was invariably synonymous with non-performance of clerical duties. In 1778 Oxfordshire had 100 non-resident incumbents to 65 residents. Of these 100, 27 were serviced by a stipendiary curate who lived in the parish. Thirty-three more had an incumbent living in the vicinity who took regular service. The remaining 40 were serviced as practicable by neighbouring clergy, and here the system might break down. (22) In Wiltshire at the same time only 90 of the 232 livings were in the hands of a resident incumbent, but a further 39 had a resident stipendiary curate. Eighty more parishes had an incumbent or curate who lived not more than five miles from the church. In most cases this meant fairly regular ministration. (23) In Devon in 1779, 159 of the 390 incumbents were non-resident. Of these livings, 56 had a resident stipendiary curate, 33 an incumbent who lived in an adjacent parish and 65 were served by a neighbouring cleric who might act as curate to the living in question. (24) Obviously, an elaborate system of make do and mend was in operation. A well-endowed rectory was more likely to attract a resident incumbent, but there were not enough of these to make residence an attractive or even practicable proposition. Dilapidated parsonages only exacerbated the problem. It could not be concealed that the ecclesiastical establishment relied too heavily upon the insecure base of an overworked and underpaid army of perpetual, stipendiary, assistant and temporary curates - men of little standing in the community who were often looked down upon or patronized by the small farmers and proprietors of rural England.

The majority of pluralists, therefore, were not the 'bloated clergy' so firmly entrenched in radical demonology. Rather more than a half of all English and Welsh livings were not rich enough to support a resident incumbent with comfort. Perhaps 10 per cent could be considered opulently endowed and some of these were held in plurality by those with already adequate incomes. Some rich pickings were more or less permanently annexed to the poorer bishoprics. The Bishop of Llandaff was also Dean of St Paul's, an office which carried about £5,000 in the 1830s - more than five times the value of the see itself. The Bishop of Rochester was also Dean of Worcester, which post doubled his income. (25) When Richard Bagot was presented to the see of Oxford in 1829 he retained the family rectories of Blithfield and Leigh in Staffordshire which together realized more than £1,200. As he was also Dean of Canterbury these three livings provided comfortably more than his bishopric. (26) Such augmentations as these, particularly when brought to the attention of the public by the assiduous John Wade in his 'Black Book' (1820) and 'Extraordinary Black Book' (1831) cataloguing pluralities, did much to concentrate the radicals' fire against the over-endowed princes of the church.

The richest ecclesiastical pickings were reserved for the representatives and clients of the aristocratic and upper gentry families. There was little question of promotion by merit except from within this elite. The clerical members of the Pretyman family, coming from well-established Suffolk gentry stock, owed their advancement largely to the patronage of William Pitt the Younger. George Pretyman had been tutor and ecclesiastical mentor to Pitt and was rewarded not only with the bishopric of Lincoln but also with rich livings in Hertfordshire. The apex of his career was his appointment to Winchester in 1820. He was reputedly worth £200,000 when he died in 1827. His influence helped to make his son Richard one of the most notorious pluralists in England. Richard held three rectories in Oxfordshire, Northamptonshire and Wiltshire and his father appointed him to three Lincoln perquisites which together realized over £3,000. He held some of these livings in plurality continuously for more than forty years. Bishop Pretyman-Tomline's other son George held the chancellorship and two prebends in Lincoln, the livings of Nettleham (Lincs.), Wheathampstead (Herts.) and Chalfont St Giles (Bucks.) and was a canon of Winchester cathedral. Nephew John held two opulent Northamptonshire rectories, yet another prebendary stall in Lincoln and the mastership of Spital Hospital. (27) Nepotism was one of the commonest reasons for what might be called 'rich pluralism'.

The leading Wiltshire pluralist in the 1780s, Nathaniel Hume, depended on the patronage of his uncle John Hume, Bishop of Salisbury from 1766 to 1782. This extended to London as well as Wiltshire, for Nathaniel had been Dean of St Paul's in the 1760s. He used the influence provided by this office to advance his nephew in the London area. It is striking that of twenty-five Wiltshire rectories which afforded their incumbents a comfortable existence twelve were held by pluralists. (28)

Ecclesiastical preferment, a cornerstone of the patronage system, was used in the eighteenth century in a restrictive fashion which served to increase the enormous gulf between rich and poor in the church. Advowson rights were employed for secular purposes. Bishops and Deans presented useful cathedral officials to rich country livings. Oxford and Cambridge bestowed the most valuable of their many livings on important college men who frequently regarded such benefices as rural retreats or retirement presents. Members of the aristocracy willingly sought advice from the bishop on candidates for their less valuable livings, but they rarely stood in need of counsel when their richer prizes fell vacant. The Earl of Pembroke, the leading Wiltshire lay patron, bestowed his most valuable living, Bishopstone, on his cousin. Two other comfortable ones were held in plurality by Pembroke's chaplain. Livings were also given to a local family which had been of service to the Earl's father and on tutors to his son. (29) It is difficult to dissent from Wade's judgment that 'One of the greatest abuses in the disposal of patronage is 'monopoly' in a few individuals of influence and connexion, sharing among them the most valuable emoluments of the Church.'

II

The value of most livings was dependent on land. This was true even of a large number of curacies which did not have the right to draw tithes. One of the most common means of endowing a curacy was by a grant of land which the incumbent could either farm or lease. Of 95 perpetual curacies in Staffordshire in 1832, 49 received the bulk of their income direct from land. A further four received a majority by a combination of land and tithes. Less than half depended significantly on cash payments from other sources. (31) Rectories and vicarages, of course, depended heavily on tithe. The tithe of all produce was the traditional means of support for men of God in many early communities. It was meant to link pastors with the productive toil of the community in symbiotic relationship. Eighteenth-century English society bore little relation to a primitive community, except perhaps in that its established ministers still relied on the old form of payment. Rectories were endowed with all the tithes of a parish both 'great' and 'small' as they became known. This division was necessitated by the institution of vicarages, probably in the thirteenth century. 'Vicarii' were appointed as deputies by the abbots of religious houses to discharge the pastoral duties of a parish. Their payment was to be a portion of the tithes paid directly to them by the farmers. (32) A statute of 1391 (33) regularized this procedure by making vicarial upkeep compulsory. After the Reformation, of course, the duties of maintaining vicarages passed to the crown and the laity when they acquired monastic lands and tithes.

Impropriators (as the lay owners of tithe were called) retained the great tithes which were usually of corn, hay and wood. The small tithes were all the rest. Although of much greater variety, small tithes were usually of lesser value and a greater nuisance to collect. The most important were the tithes of wool and of all kinds of livestock and garden produce. The division of great and small tithes, however, was not fixed and unalterable. Each vicarage had an original endowment which stated precisely which tithe rights were attached. When this endowment was lost (a frequent occurrence in the eighteenth century), local customary practice was taken as the guide. Richard Burn reminded the readers of his 'Ecclesiastical Law' that the normal divisions could be varied in three ways. (34) First, wood could be accounted a small tithe if the vicar had customarily collected it without contrary claim by the impropriator. Second, if a parish's most productive crop was one which was normally classified as a small tithe then it could be considered as a great tithe since a rector or impropriator must be assumed to have a right to the most valuable tithes in a parish. There was considerable uncertainty on precisely this point after Lord Chief Justice Hardwicke's judgment that potatoes grown in the open fields were still small tithes. (35) Third, the place of produce could be crucial. Burn held the very valuable hop tithes to be great tithes if grown in the open fields but small if grown in gardens or small allotments.

The evidence of the glebe terriers of ecclesiastical property further indicates the extent to which the hard and fast divisions had broken down. An examination was made of the glebe terriers of 131 Staffordshire parishes whose records survive in sufficient numbers to be useful as a series. (36) Of these, 42 were rectories, 34 vicarages and 55 were perpetual curacies in which livings, according to Professor Best, 'small ... as well as great ... tithes were completely appropriated ... and the incumbent was completely supported by a fixed money payment or "pension" paid to him by the impropriator'. (37) In 23 of the 34 vicarages tithe of hay was collected by the incumbent. Some terriers speak of hay explicitly as a small tithe. Elsewhere it was assumed to have been granted by the impropriator to the vicar. Even corn tithes, the most valuable of all, were not exclusively collected by impropriators. It was common for vicars to hold corn rights in parts of the parish, perhaps in one township, while the remainder were tithable to the impropriator in the traditional way. (38)

The terriers clearly show the extent to which perpetual curacies were involved in tithe collection by the eighteenth century. Fourteen of the curacies were supported in part by grants of tithe. The rector of Stoke-on-Trent had since the seventeenth century permitted the various curacies under his control to take all tithes for their own use. The 1701 Burslem terrier states that 'The Rector of Stoke-on-Trent and his predecessors to whom the Cure or Chappellry of Burslem belongs has ... given and allowed unto the Curate of Burslem all the Tyths in kind of Corn, Grain, Hemp, Flax, Wooll, Lamb, pigs and geese annually arising within the liberties of the said Township ... together with the Easter Roll and Surplice Fees.' Such provision was exceptional. It was more usual for a portion of the tithes to be granted. At Maer, for example, Mrs Elizabeth Ashe donated all the corn tithes except those arising from old demesne land, and one or two attached cottages. She collected small tithes herself.

The attraction of alienating some part of the tithes to a curacy is evident since tithe was difficult to collect and the collection of small sums over a large area was sometimes not worth the expense and inconvenience. A resident curate would at least have the advantage of personal knowledge of his parish and parishioners which an absentee impropriator could not possess. It might additionally be cheaper for an impropriator to endow a curate with some portion of the tithe than to provide fixed cash payments. The first half of the eighteenth century saw generally falling or depressed prices, at least after 1720. Tithe was viewed with less covetousness then than later.

Tithe payments were the cornerstone of most rectorial incomes. In Staffordshire 32 of the 41 rectories received more than half their income from tithe, and 23 of these more than three-quarters. Vicarages often suffered from the depression of small tithe revenues near towns and had to seek supplementation elsewhere, but a third of them still received more than three-quarters of their income from this source.

Land was much more desirable property than tithe, but until about the middle of the century the number of rectories and vicarages enjoying large glebes was not great. This situation was transformed, however, especially in midland and eastern England, by the parliamentary enclosure movement which got under way in the late 1750s. The effects of enclosures on the income and status of the clergy are examined below, (39) but it is pertinent to remark here that there was in this period a decisive shift in the source of income of many of the better endowed clergy. Many gratefully exchanged the duty of tithe-gatherer for the more pleasant and socially acceptable one of substantial landed proprietor when tithe was exonerated by allotments of land in lieu.

Despite developments in some areas at enclosure, however, tithe remained the crucial source of income for the English clergy. It will be argued that tithe was an irritating and harassing levy, as unpopular with many receivers as it was with most payers. It was no doubt demeaning for a rector or vicar to appear in the guise of a tax collector. It was undoubtedly detrimental to a clergyman's social standing and pastoral relationships if he was involved in one of the all too frequent tithe disputes. For some it would not be too much to say that tithes stood between the clergy and respectability in the eyes of the local leaders of the community.

By no means all tithe owners in the period were clergymen. Approximately one-third of all tithes were held by lay impropriators. There had been instances as early as the twelfth century of laymen appropriating clerical tithes to their own use, but they became much more commonly lay property as part of the enormous property redistributions which followed the dissolution of the monasteries during the Reformation. Monastic property forfeit to the Crown in the 1530s was during the next thirty years or so granted or sold outright to administrators, notables and court favourites. The tithes thus demised became private property which could thereafter be re-sold, leased or bought at will. Impropriators were mostly men of substance and influence, at least at the local level. While the largest landowners usually had substantial tithe holdings, country squires frequently held the tithes of their own and adjoining lands. Thus the Sneyd family of north Staffordshire, with a comfortable income both from land and coal workings, held the impropriate tithes of the parishes of Keele and Wolstanton, which they enjoyed with the ownership of both manors and the patronage of both livings. A similar domination was exercised by the Elde family in Seighford. (40) Commonly also, an impropriator was the dominant landowner of the parish. Impropriators, having no direct pastoral oversight, could afford to regard their property in purely business terms, and there was a popular belief that laymen were harsher taskmasters than the clergy, both in their demands for high compositions in lieu of tithe, and in their readiness to go to law if these demands were resisted.

During the eighteenth century the disparity between rich and poor in the church became greater. In some areas enclosure made clerics into influential public figures, but throughout the country agricultural profitability significantly increased in the latter part of the century. Those who had glebes to let could perhaps double their rental income in ten or fifteen years. If they farmed for themselves, their rewards also increased. It is not surprising that there was pressure to improve tithe values. Tithe naturally became more valuable as the land was rendered more productive, and the church embarked on a campaign to realise the full improved value of these tithes. Attempts were made with considerable success to tighten up collection procedures and to challenge moduses (small customary payments) which might not be valid in law. Church leaders were determined to ensure that the full share of improvement was received. The success of this campaign served further to widen the rift between rich and poor, since only those who possessed valuable tithe rights could improve them, and corn tithes improved with more swiftness and certainty than small tithes. Curacies generally were left behind, and stipendiary curates did not find that their employers raised stipends sufficiently to keep pace with their more fortunate colleagues. Curates were severely hit by the general price inflation of the 1790s. Bishop Hurd discovered at the end of the century that while forty curates received stipends of £50 or over in the diocese of Worcester, no fewer than 113 still existed on £30-£50. Even as late as 1830, more than a third of all curates received less than £60 per living. The average salary of curates in 1835 was estimated at no more than £81. (41) Economic pressure to hold livings in plurality still remained strong, although the moral climate had moved decisively against it.

By means of plurality or by adding the post of schoolmaster to that of parish priest, most curates were earning at least £60-£70 a year at the end of the eighteenth century. At this level, the curate's wages were roughly equal to, or a little below, those of a superior village craftsman or a cotton spinner in one of the new factory towns of south-east Lancashire. It should be remembered, however, that his outgoings were likely to be heavier, since he had appearances of a sort to keep up, and was expected to contribute as liberally as might be to the various village charities. A salary of £30-£50 a year would give a curate earnings equivalent only to those of a hard-pressed agricultural labourer in the south of England. (42) Few curates survived on £30 a year, though many were forced to resort to plurality and extra duties to avoid it. The ecclesiastical system was just flexible enough to permit the lower orders of the English clergy to avoid the indignities of poverty visited on discontented French vicars and curates with their 'portions congrues' of 750 livres and 300 livres respectively, and no prospect of amelioration short of revolution. (43) Nor, since nearly all English clergy were graduates of the ancient English universities, were they so ignorant. A sharp contrast may be drawn between the French peasant-priest, of the same rank as his flock and with strictly limited horizons, and the English perpetual or stipendiary curate with a university education and, more often than not, a consummately stifled ambition. Many were intensely frustrated that the patronage network seemed automatically to exclude them from proper preferment. Pluralist clergy were worked hard, for the most part, and few found the spare time to indulge the classical, antiquarian or scholastic tastes which set apart some of their more favoured colleagues in deaneries or rectories as distinguished men of letters. Professor Sykes is undoubtedly right to insist that the eighteenth-century church was not intellectually moribund, but its distinctive intellectual contribution could only come from that minority of its clergy with time on its hands which money could buy and the talent to employ it productively. Men of talent in poorly-endowed curacies might come to the notice of an influential patron - some strove officiously to ensure that they did - and be raised to an enviable living. Just enough instances could be cited to perpetuate the myth of a career open to talent. The vast majority of curates, however, lived out their lives in not-so-genteel poverty, the height of their ambitions being promotion to a moderate and undemanding vicarage as solace for their declining years.

By contrast, most rectories more than kept pace with rising prices, and their occupants were able to enjoy not only a higher income but increased leisure. The clergyman with a large glebe could indulge his tastes in various directions. He could join the local hunt. He could acquire knowledge of the new agricultural techniques while leaving most of the spadework to his tenants. He could receive and contribute to the growing number of literary and specialist agricultural magazines. In many cases he could converse on equal terms with those he or his predecessor would have considered his social superiors only thirty or forty years before. He could even aspire to social as well as spiritual leadership of his local community.

Perhaps the most telling evidence for the growth of 'respectability' by the better-off clergy at the end of the century is the increasing use of clergymen as magistrates. Justices of the Peace were the natural leaders of local society. In a country still much less dominated by either London or central government than is suggested by the space devoted to them in general textbooks, a magistrate was a figure of real influence. In 1700 most JPs were the solid representatives of rural England, substantial proprietors and county squires. The aristocracy and bishops were automatically included in the county lists of magistrates but most of the active work of supervising local affairs and administering justice was done by the squirearchy. As the outward and visible sign of status, a place on the bench was much sought although unpaid. During the early part of the century little use was made of the clergy in this direction. Walpole feared, or affected to fear, the ordinary country parson's susceptibility to Jacobitism throughout his career, and kept the clergy out of local administration as far as possible. In 1732 legislation was passed restricting membership of the bench to those possessed of property worth at least £100 per annum, and this effectively debarred many clergymen anyway. (44)

The situation began to change after about 1750. With the threat of Jacobitism effectively dispelled by Culloden, and clerical incomes rising for the more favoured, beneficed clergy seemed an altogether sounder bet. In 1761 just over 11 per cent of all magistrates were clerics with particular concentration in counties such as Oxfordshire, Cambridgeshire and the Isle of Ely where endowments were lavish thanks to the patronage of the two universities. It is interesting to observe, however, that in Walpole's old stamping ground of Norfolk only two of the 192 JPs were clergy. (45) During the rest of the century the number of clerical justices rose significantly. The 'squarsons', as they became known, were recognized as among the most conscientious and assiduous attenders to judicial duties at a time when the tasks of parochial administration were increasing. By 1832 the proportion of clerical magistrates had almost doubled to 22 per cent. In Lincolnshire, Cambridgeshire and Bedfordshire it was over 40 per cent. (46) In terms of active membership, squarsons were in the majority in counties of the midlands and east where parliamentary enclosure had been heaviest. Clerical magistracy was a frequent target of attack by radicals and Whigs who took much delight in pointing up the conflict between the squarson's pastoral concerns and his judicial functions with new game laws to enforce and poor law administration ever more difficult. The clerical magistrates were much criticized but they had undoubtedly attained a new rank in society. It was argued in the early nineteenth century that local administration would grind to a halt in some counties if the squarsons did not bear their heavy burden. In the persons of the 'parson justices', church and state were bound ever more tightly in the face of radical agitation for the reform of both.

This union was at the expense of growing rifts within the church. Whereas at the beginning of the eighteenth century princes and prelates were clearly differentiated from the rest in terms of income, influence and social position, by the end there were much clearer dividing lines between parochial incumbents than there had been. Rich rectors pulled away from their less favoured colleagues, and Swift's cutting analysis of the expectations of 'an English vicar of £20 to £60 a year' remained relevant to a much more clearly defined sector of the clergy at the end of the century. By then, of course, an income considerably in excess of £60 was needed to avoid the not so genteel clerical poverty he describes: (47)

If he be the son of a farmer it is very sufficient, and his sister may be very decently chambermaid to the Squire's wife. he goes about on working days in a grazier's coat: and will not scruple to assist his workmen in harvest time. His daughter shall go to service, or be sent apprentice to the seamstress in the next town, and his sons are put to honest trades.

Contrast the rector with profitable glebe and a social position to keep up. He would pay in order to educate his children out of the parochialism to which Swift accurately consigned the poor vicar. He would entertain on a reasonably lavish scale to assert his status as one of the pre-eminent figures in the local community. Many clerical farmers and landlords were accorded somewhat grudging respect by the gentry for an increasingly hard-headed attitude to business and land management. There were more clergy with a working knowledge of agricultural profit maximization at the end of the century than there had been at the beginning. Some undoubtedly remained a soft touch when it came to negotiating tithe compositions or renewing a lease, but among the well-endowed they were thinner on the ground. Their social intercourse with local elites had taught them more than rustic social graces.

The poorer clergy with neither rising incomes nor rising expectations were left on a limb. Archdeacon Paley's defence of the disparity of clerical incomes in 1782 seemed more like a rationalization than a justification. 'The distinctions of the clergy ought, in some measure, to correspond with the distinctions of lay society, in order to supply each class of people with a clergy of their own level and description, with whom they could associate upon terms of equality.' (48) The gulf between rich and poor was most overtly displayed by the state of parsonages. While rectors were busy rebuilding or extending their dwelling houses at the end of the century, most curates had to be content with dilapidated parsonages or no dwelling at all. Until the government took a hand in the early nineteenth century in the shape once more of Queen Anne's Bounty they had no cash to spare to emulate the example of their richer colleagues.

The problem of tithe, while doing little to reconcile the contrary interests of rich and poor in the church, at least posed similar problems for both. The policy of improvement exhorted on all clergy by the church dignitaries was strenuously resisted by the farming interest, and since most English living were dependent at least to some extent on tithe collection the issue became a burning one. The church, which owned roughly two-thirds of all tithes after the Reformation, bore the brunt of the attack on a system which seemed ever more anachronistic as the economy developed and the industrial revolution dawned.

Chapter 1

NOTES

1. G.V. Bennett, 'White Kennett, 1660-1728, Bishop of Peterborough' (1957), pp. 225-7. N. Sykes, 'From Sheldon to Secker' (Cambridge, 1959), pp.13-15, 217-18. For details of confirmation tours see N. Sykes, 'Church and State in England in the Eighteenth Century' (Cambridge, 1934), pp.429-36.
2. M.G. James, 'The Charity School Movement' (Cambridge, 1938), pp.36-84. For a local study of the influence of the church on education, see A. Warne, 'Church and Society in Eighteenth-Century Devon' (Newton Abbot, 1969), pp.129-47.
3. The study of ecclesiastical administration in the eighteenth century has largely ignored the question of the continued use of the church courts. Much research is needed before conclusions emerge, but it is clear to anyone who studies ecclesiastical cause papers that the courts retained a greater vitality than has been assumed by, among others, J.E.C. Hill, 'Economic Problems of the Church' (Oxford, 1956), p.349.
4. By 53 Geo. III c.127. G.F.A. Best, 'Temporal Pillars' (Cambridge, 1964), p.191.
5. In the debate on Fox's Bill to repeal the Test and Corporation Acts, 2 March 1790. 'Cobbett's Parliamentary History', xxviii (1789-91), col. 405. The Bill was lost by 294 votes to 105.
6. N. Sykes, 'Edmund Gibson, Bishop of London, 1669-1748' (1926) and N. Sykes, The Duke of Newcastle as ecclesiastical minister,'English Historical Review' lvii (1942), 59-84.
7. Sykes, 'Church and State ...', pp. 61-5.
8. An 'in commendam' living was one in which the stipend and perquisites were enjoyed without performance of duties.
9. Sykes, The Duke of Newcastle as ecclesiastical minister, loc. cit. 81.
10. A useful summary of the value of the sees immediately before the reorganization of 1836 appears in Best, op. cit. p.545.
11. T.B. Macaulay, 'The History of England' 4 vols (Everyman ed., 1906), i, pp.245-7.
12. Sykes, 'Church and State ...', p.212. For Queen Anne's Bounty, see A. Savidge, 'The Foundation and Early Years of Queen Anne's Bounty' (1955) and Best, op. cit. pp.11-34 and 78-136.
13. Francis G. James, 'North Country Bishop. A Biography of William Nicolson' (New Haven, 1957), p.127.
14. D.M. McClatchey, 'Oxfordshire Clergy, 1777-1869' (Oxford, 1960), p.13.
15. E. Halévy, 'England in 1815', 3rd ed. (1961), p.397.
16. A. Tindal Hart, 'The Curate's Lot' (1970), pp.116-17. Chapter v of this work contains a modest catalogue of such success stories.
17. Sykes, 'Church and State ...', p.207.
18. McClatchey, op. cit. pp.42 and 53.
19. Mary Ransome, ed., Wiltshire Returns to the Bishop's Visitation

Queries, 1783, in 'Wiltshire Record Society Publications', xxvii (1972), 11.
20 Quoted in Alan Armstrong, 'The Church of England, the Methodists and Society, 1700-1850' (1973), p.28.
21 PP(HC) 1808, ix, pp.237-60 and 1809, ix, pp.23-32.
22 McClatchey, op. cit. p.31.
23 Ransome, ed., loc. cit. 9.
24 Warne, op. cit. p.42.
25 Best, op. cit. p.197.
26 CCF NB20/38 and 206.
27 G.F.A. Best, The road to Hiram's Hospital, 'Victorian Studies', v (1961-2), 138-40 and McClatchey, op. cit. pp.43-4.
28 Ransome, ed., loc. cit. 11.
29 Ibid. 12-13.
30 'The Extraordinary Black Book' (1831), p.22.
31 CCF NB20, Staffordshire parishes.
32 W. Easterby, 'The History of the Law of Tithes in England' (Cambridge, 1888), pp.26-7.
33 15 Ric. II c.6.
34 R. Burn, 'Ecclesiastical Law', 4 vols, 8th ed. (1824), iii, p.409.
35 Smith v. Wyatt. The case is fully reported in H. Gwillim, A Collection of Acts and Records ... Respecting Tithes', 4 vols (1801), ii, p.777.
36 For a fuller discussion of the value of glebe terriers see E.J. Evans, Tithing customs and disputes: the evidence of glebe terriers, 'Agric. Hist. Rev.' xviii (1970), 17-35.
37 Best, 'Temporal Pillars', p.17.
38 See for example the terriers of Hanbury, Ilam and Sandon, LJRO B/V/6.
39 See below, ch. 5, sect. IV.
40 LJRO B/V/6, Keele and Wolstanton and A/V/1/2, 1830, pp.80 and 138.
41 Sykes, 'Church and State ...', p.209.
42 S. and B. Webb, 'English Local Government' 8 vols (1906-29), i, p.324.
43 On the incomes of curates see Best, 'Temporal Pillars', pp.16-18 and 207-14, and Hart, op. cit. pp.101-9. For labourers' wages, see J.D. Chambers and G.E. Mingay, 'The Agricultural Revolution, 1750-1880' (1966), pp.136-7 and P. Mathias, 'The First Industrial Nation' (1969), pp.217-21. On skilled workers, see E.P. Thompson, 'The making of the English Working Class' (1963), pp.235-9 and G.H. Wood, 'History of Wages in the Cotton Trade during the last Hundred Years' (1910), p.28.
44 A. Soboul, 'The French Revolution, 1787-99' (Eng. lang. ed. 2 vols, 1974), i, pp.41-2. A useful corrective against the over-simple view that there was no 'middle' to bridge the gap between 'high' and 'low' in the French church may be found in C. Berthelot du Chesnay, Le clergé diocésain francais du 18e siècle et les registres des insinuations ecclésiastiques, 'Revue d'Histoire Moderne et Contemporaine', x (1963), pp.241-69.
45 PRO, C234/1-99.

15 Chapter 1

46 PP(HC) 1831-2, xxxv, pp.231-72. For a fuller discussion of the development of clerical magistracy in this period see Eric J. Evans, Some reasons for the growth of English rural anti-clericalism, c.1750-c.1830, 'Past and Present', 66 (1975), pp.84-109.
47 Quoted in C.J. Abbey and J.H. Overton, 'The English Church in the Eighteenth Century' 2 vols (1878), ii, p.18.
48 Quoted in G. Kitson Clark, 'Churchmen and the Condition of England, 1832-1885' (1973) p.30.

CHAPTER 2

THE NATURE OF THE TITHE PROBLEM

I

Tithe was a most irksome and unpopular tax. Its unpopularity derived from several causes. It was uncertain in incidence, and subject to violent fluctuations. Its assessment and collection were based on an amalgam of custom, precedent and case law complex enough to baffle even the lawyers who waxed fat on the numerous disputes brought before the courts. The basic form of collection - tithing in kind - appeared absurdly out of date by the middle of the eighteenth century and was being rapidly superseded by money payments. Even with this reform effected, however, tithe remained an awkward duty to administer. It required regular valuations of land and property to ensure fairness. In addition, it bore almost exclusively on the agricultural interest. As fortunes from commerce and industry grew in the early eighteenth century, the inability of the tithe owner to extract his tenth from these quarters was the subject of much adverse comment from farmers and landowners. It seemed unjust that the wealthy London banker should escape while the fields of Norfolk or Bedfordshire remained open to the full ravages of the titheman. Within the agricultural sector also, tithe operated as a differential tax. There is strong evidence that the arable lands of England, more labour-intensive and in need of heavier initial expenditure before they yielded their full profit, were harder hit than dairy or pasture lands. Tithe was a tax on the gross, rather than the net, produce. It was, in short, a tax on yield.

It is easy to appreciate why tithe seemed appropriate to primitive agrarian societies. Land and livestock were open to public gaze, and a minister might legitimately claim to share in the economy by subsisting on a small part of the fruits of his community's labours. A tenth part of the land's produce and a tenth of the livestock nourished by that produce was the basis of payment not only in early Jewish society but also in pagan communities. (1) Although the New Testament gave no such sanction, (2) tithing was normal in most early Christian communities. In pre-conquest England, the treaty made in 900 between Edward, King of Wessex and the Danish King Guthrum included penalties for non-payment of tithe. This sanction was strengthened in 944 when the National Synod of the English Church imposed the penalty of excommunication on defaulters. (3) By the end of the twelfth century, tithe was paid not only to the church but also to laymen holding leases from the monasteries. Monasteries, which owned about a third of English tithes before the Reformation, frequently found it convenient to farm out a portion of their holdings. There are even instances of influential noblemen, like Robert Earl of Leicester in 1168, appropriating such tithes to their own use and claiming them as freehold possessions. (4) Tithe could therefore be claimed as lay property before the Reformation, despite the clear perversion of the uses for which the duty had been instituted. The grants of monastic property from the middle of the sixteenth century, of course, greatly extended this practice, 'giving in many cases', as William Cobbett was to remark, 'thousands of pounds a year to a layman, who never sees the parish and a few pounds a year to a clergyman who does whatever clerical duty is done in that same parish'. (5) When laymen owned approximately a third of all tithes it was difficult to see them as anything more than pieces of property to be safeguarded or marketed for maximum profitability. By the sixteenth century also the old triple division of tithes which ensured that a portion of tithe revenue went towards the upkeep of the poor and the fabric of the church as well as the maintenance of the clergyman, had fallen into disuse. (6) Tithe, thus divested of mystical and charitable significance, became from the Reformation onwards fair game for vexation, evasion and dispute.

The payment was classified both according to type and value of produce. There were three kinds of tithe separated by produce. Predial tithes arose directly from the ground - corn, hay, wood and fruits. Mixed tithes derived from livestock nourished by the ground. Personal tithes encompassed 'such profits as do arise by the honest labour and industry of man'. (7) These included wages and profits from trade and commerce. As has been seen, tithes were also divided between great and small, the more valuable great tithes being generally payable to rector or impropriator.

Tithe was not payable on all lands. Old monastic land and forest lands in the occupation of the crown were considered exempt as were lands deemed naturally barren. Such exemptions, though they frequently figured in tithe litigation, (8) paled into insignificance beside two partial exemptions guaranteed by statute after 1549. As a stimulus to agricultural improvement land previously waste was exempted from tithe for the first seven years of cultivation. (9) The same legislation also limited the right to take personal tithe. Commercial developments had placed a great strain on personal assessments. Profits from trade were in theory liable to personal tithe, but the problems of isolating and assessing a merchant's profits accurately precluded any effective impost. The statute largely rationalized existing practice by demanding evidence of payment for at least forty years before personal tithes could be enforced.

There was, however, a new principle involved here. For the first time the law had intervened to circumscribe the absolute right to take a tenth. Christopher Hill has seen this legislation as 'disastrous for the church'. (10) As the statute in many instances denied only the right to unenforceable contributions this judgment may be questioned. Even before 1549, personal tithe amounted to an insignificant fraction of the whole.

The most important battles were to be fought over predial and mixed tithe, but personal tithes do not disappear entirely from the story. Occasional references are found in terriers and account books to customary payments for forges or the skills of 'hammermen' in the iron-working areas of south Staffordshire. (11) As late as 1839, the vicar of Uttoxeter estimated that most of his income derived from personal tithes or small customary payments in lieu. (12) Personal tithes also caused frequent stirrings in Devon and Cornwall fishing villages at the end of the eighteenth century, while the radical press was roused to fury in the 1830s by an attempt to tithe a Yorkshire labourer's wages. (13)

There was a yet more important exemption from tithe available to many landowners. This was the 'modus', or small customary payment made in lieu of the full demand. Plowden defined a modus as a 'peculiar manner of tithing' subsisting 'from time immemorial'. Lord Chief Justice Hardwicke said in 1747 that it was 'nothing more than an ancient composition between the lord of a manor and the owners of the land in a parish and rector, which gains strength by time'. (14) Moduses, which offered the greatest challenge to the realization of a tithe owner's full income, were of two types. A parochial modus was a payment valid throughout the parish for a particular crop or animal. A payment might be made of 1d or 2d per acre in lieu of tithe hay, or 1d in lieu of a tithe colt or of eggs. Farm moduses exonerated all the tithes of a particular estate on payment of a small sum. These originally related to medieval agreements between the lord of a manor and the rector of his parish. In Abbots Bromley in the early nineteenth century the vicar had to content himself with only £2 12s 4d from 1,390 acres of prime land held by three leading figures, the Earl of Dartmouth, the Marquis of Anglesey and William Sanders. (15) Sir Charles Chester of Chicheley (Bucks.) was able in 1776 to prove unbroken payment of small moduses of 10s in lieu of all tithes from 380 acres and 6s 8d in lieu of 172 acres when the vicar of Lavendon was trying to establish a more realistic payment. (16) If farm moduses usually pertained to aristocratic or gentry estates, the prevalence of parochial moduses seems to indicate old compromises over tithes of lesser or uncertain value which were in any case awkward and expensive to collect. Glebe terriers frequently refer to moduses of a few pence in lieu of tithes of milk, garden produce and hay. Of terriers from 87 Staffordshire parishes which provide information about tithing customs, 67 include moduses of 1d, 1½d or 2d from each cow in lieu of tithe milk. Milk was a product at once difficult to collect and of uncertain value which posed enormous problems of prompt marketing and efficient distribution. With scattered dairy farms it was an impossible task even for a tithe owner prepared to employ a small army of collectors. Thus fixed payments became the rule and these formed the basis of moduses which tithe owners were desperate to break in the second half of the eighteenth century.

Tithe of garden produce had also been of little commercial value and liable to similar ancient agreements; but as the eighteenth century progressed certain areas flourished as market garden centres supplying the growing commercial and industrial centres. It was estimated by land surveyors at the end of the century that the value of tithes from market gardens around Liverpool, in south-east Staffordshire supplying the Birmingham market and in south Essex which was one of many provisioning centres for London, approached 10s or 12s an acre. (17) Here parochial moduses were a formidable obstacle to the proper tithe income which impropriators and rectors considered was being unjustly withheld from them. Many, if not most, of the tithe disputes which dragged on for years in ecclesiastical or equity courts arose out of the determination of impropriators or incumbents to break the stranglehold which moduses imposed on their fortunes.

As more disputes came before the courts an impressive array of case law became available to enable the validity of a modus to be established. By 1806, Plowden could suggest six rules to test the payment. (18) First, it must be fixed as to amount and unaltered. Second, it had to be shown that, originally, the payment would have been to the benefit of the incumbent. On the other hand, it must be sufficiently small to have been feasible at the time of the limit of legal memory (i.e. before 1189). Third, payments which were 'rank' (too large) were inadmissible. (19) Fourth, a modus could not be a smaller quantity of the tithable product compounded. It was invalid to plead that a tithe owner held a small meadow in lieu of the tithes due from a larger one. Fifth, payment of one tithe could not discharge another. A modus of, say, 4d could be in lieu of the tithe of milking cows, but not of barren cattle fattened for the market at the same time. Lastly, a modus must be of equal duration with the tithe it was claimed to cover. The King's Bench laid down that 'A modus ought to be as certain as the duty which is destroyed by it.' (20)

This brief glimpse into tithe law and precedent must serve to indicate the uniquely arcane complexities of the subject. It shows also that although a small modus for a large crop could be ruinous to the interests of the tithe owner, a heavy burden of proof was laid on those who claimed this right. If the full rigour of Plowden's tests had been consistently applied, few moduses would have survived the onslaught of the late eighteenth century. In practice, however, a modus was frequently more easily established. It was not necessary to prove fixed and unalterable payment back to 1189. In the Claverdon (Warwickshire) tithe dispute of 1785, Sir Henry Gough's counsel successfully contended that a modus need have been in existence only since 1570 when a statute was passed limiting the powers of leasing clerical tithes. (21) The Lord Chief Baron of the Exchequer went further when he gave judgment in the Cheadle (Staffs.)

tithe dispute in 1826: (22)
> It cannot be expected that any testimony should be produced that the lands ... were cultivated at or before the year 1189, nor that the payments insisted upon were then made. It would be nearly as reasonable to require the actual production of that which every case supposes, the deed of composition executed between the landowner and the parson, patron and ordinary. From the nature of the fact, it can be established as presumptive evidence only ... that is, the usage, as far back as can be reasonably traced of the payment being made on one side and of tithes in kind not being demanded on the other.

It was frequently the case that the evidence of the oldest inhabitants in the parish, plus receipts for a modus stretching back for two or three generations, would be sufficient to establish a modus at the end of the eighteenth century. Frequently also, the issue was decided by factors other than the strict merits of the case, such as the power of the purse. (23)

II

Moduses provided one large bone of contention between tithe owners and payers. The uncertainty of customs and norms concerning collection was another. Common and ecclesiastical law alike upheld the right of the tithe owner to take his dues, but the custom of the parish dictated the precise manner of collection. The repository of customary wisdom in this matter was the glebe terrier which the incumbent drew on and his churchwardens countersigned to signify assent. (24) Here tricky issues of right were decided when, for example, fewer than ten animals were produced. The terrier of Pattingham (Staffs.) explained local procedure with regard to tithe of lambs: (25)

> The custom of tithing lambs is this, the owners first chuse two & then the Vicar takes his tithe & then the owner takes out seven more to make them ten & so on till all are tithed. If there be seven od ones ... the Vicar has one ordinarily allowing 3d a lamb or reserves them for the increase of the insuing year.

At Bishopside, near Ripon (Yorks., WR) the following was the practice for tithing corn and wool: (26)

> The Tytheman to take Evrey tenth stock, Hattock or Sheafe of Evrey sort of grane - if in two closes of Wheate Evrey tenth and if any less than ten, the Remainder of ten to be counted on the Second Close and the same of Oats, Barley or Pease ....
>
> Tythe Wooll
>
> The Tything Man to take Evrey Tenth, Seaventh or Sixth and Evrey fifth fleece to be Divided in two, the owner to chouse the first, the Tytheing man the Second .... The Farmer is to give Notice to ... The Tytheing Man .... Twenty Four hours if Required. The Tytheing Man is to let the farmer know before he begineth to Tyth, and to set a Green bough in Evrey Tenth Stook Hattock or Sheafe.

Chapter 2

Unless a specific custom was in operation to the contrary tithe was due in kind. The acceptance of monetary compositions was entirely at the discretion of the tithe owner. This right to collection in kind, which remained until tithe commutation in 1836, was a major source of friction. Collection in kind could be a frighteningly complex business, and farmers could conspire at need to make the business both acrimonious and unprofitable in some circumstances. There were powerful incentives before 1836 for both sides to agree on compositions in lieu. Nevertheless, tithing in kind retained a surprisingly tenacious hold. Most great tithes had been rendered in kind at least until 1640. (27) Monetary compositions were steadily introduced thereafter, but large areas of the country continued to pay their tithes in kind.

It is somewhat misleading to say that even as late as the end of the eighteenth century 'comparatively little tithe was collected in kind'. (28) This impression, which was originally given by the Board of Agriculture reviewers in the 1790s, requires considerable qualification. (29) Their evidence suggests that the practice was confined to the extreme north-west, parts of the south coast, particularly Hampshire and Kent, and in the east, Cambridgeshire and Suffolk. In the midlands they agreed with William Marshall who had stated that he came across one example only in that area - Bosworth Field (Leics.). (30)

While the agricultural writers were preparing their reports, Frederick Morton Eden was beginning to collect information about the extent of poverty in England in a pioneering, if amateurish, social survey. (31) He solicited replies to a questionnaire which, while naturally concentrating on poor law practices, was concerned also with the state of agriculture with specific reference to employment prospects. Included here was a question on tithing practices and the replies, admittedly from a fairly small sample of parishes, suggest that tithing in kind was by no means unknown, even in the midlands. Of 115 replies from towns and villages which answered the question on tithe, 34 noted that a substantial portion, if not all, tithes were still taken in kind. As tithe had been exonerated by allotments of land or money payments at enclosure in 14 places, the overall impression is given that payment in kind was by no means uncommon. The returns confirm that Cumberland (where 9 of the 10 parishes tithed in kind), Westmorland (2 of 3) and Kent (5 of 8) were the main centres of the old practice; but it survived elsewhere. The Chester correspondent where composition was the rule, replied that 'in the neighbouring parishes, they are, generally, taken in kind'. This was confirmed by the other two of the three replies from Cheshire. (32) At Esher (Surrey) a composition was currently being paid, but in a period of inflated rents and profits the farmers were apprehensive that 'next year, the composition will be raised, or the tithe be taken in kind'. (33) Eden's replies suggest that the practice was by no means uncommon in Bedfordshire, Lancashire, Lincolnshire and Shropshire. In most of the midland counties, enclosure had intervened and tithe exoneration had been common.

The impression is strengthened by evidence collected when

William Pitt considered tithe reform in 1791-2. He authorized
the circulation of a questionnaire which asked about tithing
practice throughout the country. Replies were received from 27
counties. In no fewer than 12 of these - Berkshire, Buckinghamshire, Cheshire, Durham, Hampshire, Huntingdonshire, Kent,
Lancashire, Shropshire, Somerset, Surrey and Wiltshire - tithing
in kind was reported to be a common practice. (34) The Somerset
correspondent was even able to report that 'The Tythes of Corn
in this Neighbourhood are in many Places paid in kind by choice
and set out ... with great exactness.' It is clear that Ernle
underestimated the extent of these payments. They were normal
in most of the north-west and in many parts of the south from
Somerset in the west to Kent in the east in addition to being a
fairly frequent occurrence in parts of the north-east and even
in the east midlands. Nor, as is clear from this evidence, was
in-kind payment a feature merely of agriculturally backward
areas where rents were low and profits slender. It remained an
important factor in much of the country when the tithe system
came under its severest attack.

An important distinction should be made between tithe normally
collected in kind and exceptional demands made by a tithe owner
wishing either to establish new claims or to prepare the way for
increased compositions. The power to insist on payments in kind
was frequently used as a lever to extract higher payments. When
a dispute broke out it was normal for the tithe owner to terminate
his compositions and revert to tithing in kind. There was
undoubtedly an increase in these tactical demands at the end
of the century. The 'in kind' parishes from Eden's survey all
seem to have been paying in this way as a matter of course.
Tithing in kind was prevalent in a significant minority of
cases and operated as a real or potential threat in many others.
When tithe was assessed for the income tax in 1813 it was
estimated that about 18 per cent of the value of all tithes was
still taken in kind. (35) Those who argued that the tithe system
was a disincentive to agricultural improvement relied heavily
on evidence from parishes in which tithes were taken in kind.
It is important to realize that by 1800 this method of payment
was not freakishly uncommon.

Of course, in most cases it was much more convenient and
probably in the long run more profitable for money compositions
to be agreed. Insistence on payment in kind might be regarded
as a provocative act and leave the tithe owner open to reprisals.
The vicar of St Mary's Lichfield sourly noted in his tithe
book for 1773: (36)

> As the gathering in kind of wooll and Lamb, of Calf and
> Milk and seperating (sic) & distinguishing of land agisted
> or depastured by unprofitable cattle would be attended with
> endless trouble, as well as continual Quarrels with the
> persons from whom due, the Vicar in lieu thereof takes a
> Composition of one shilling and sixpence an acre for all
> land depastured or grazed without exception.

A tithe payer wrote enviously to a friend in Scotland, where tithes
(or 'teinds') had been redeemed from the middle of the seventeenth
century: (37)

> In many places it is the custom for the tythe-owner to
> require 24 hours to go and set out the tythes, by which
> it frequently happens that though a field of corn be per-
> fectly fit for leading and stacking yet the cultivator
> is prevented from embracing the opportunity - and before
> the expiration of 24 hours the rain comes; and if a series
> of wet weather ensues, the crop is very often materially
> injured ....
>   Another hardship is that the courts of law have deter-
> mined that after the crop is tithed and the farmer has taken
> his part away, the tithe owner may let his share remain in
> the field, and thereby prevent the owner from turning in any
> stock to depasture in the field or to plow the land for any
> other crop which he might wish to put in immediately ....
>   Every farmer who knows the value of good fold yard dung
> as a manure must materially feel the want of one tenth of
> his produce where tythes are drawn in kind- and where it
> happens on poor land, the loss is irreparable.

Clearly tithing in kind required mutual harmony in the best of circumstances. Except in a small, compact and flat parish the procedure of gathering in kind would be lengthy and costly. A full-time collector was necessary, supplemented by several assistants throughout the hay and corn harvests and at shearing time. A team of horses and waggons was also a prerequisite and a large tithe barn was required for storage. (38) As the farmer must inform the tithe owner when his crops would be ready for collection it was extremely difficult to plan a tithing tour in advance. There were also problems of disposal. Tithe owner must become farmer or merchant and join the haggling to get a good price. The task could, of course, be entrusted to the titheman, but only by incurring extra expense. If the parish was at a distance from the nearest market the problem was further magnified. John Middleton wryly commented on the difficulties of the vicar of Battersea who attempted to take his tithe of garden produce in kind. He continued the experiment for three years 'during which time nothing was more common than to meet his carts in the streets retailing his tithes with a person in each, vociferating 'Come, buy my Asparagus: Oh, rare Cauliflowers!' (39)

The collection of tithes in kind was invariably expensive. A witness before the 1833 Select Committee on Agricultural Distress observed: 'There is more difficulty in collecting the tithes than in receiving the rest of an estate'. (40) John Cramp, a tithe collector on the Isle of Thanet where payments in kind were normal until Commutation, said that he deducted a minimum of 25 per cent for collection expenses: (41)

> These calculations are made in a part of the country where
> every facility exists for collecting the tithes; the
> fields free from fences of every kind, and waggons crossing
> in the most direct way from one part to another, and the
> country a complete level; and all the roads good for the
> easy conveyance of the produce to and from the tithe barn.

If the parish was some distance from market or tithe barn, across bumpy roads in hilly country this proportion might be almost doubled. At Commutation, assistant tithe commissioners regularly deducted as much as 40 per cent. John Matthew, for example, deducted two-sevenths of the total produce in calculating the value of the great tithes and two-fifths for the small. (42)

Tithing in kind invited a war of nerves between collector and farmer. To priest and parishioners alike, the remarks of an anonymous defender of the church establishment in 1782 that 'the greatest harmony subsists between the incumbent and his parishioners' where tithes were taken in kind must have seemed no more plausible than his conclusion that 'Were the clergy compelled to take their tithes in kind, the universality of the practice would be very effectual in silencing murmurs and discontent.' (43) There seemed to be no lack of cunning expedients devised by farmers who resented the practice. Charles Bill of Alton warned that the parishioners would 'give as much trouble as they could in collecting the Tythes - perhaps they intended to throw out every 10th Sheaf as they were reaped in which case they might have made them as small as they pleased'. (44) A Hampshire farmer informed the tithe owner that a crop was ready for tithing. The tithe owner arrived with his servants, horses and waggons only for the farmer to present him with a single turnip, requesting him to return later when he might have another. (45)

John Skinner, rector of Camerton (Somerset) had trouble in the 1820s in taking tithes from one of his own churchwardens, a farmer named Skuse. As he noted in his Journal for June 1828: (46)

> On walking into the field after dinner I found my men at a stop there being six rows fit for tything, and Skuse would not tythe it because his men were unloading, and there were only a few cocks - not a quarter of a load - for them to carry. As I had received notice for tything in the morning, I desired Heal to take some boughs and tythe the six rows in order that he might take another load to the mow. Skuse came running like a wild bull, and bellowing as such, snatched the boughs out of my servants' hands, and said that no one should tythe but himself. I desired Heal to persevere, and get some other boughs; I also told George to leave the cart and witness what was going forwards. Skuse collared Heal and pushed him beyond the first row of cocks, and his son took George by force in his arms, and notwithstanding his struggling, threw him also beyond this barrier, which he had a right to keep, and neither my people nor myself had a right to be there. Seeing the party ripe for an assault, I desired my men to leave the field with the cart, and told my son, loud enough for Skuse to hear, I would not take tythes so put out, and have my men assaulted for doing their duty.

When the vicar of Ilam (Staffs.) attempted in 1830 to take tithe in kind from a farmer called Harris who had refused to pay either tithe or composition, he found that the tithe road had been blocked. The next month a request was met by the farmer's waking the vicar at 5.30 a.m. with notification that the tithe could be drawn. In 1831, Harris set out some tithe in minute quantities at irregular intervals, and refused other requests entirely. (47)

Chapter 2

At Aston (nr Birmingham), still partly an agricultural parish in the early nineteenth century, disputes arose over milk tithe. Richard Fowler, a leading local landowner, determined that if the vicar were set on imposing this new obligation he would retaliate by putting maximum difficulties in the way of the vicar's collectors. He wrote to the vicar in 1828: (48)

> Take Notice, I shall from and after this date set out tithe Milk as it arises - Counting from this time the first tenth Meal will become due on Friday evening the 12th inst. At 6 o'clock in the evening of that day I shall set it out in a field of land called Bromford Meadow my usual place of milking, and also the following Mornings Meal of Milk Saturday the 13th. Inst. at 6 o'clock in the morning and continue to set out every subsequent Evening and Mornings Milk as it becomes due.

All of the trouble and collection and disposal of a highly perishable commodity were laid on the vicar who would not find it worth his while making special arrangements to collect such small quantities regularly. Fowler and the vicar, George Peake, were practised antagonists. During the potato harvest of the previous year, Peake's tithe collector had to make five journeys in four weeks to take tithe of small quantities, varying from ¼ peck to one peck on each occasion. Peake was forced to agree a composition for the remainder of the crop. (49) In 1777 the parishioners of Fortworth (Glos.) received notification from their rector, Dr Bosworth, of his intention to impose milk tithes in kind. Parishioners called each tenth day, when the rector claimed his milk, 'Devil's Day', and an enterprising milkmaid expressed her disapproval of the new arrangement by adding urine to the milk before she handed it over. The rector's experiment was quickly discontinued. (50)

Personal antagonisms, of course, could be exploited in disputes over tithe. In 1808, a Somerset farmer wrote to Cobbett's 'Political Register' to explain how the expedient of tithing in kind could be used as a weapon: (51)

> I beg leave to state the case of a very industrious honest, worthy friend of mine, residing in the western part of the country. The great bashaw Tythe Monger who is a layman has been in the practice of taking his tythes in kind, and from an election pique he harboured against my friend ordered his men whom he sent to collect his tithes, to treat him with every kind of insult and indignity; accordingly when they first came to collect their tithes they let their horses loose in a fine field of wheat, to eat and trample my friends corn, while they loaded their carts; and at another time they left open a gate which they passed through, and let a number of cattle into another field which was not cut, and did considerable damage; at another time broke open a gate, and went into another corn field, and carried away what they thought proper before the tithe was set out, and when my friend went to remonstrate, and pray they would discontinue to harass and injure him in such manner, he received no other apology than that the most heinous curses and scurrilous abuse, which was too much for

John Bull to take and he gave one of the fellows who was the most abusive and impertinent, a box under the ear.... And for this great assault the great tithe-monger has actually instituted a suit against him which is now pending in a court of law.

There were many pressures on tithe owners, therefore, to take compositions rather than insist on their ancient rights. Tithing in kind remained of occasional value to a new incumbent anxious to alter the compositions of his predecessor (52) or when parishioners refused to accept new assessments or valuations. (53) In such cases, the demand of tithe in kind was frequently the prelude to a legal tussle. By the beginning of the nineteenth century, however, few would have disagreed with the heartfelt, if ungrammatical, conclusion of a Great Marlow farmer. 'There is (sic) many unpleasant things happens in taking the Tithes in kind after the Farmer have done his best for his Crop to have the tenth taken by the Rector or the Layman as taking the Tithes is the greatest evil in the country....' (54)

A similar impression was given to the Select Committee on the operation of the Poor Laws in 1834. Ashurst Majendie stated that in Northam (Sussex) 'Tithes in kind are a principal cause of the bad feeling which exists in this parish' while in Hornchurch (Essex) 'Tithe in kind has been a fruitful source of animosity and litigation in this parish from the year 1801 to the present time.' Alfred Power confirmed that in Selbourne and Headley (Hants) the system 'is a frequent subject of dispute, and a cause of much ill feeling'. (55) A correspondent to the 'Monthly Magazine' in 1798 had drawn the obvious conclusion about the significance of tithing in kind for the effectiveness of pastoral ministration. 'Very few clergymen in England who take tithes in kind retain the good opinion of their parishioners, and therefore have but little prospect of ministering to their religious improvement.' (56)

III

It is not surprising that most tithe was paid in cash by the end of the eighteenth century. Payments by composition, however, were not free from controversy. The wide variations in assessment ensured that some tithe owners got much nearer their tenth than others. Those who could afford it usually decided to commission yearly valuations. An experienced valuer, preferably with local knowledge, was employed to inspect and value tithable produce in the fields. A cash demand was sent to the farmer, who either paid or submitted to collection in kind. Such a practice was invariably followed at Leigh (Staffs.) where the rector was always a member of the wealthy Bagot family. The parishioners declared in 1813: (57)

> The Rector & his predecessors have always resided at
> Blithfield ... & have always employed a person resident
> in the parish of Leigh as Tythman. In June every year,
> the Tytheman goes round the parish & enquires of the
> different farmers what Cows they have kept, what Calves

have been born, what sheep etc. & how many acres of wheat,
oats etc. Grass etc. are growing on their respective
farms. Everything is reckoned up to the time the question is
asked.... On the Monday after Advent Sunday the Parishioners
account with the Rector for the tythes & compositions according
to the acct. taken in the June preceeding.

The advantage here was that an accurate assessment was made.
Accounting could be a smooth process, particularly if the tithe
owner was prepared to make abatements if the crops suffered damage
at any time after valuation until harvest. The disadvantages were
clear. Parishioners might resent a yearly inquisition, and the
system was expensive to operate. The tithe owner had to calculate
whether his additional receipts justified the extra expense. In
remote, hilly or rough grazing districts the method was an extravagance. In any case, yearly valuations were beyond the means of
all but the most opulent tithe owners. At Leigh, for example,
the rectory was worth £800 a year, and nearly £700 of this came
directly from tithes. (58) Similarly, the Marquis of Stafford,
whose son was to marry into a Scottish fortune and became, as
1st Duke of Sutherland, one of the richest men in the kingdom,
found that it paid to employ the experienced land surveyor and
enclosure commissioner John Bishton to value his tithes in
Codsall. (59) The Dean and Chapter of Durham made use of yearly
valuations to collect the tithes of Lowick and Stannington
(Northumberland). (60)

Yearly valuations were too costly for most parochial incumbents,
but a valuation was a useful insurance when disputes threatened.
At Hambledon (Bucks.), for example, the rector employed a
Mr Trumper to value his tithes over nearly 4,500 acres in order
to set new compositions for his recalcitrant parishioners. (61)
The vicar of Garstang (Lancs.) had a new valuation made of
Claughton township in 1828 before instituting a series of new
claims against 75 parishioners living in the township. (62)

A cheaper, but less accurate, alternative to yearly valuations
was provided by the tithe owner's setting a composition value
per acre on each crop. Wheat tithe at the end of the eighteenth
century might be payable at 7s or 8s per acre, oats and barley
at 4s to 5s, with pasture and other livestock tithes at varying,
but usually much lower, rates. At Midridge (Durham) in 1774,
the agents of Lady Legard took tithe from ten occupiers at a
fixed rate of 7s per acre for wheat, 4s for oats, 2s 6d for
meadow land and 2s for pasture. (63) Such rates were levied with
prevailing rental values in mind. Indeed, in many cases tithe
compositions were assessed at a fixed proportion of the rent.
George Smallpeice, a 500 acre farmer from Guildford, told the
Select Committee on Agricultural Distress in 1836 that he paid an
overall composition of 5s per acre for his tithe and that this
amounted to between a third and a quarter of his rental on
arable land and about one-eighth on pasture land. Robert Babbs,
who farmed nearly 300 acres in Essex, paid 5s 6d per acre on top
of an ordinary rent of 14s. (64) In 1821 William Ilott paid
£125 rent for a 100 acre farm in Blandford (Dorset). His tithe
composition was an additional £31 5s 0d - virtually a quarter of
the rent. (65) Such examples serve to remind that tithe was a

tax on the gross produce. A parochial valuation which set uniform rates, of course, meted out rough justice to farmers. It penalized the improver who had sunk large amounts of capital into his land, and it bore less heavily on those whose lands were naturally fertile and required less additional capital to yield a rich crop. This was a source of some discontent, allayed only by the knowledge that levels of composition set by this method were usually considerably lower than was possible with individual valuations. At Church Eaton (Staffs.) in 1814, Rev. George Talbot's tithe valuer assessed the value of tithe wheat from a hundred-acre farm at 15s per acre, when the general value of tithe corn in Staffordshire barely reached 8s. (66) John Lake, a farmer from Bapchild (Kent) reported in 1821 that during the wartime boom wheat had realized as much as 30s per acre for tithe, but only when in lay hands. (67)

The cheapest method of setting compositions in lieu of tithe was probably to agree on a particular sum for a number of years. Not surprisingly, this method was adopted by many of the poorer clergy. In vicarages not endowed with great tithes, the system worked moderately well as most small tithes were less price-sensitive than corn tithes. Even here, however, collection could be irksome. Rev. John Pedder, vicar of Claughton nr Garstang found tithe collection at the end of the eighteenth century 'tiresome, independently of there being scarcely so much raised from small tithes and Easter Dues as will defray expenses'. (68) When agreements were made for a term of years an option was usually retained to alter the sums involved in exceptional circumstances, such as a very bad summer or a change in land use. Many parochial incumbents paid for a fresh valuation when they entered their livings and made these the basis of their receipts thereafter. Assistant tithe commissioners in the 1830s and 1840s frequently pointed out that although impropriate rent charges were usually easily ascertained because there had been annual tithe valuations, vicarial tithes were often based on long-standing compositions which might bear no relation to current tithe values. George Ashdown stated in 1838 that receipts for the vicarial tithes in Wolstanton had been unchanged since 1801. (69)

There is no doubt that many clergy feared to take on those more powerful than they in tithe wrangles, preferring to settle for low compositions rather than stir up trouble. In some instances parishioners, fully aware that a change of incumbency might mean higher compositions, tried to guard against the possibility by attempting to influence the choice of a new man. During the long tenure of Rev. Benjamin Adams, the inhabitants of Barlaston had enjoyed artificially low tithe compositions. When Adams died in 1834 a leading inhabitant, Mrs Adderley, opened negotiations with a poor curate named Barton who was to succeed Adams on condition that he continued to take tithes at the old rate. The patron, the Duke of Sutherland, however, preferred another candidate, one William Oliver. Oliver's first action was to employ a leading surveyor to value the tithes. The valuation would have trebled the value of the living. The parishioners of Barlaston refused to accept his view and the

Chapter 2

parish was plunged into twelve years of tithe strife. (70)

At Ripley (Yorks.) the patron, Sir John Ingilby, took a direct hand in such matters. He warned his nominee to the living in 1759 that a rise in tithe compositions would be unacceptable, and the wretched man was forced to sign a declaration of his intention not to disturb his prospective flock with additional tithe burdens. (71) Jane Austen's William Collins, presented to a valuable rectory by the beneficence of his patron, Lady Catherine de Bourgh, may be a prime parody of the deferential clergyman, but one may readily appreciate the dependence of even many well-endowed clerics. (72) The weakness of many clergy of humbler station should not be underestimated. It was frequently reflected in their tithe income. They often took what they were permitted rather than what the law allowed them. Thomas Greene, MP for Lancaster in the 1820s, was frequently reminded of this fact in his deliberations over possible legislation. John Thirkins reminded him in 1828: 'I do really think I don't get much more than a fourth part of my dues & if I collected the tithes in kind the land occupiers would harass me to death.' R.B. Podmore indicated that he was 'in the habit of compounding for the Tithes of 10,000 Acres of Land at about "one half" of their value'. (73) The vicar of St Mary, Lichfield, believed that 'it being impossible for a peaceably disposed clergyman to get his due', he might have to accept a reduction on an income of £500 although he believed the 'real value may be £1,000'. John Simpson, vicar of Alstonfield in the 1830s said that he had 'agreed not to raise or alter the compositions with the present occupiers of land & who now pay abt. the half of what is due'. (74) William Jones, vicar of Broxbourne and Hoddesdon (Herts.) in 1803 was 'confident that I am defrauded by many of my parishioners of various vicarial dues and rights to which the laws of Heaven and earth entitle me'. (75) Thomas Greene himself was well aware of the situation. He had written a circular to all Archbishops and Bishops in August 1827 as his first shot in a campaign to persuade leading churchmen that tithe reform was essential in the interests of the established church just as much as of overburdened farmers: (76)

> To your Lordships, I need not dwell upon the inconvenience of the present mode of collecting tithe; it is g nerally felt & admitted both by the clergy & the landowners, and, I believe, I am justified in asserting that under it, Incumbents do not receive one half of what they are legally entitled to & even that half is too often paid grudgingly & with ill will. Much of this evil, I conceive, arises from the great uncertainty in many parishes of the titheable matter and of the value of that which is ascertained. A clergyman entering upon a living finds himself in the very disagreeable situation of having to make a bargain with persons necessarily more conversant with business of this nature than himself & has the additional difficulty to overcome of treating with those whose good will it is of the greatest importance for him to secure in furtherance of the due discharge of his general duties.

Quite apart from the problems of many clergymen who had to deal with powerful adversaries, there were long-term disadvantages in accepting valuations which were only rarely revised. Prices, particularly of arable produce, fluctuated more dramatically between about 1790 and the passing of the Commutation Act of 1836 than at any time in the previous century. (77) A valuation made in a high price year with land demand buoyant seemed punitive when prices dropped, as they generally did after 1813. Even seven-year valuations seemed blunt instruments, especially as adjustments to tithe revenue tended to lag behind developments elsewhere in the agricultural market. There was much criticism of arrangements for commutation, which incorporated valuations based on such averages, for precisely this reason. During the boom of the French war period (1793-1813), rental values approximately doubled. (78) Tithe, after a slight lag, increased in a similar or slightly lesser proportion. George Brown George, a Norfolk farmer, informed the Select Committee on Agricultural Distress that while his rental had increased from £80 to £130 between 1791 and 1819, his tithe had risen from £14 9s 0d to £29. In the same period, his poor rate contribution had increased from £8 to £60. John Rodwell of Barham (Suffolk) fared rather better. While his rent of 373 acres of good quality land rose from £300 to £500 between 1798 and 1820, his tithe increased from £52 17s 4d to £75 and his rates from £23 13s 4d to £50. Edward Wakefield, an Essex land agent, believed that the price slump of the post-war period was reflected earlier in rents and prices than in tithes, which had often been revalued towards the end of the boom. (79)

The evidence of these Select Committees needs some qualification, since it was drawn in large measure from the corn-growing areas of the south and east of England. Evidence from the midlands and north, however, points to a similar conclusion. Between 1796 and 1812, Rev. George Talbot's income from tithe in Hopton, near Stafford, increased from £205 to £447. (80) Sir Edward Littleton's tithe rent in Penkridge, Cannock and Shareshill increased from £1,268 to £2,475 between 1797 and 1812. (81) The Stafford tithes in Codsall totalled £165 in 1796 and had risen to £276 by 1812. (82) In Northumberland, Matthew Ridley's tithes at Stannington had averaged only £348 in the 1780s. In the 1790s this rose to £494, and in the first decade of the nineteenth century they realized an average of £717, with a peak of £856 in 1805. (83) The tithes of St Nicholas, Newcastle-upon-Tyne were worth £602 in 1781, £702 in 1790, £1,136 in 1798 and £1,501 in 1802. A peak of £1,876 was reached in 1806. (84) On a predominantly arable farm in Cheshire, evidence for the post-war depression in tithe values is strong. There, tithes were let to the respective farmers for an average of £1,826 between 1810 and 1816. Between 1817 and 1823 this average dropped to £1,471, and the pattern was maintained in the later 1820s with the averages standing at £1,348. (85)

Such accurate pictures of prevailing boom or slump in tithe values, of course, was only possible with yearly valuations. Many incumbents complained during the wars that their receipts were not matching the undoubted increases in farming profits.

To take just one example from many which tell a similar story, John Riland, rector of Sutton Coldfield (Warwickshire) throughout the period of boom and relative slump (1790-1822) was convinced that he had been systematically short-changed by his parishioners. In April 1796 he wrote that while his tithe wheat was worth £1 an acre, he was receiving only 6s so that 'between the Pay to me and the Worth to me and to the Farmer, there is no tolerable Proportion. The tithe was, by no Means, at or near to an Equivalent, as in all Fairness it ought to be'. He threatened the usual remedy for falling receipts of letting the tithes to laymen, some of whom had already approached him convinced that they could make far more of them than the rector had done. In 1801 he reminded his parishioners that, although he had reduced his tithes in 1793 when a long drought had diminished yields, the farmers had not reciprocated by volunteering higher payments when they could afford them. 'For the first seven years of my residence amongst you here, the Tythe-wheat only was worth £1,600 out of which you had £1,000 and I only £600.' (86)

Such recrimination was common, particularly among those who did not have their tithes valued yearly. Conflict was sharpest also on arable lands. Corn growers felt the tithe system pinching hardest, particularly if they occupied second or third quality lands. The rewards of improved arable farming, reflected in rocketing prices and rentals, obviously attracted many at the end of the eighteenth century, but improving farmers would need to know the local tithe policy. If tithes were collected strictly, or by yearly valuations, such a tax on the gross produce could eat away much of the profit earned only after considerable initial outlay. Much of the battle over tithes would be waged on the corn lands where the stakes were highest.

IV

Tithe, then, was collected in a variety of ways, none of them satisfactory. Once collected, tithe was liable to a variety of taxes. It was in this respect little different from any other form of landed property. Tithe was rated to the land tax, property tax, income tax (after 1799) and, most important of all, poor rates. There is some evidence that as poor rates increased in the early years of the nineteenth century, attempts were made by some proprietors to shift part of the increased burden on to the tithe owner. It was not difficult to find incumbents who believed themselves to be over-rated. Influential parishioners in the select vestry might be tempted to be revenged on a stern tithe owner by rating him to the hilt. William Cobbett approved the efforts of farmers who 'have had the sense and spirit to rate the tithes to the "poor rates". This they ought to do in all cases, whether the tithes be taken up in kind or not'. (87) A defender of the church establishment wrote to Cobbett in 1808 complaining that too many new incumbents who raised tithe compositions found

themselves penally assessed to the poor rates for their impudence.
(88) John Norcross, rector of two Carmarthen parishes, tried in
1828 to increase his tithes, only to be threatened by his
parishioners that if he did so he would be overwhelmed with
'enormous poor and other Parochial rates'. Philip Nevill
Jodrell, incumbent of Yelling nr Caxton had to go to law to
reduce a poor rate assessment which saddled him with a payment
of almost £200 from an income of £450. (89) An anonymous
Norfolk rector, anxious to accede to the request of the pro-
establishment 'British Magazine' for evidence of tithe to put
the record straight in the face of the radical onslaught of
the 1830s, pointed out that a poor rate of £125 was levied on
a notional tithe value there of only £345. He was therefore
perforce contributing well over a third of his income to the
upkeep of the poor - and one of the main planks of the radical
argument seemed to him to collapse, since the radicals argued
that tithes were being misappropriated. The Norfolk clergyman believed that it was the general experience for tithe owners
to be over-rated to all parochial assessments. (90)

John Tomlinson, rector of Stoke-on-Trent, fought a long
battle in the 1820s with Thomas Swynnerton of Butterton Hall
over the question of rating. Tomlinson argued that the combination formed against him under the leadership of Swynnerton
had been motivated by his attempts to improve his tithe
revenues. It was Tomlinson's contention that the select
vestry deliberately under-valued collieries, water-works and
other property while the tithe was 'worked-up'. He issued a
pamphlet, alleging corruption in the vestry, and blaming the
malevolent influence of Swynnerton. 'It seems that Tithes are
at one value in Stoke Vestry, for the purpose of being rated
to the Poor, and of another, but reduced value, when the same
parties have to pay on Tithe Rent Days.' (91) Swynnerton stood
'in the situation of an Irish absentee Landlord ... drawing
all out and spending nothing in it. Why, then, is he, and
certain other persons allowed to persecute me at the public
expense?' Tomlinson alleged that tithes were rated 'in a
double proportion to land'. (92) The rector brought his grievance
to Quarter Sessions where his rating was reduced from £1,322
to £1,140. (93) Tomlinson was fortunate in having the means to
plead his case in the appropriate quarters. His rectory,
worth £3,000 a year after the improvements which had made him
so unpopular, supported him much more substantially than most
livings did. It seems likely that threats from the vestry
deterred incumbents less fortunate than Tomlinson from pursuing
tithe demands in the teeth of entrenched local opposition.

It seems safe to assume that few incumbents were other than
fully rated to the various parochial charges. Another, though
ostensibly more pleasurable, expenditure attached to the
ownership of tithe in many parts of the country was the tithe
feast. In view of the frequent difficulties of assessment and
collection, this was a somewhat ironic celebration. The feast
was usually held annually after the tithe audit. The vicar of
Cumnor (Berks.) explained the prevailing situation in his
parish: (94)

> It is a custom here for the parishioners, all those that
> pay the vicar any tithes, immediately after prayers in the
> afternoon of Christmas Day to repair to the vicarage,
> where they are entertained with bread and cheese and ale.
> They claim on this occasion four bushels of malt, brewed
> into ale and small beer, two bushels of wheat made into
> bread and half a hundred weight of cheese. The remains of
> the ale, small beer and cheese are divided the next day
> after morning prayer to the poor of the parish.

At Weston Longville (Norfolk), Parson James Woodforde gave an annual feast in early December. Woodforde, a convivial and outgoing figure, noted in his Diary that his parishioners usually enjoyed themselves hugely at his expense. In 1776 he recorded: (95)

> My Frolic for my People to pay Tithe to me was this day. I
> gave them a good dinner, surloin of Beef roasted, a Leg of
> Mutton boiled and plums (sic) Puddings in plenty....
> Every Person was well pleased and were very happy indeed.
> They had to drink Wine, Punch and Ale as much as they
> pleased.

The 'frolic', however, was not always so pleasant. Even Woodforde had his tithe troubles. On occasion the parson's ample cellar revealingly loosened his parishioners' tongues. In 1782 a farmer named Forster 'behaved so insolent towards me that I don't intend to have him ever again at my Frolick'. The next year, Forster was told that his tithe would be drawn in kind. Perhaps this had the desired salutory effect, for by December Woodforde was observing, 'We had this year a very agreeable meeting here, and were very agreeable - no grumbling whatever'. (96) Of course, Woodforde was no grasping parson, and he seems to have taken the path of easy accommodation readily enough. It is significant that, immediately on arrival at Weston Longville in 1803, his successor doubled the tithe composition. (97)

The tithe feast was not an impossible burden for impropriators or clergy to bear, of course, although some farmers clearly took the opportunity to down as much free ale as possible. Where the feast was a traditional feature of the village year, any attempt to shirk the responsibility met with a quick response. A petition from six inhabitants of Cauldon (Staffs.) early in the nineteenth century put the point forcibly: (98)

> To Mr James Burnett: Grindon
> We the principal tithe payers in the parish of Cauldon
> do desire that Mr Burnett will take it into his consi-
> deration and allow them to meet him in some respectable
> room in their own Parish when they come to pay him
> Tithe ... and allow them there to have a slice of Beef
> and a quart of Ale; and not come round like a collector
> of Taxes as he has done of late.

Charges on a tithe estate were usually heavy in total. Tithe was unlikely to be under-assessed for any levy and when poor rates virtually quadrupled between 1775 and 1818 this bore as heavily on tithe owners as proprietors. Rev. Thomas

Cockayne, absentee rector of Burnham (Essex), made the reason for his first application for increased compositions for ten years in 1806 his growing tax burden. He was particularly concerned at the triple assessments and income tax in the late 1790s, and informed his agent, 'I have proofs before me that my living is less by sixty pounds & upwards than it was at the time of my composition.' (99)

One further problem remained - the great difficulty experienced by many tithe owners, lay as well as clerical, in making people pay even the reduced value of the tithe for which many of them were happy to settle. The evidence does not entirely support Professor Best's view that 'The farmer who grumbled exceedingly in paying the parson paid his tithes to the squire as a matter of course.' (100) Even when the impropriator was not the squire but a member of the aristocracy a full realization of the assessment values was by no means assured. Few impropriators had such a formidable array of local agents, solicitors and collectors as the Marquis of Stafford, yet he experienced many problems in collecting his tithes. The Marquis's Staffordshire agent, Geroge Lewis, wrote to his commissioner, James Loch, in May 1824: 'I agree with you that tithes are a very unpleasant property for anyone that has to deal with them.... I assure you I have got characters to deal with that would object to pay if only half was demanded.' (101) From Trentham, William Lewis wrote of the situation in Codsall. The tithes (102)

> have been collected with a great deal of trouble this and the past years, and the same have been valued fairly. The tenants are disposed to give much trouble & the only way to bring them to their senses is to let the Tithes for 3 years to a person who will collect them strictly.

The shrewd Loch was unwilling to prejudice the Stafford interest by this course of action. He knew that it would only exacerbate the situation by provoking the tenants to use the many expedients open to them to delay matters still further. He was even prepared to condone a few bad debts, rather than provoke tithe litigation. As a result, the Codsall arrears mounted. A running list was kept from 1829 to 1849, by which time they totalled £178 16s 6d, or about one and a half times the yearly tithe value. (103) Often the marginal comment 'irrecoverable' appears in the account book. By 1842, the agent calculated that only some £77 of the £220 outstanding seemed likely to be recovered. In 1840, for example, four proprietors gave their reasons for non-payment as follows: (104)

William Illage (arrear £1)	'Says the Duke has no right'
John James (arrear 3/6)	'Says he was overcharged'
William Johnson (arrear £1.2.0)	'has taken the benefit of the Insolvency Act'
John Grosvenor (arrear 3/6)	'says he will not pay'

Sir Edward Littleton had similar problems in Penkridge. In 1797, £316 of his tithe worth £1,268 remained unpaid. Although arrears fluctuated from year to year and his agents instituted periodic purges against bad debtors, the average arrears ran at about 12 per cent of the total assessment. (105) On Lord

Cavendish's estate in Cartmel in 1802 no fewer than 106 tithe payers were in arrears to a total of £182; 18 of these had payments which had been outstanding for ten years. (106) It is perfectly true, of course, that landlords permitted arrears of rent to accumulate rather than lose good tenants in bad years. (107) Tithe owners, however, found collection problems in both good and bad years, and usually found themselves last in the queue when outgoings were budgeted.

In Aston (Warwickshire), where there were many disputes, the situation was worse, although the great tithes had been leased to tithe farmers, who were supposedly the strictest collectors of all. In 1821, the lessees, Messrs Robins & Fowler, were able to collect only £269 16s 0d of the £437 0s 9d due - arrears of 37.7 per cent; 20 per cent remained unpaid nine months later. Not even the inducement of a 10 per cent reduction for prompt payment - an expedient to which many collectors were driven - had much effect. The tithe arrears in Aston between 1828 and 1847 totalled £984 13s 1d, the equivalent of a full three years' dues. (108)

It is easy to understand why George Lewis considered tithe 'a very unpleasant property'. The unpleasantness was on both sides. The payer considered the tithe a burden, but he was not entirely defenceless against it. Many owners had to live with evasion, prevarication, concealment and sometimes downright refusal. As clerical tithes after the Reformation were inalienable, there was no way out for the clergy; but laymen could sell their tithes in the same way as any other piece of property if a purchaser could be found. This was often difficult. It was easy enough to obtain a lessee for a fixed term, but by the end of the eighteenth century, as the unpopularity of the payment increased, few wished to buy a bed of nails. As early as 1726, John Vernon had argued that tithes were 'what no person desires to buy but to free their own estates from lay demands of'. (109) For many impropriators, this offered the only hope of solution. Landowners were happy enough to buy the tithes of their own estates in order to let their farms tithe-free at a higher rental. To owner-occupiers, the attraction was also considerable, if the price were right. The owner of the Norton-in-the-Clay (Yorks., NR) tithes was prepared to sell his property to the respective owners in 1765 but 'wd. not chuse to ratifie any of the bargains till he had disposed of the whole tythes of that township to prevent the inconvenience he might suffer by having the tythes of perhaps one or two farms only left upon his hands'. (110) Tithes were sold to the respective landowners in Chesham (Bucks.) in 1800, though many considered 25 years purchase too steep a price. (111) In Preston Patrick (Lancs.), great difficulty was experienced in selling the tithes as a block in 1797, and they were eventually offered to the landowners with varying success. (112) John Tomlinson went to the extraordinary length of obtaining a private parliamentary Act in 1827 to enable him to sell portions of the Stoke-on-Trent tithe and glebe. The proceeds went to the improvement of his rectory. (113) The tithes were sold for between £10 and £15 an acre, and by 1840 about £50,000 had been raised from tithe and glebe together. (114)

James Loch believed that the sale of tithes was a solution to collection problems in Codsall. Lewis wrote confidently to him in 1831: 'I mean to offer the Tithes to the different proprietors of the lands, (and) if they refuse to dispose of them, to anyone else that will purchase. There may be some foolish enough to object but I know that customers will be found for the whole.' (115) This expectation proved much too sanguine. Lewis could only dispose of 10 per cent of the Stafford tithe interest in Codsall. No doubt the remaining landowners preferred to pay the very moderate compositions which were demanded. When commutation was effected in 1848 the Sutherland tithe holding had been reduced only from 1,116 acres to 791. (116)

The partial success of the policy of tithe sales, however, is confirmed by the evidence of the commutation awards. (117) In many cases, landowners who owned their own tithes merged the two properties, thereby making them free of any rent-charge. In Staffordshire, mergers were effected in 79 of the 272 tithe districts. Mergers covered a total of 141,680 acres - 21 per cent of the total acreage. (118) Many of these mergers were effected by the largest landowners and impropriators, such as the Earl of Lichfield who merged all of his lands and tithes over 1,582 acres in Ranton and Ranton Abbey, or Lord Hatherton who merged 6,461 acres in Penkridge. A considerable number, however, were made by small owners who had recently bought the tithes of their own lands. In the twelve tithe districts of Leek, over 460 small proprietors merged their tithes. In Horton, 2,395 acres were merged by 21 owners, and in Walsall, 51 owners merged a total of 3,505 acres. Where land and tithe owners did not take the opportunity of making declarations of merger, they left the assistant tithe commissioners with very complex apportionments. In Rocester, for example, John Rawlinson had to make an award of £488 rent-charge on 91 landowners, most of whom already owned their own tithes. In general, however, most of those who were qualified to merge land and tithe did so, thus significantly simplifying the business of commutation.

The tithe problem, therefore derived from its unwieldiness, complexity and uncertainty. It was a valuable, though vexatious, property, and the system required a great degree of goodwill on both sides to function with even passable efficiency. With tithe rights frequently so uncertain, this goodwill was increasingly strained as the pace of agricultural change quickened at the end of the eighteenth century. New crops and crop rotations appeared and the yields of the old crops were often greatly improved. The law indubitably entitled the tithe owner to a share in the fruits of these improvements; but new claims seemed to infringe the canons of customary observance which had preserved the viability, if never the popularity or efficiency, of the system since the Reformation. Disputes and rancour increased. The rationale of the system was subject to a critique more searching and radical even than that imposed during the Puritan Revolution of 1640-60. (119) Even in these conditions, many tithe owners realized that the discretion of a lower income amicably arranged was better than the doubtful valour of a lengthy battle against entrenched positions, guarded by an assumed customary right. For those who rejected this analysis, the opinions of the fertile breed of tithe lawyers were siren voices to lure the aggrieved on to the rocks of litigation.

NOTES

1. John Selden, 'The Historie of Tithes' (1618), ch. ii, sect. ii and ch. iii. Jacob promised God at Bethel 'of all that thou shalt give me, I will surely give the tenth unto thee'. Genesis, xxviii, vv.21-2. God also instructed Moses and the Israelites that 'whatsoever passeth under the road the tenth shall be holy unto the Lord'. Leviticus, xxvii, vv.30-3.
2. Christ's only reference to the payment was hardly a flattering one: 'Woe unto you, scribes and Pharisees, hypocrites because you tithe mint and anise and cummin; and have left the weightier things of law; judgment and mercy and faith'. Matthew xxiii, v.23.
3. R.J. Phillimore, 'The Ecclesiastical Law of the Church of England', 2 vols (1873-6), i, p.451. W.E. Tate, 'The Parish Chest' (Cambridge, 1960), p.134.
4. G. Constable, 'Monastic Tithes from their Origins to the Twelfth Century' (Cambridge, 1964), p.110. The practice was not uncommon. The bishop of Carlisle sold tithes in Warkworth as freehold property to Sir Henry Percy in 1333. Cumberland RO Register of John Kyrkby, p.289.
5. W. Cobbett, 'A History of the Protestant Reformation in England and Ireland', 2 vols (1829), i, para. 328.
6. W. Blackstone, 'Commentaries on the Laws of England', 4 vols (Oxford, 1765-9), i, ch. ii. Religious houses were enjoined by a statute of 1391 (15 Ric. II c.6) to put a proper proportion of their tithe revenue to the use of the poor.
7. Phillimore, op. cit. i, p.1,484.
8. It is not intended here to dwell on the technicalities of tithe law. The best studies of this complex subject are F. Plowden, 'The Principles and Law of Tithing' (1806) and R. Burn, 'Ecclesiastical Law', 4 vols (1763-5), iii, pp. 373-502. For a more modern account, see P.W. Millard, 'The Law of Tithe Rentcharge', 2nd ed. (1926).
9. 2 & 3 Edw. VI c.13.
10. J.E.C. Hill, 'The Economic Problems of the Church' (Oxford, 1956), p.91. For personal tithes in the sixteenth century see A.G. Little, Personal tithes, 'English Historical Review', lx (1945), pp.67-88.
11. See the Wombourn terriers, LJRO B/V/6. This topic is more fully discussed in E.J. Evans, Tithing customs and disputes, 1690-1850: the evidence of glebe terriers, 'Agric. Hist. Rev.', xviii (1970), pp.17-35.
12. PRO IR 18/9528. Report of the voluntary agreement for commutation at Uttoxeter.

38 Chapter 2

13 See below, chapter 4, sect. IV.
14 Plowden, op. cit. pp.198 and 176.
15 PRO IR 29/32/1.
16 Bucks. RO D/C/2/107. Matthew Barton to Charles Chester, 1 April 1776.
17 LJRO Tithe Book of St Mary, Lichfield, Dean and Chapter Muniments, Cupboard 8/6. Lancs. RO DDM/11/60. See also the Hornchurch tithe dispute, reported in 'British Magazine', i (1832), p.387.
18 Plowden, op. cit. pp.198-207.
19 Thus a modus of £4 10s 0d per annum from a farm valued at £30 was held to be rank, as were moduses of 2s 6d per acre for corn and 1s for hay. H. Gwillim, 'A Collection of Acts and Records ... respecting Tithes', 4 vols (1801), ii, p.708; iv, p.1,323; ii, p.645.
20 Plowden, op. cit. p.205.
21 Gwillim, op. cit. iii, p.1,294.
22 Staffs. RO D239/M4624. For a full report of the judgment, see E. Younge and J. Jervis, 'Reports of Cases argued and determined in the Court of the Exchequer', 3 vols (1828-30), i, pp.135-54.
23 See below, chapter 3, sect. III.
24 D.M. Barratt, ed., 'Ecclesiastical Terriers of Warwickshire Parishes', 2 vols. Dugdale Society Publications xxii and xxvii (1955 and 1971).
25 LJRO B/V/6, Pattingham 1698. For more examples of specific customs see Evans, loc. cit. pp.20-2.
26 LCA Ingilby Records, 2741.
27 Hill, op. cit. p.95.
28 Lord Ernle, 'English Farming Past and Present', 6th ed. (1961), p.341. J.D. Chambers and G.E. Mingay largely echo his conclusions in 'The Agricultural Revolution, 1750-1880' (1966), p.46.
29 Ernle abstracts their conclusions in an appendix, op. cit. pp.504-6.
30 William Marshall, 'Rural Economy of the Midland Counties', 2 vols, 2nd ed. (1796), i, p.18.
31 F.M. Eden, 'The State of the Poor', 3 vols (1966, facsimile reprint of the original 1797 ed.).
32 Ibid. ii, p.34.
33 Ibid. iii, p.712.
34 PRO, 30/8/310 ff.1-12. I am indebted for this reference to Mr Alan Booth of the University of Lancaster.
35 PP(HC) 1814-15, x, pp.85-97. The total figures were: Tithe £2,353,000. Taken by composition, £1,932,000. In kind, £421,000. Thirty-one per cent of the land of England and Wales was either wholly or in part exempt from tithe payment. Peel used the 1813 figures as the basis for his calculations when considering the question of coluntary commutation in 1834. BM Add MSS 40408 f.228.
36 LJRO Dean and Chapter Muniments, Cupboard 8/6.
37 'Farmers Magazine', iv (1803), pp.72-3.
38 It is interesting to note, however, that new tithe barns were being built as late as the second half of the eighteenth

century. In 1760, the rector of Almondbury (Yorks., WR) received an estimate of just over £35 for the erection of a tithe barn, Lancs. RO DDX 22/184. The tithe survey of 1767-9 indicated that tithe was still being drawn in kind at this date, ibid. DDX 22/185.
39 John Middleton, 'A General View of the Agriculture of the County of Middlesex' (1798), p.59.
40 S.C. Agric. Distress, PP(HC) 1833, v, clause 2013.
41 Ibid. 1836, viii pt. ii, p.14.
42 PRO IR 18/9357 and 9377.
43 Anon., 'Observations on a General Commutation of Tithes ...' (1782), pp.6-7. Goldsmiths' Library, University of London (GL 1782).
44 Staffs. RO D554/42.
45 Ernle, op. cit. p.341.
46 H. Coombs and A.N. Bax, eds., 'Journal of a Somerset Rector' (1930), pp.166-7.
47 LJRO B/A/19. Letters of John Mott, 12 July, 3 August 1830 and 4 November 1831.
48 BRL Jewel Baillie MSS 77c 1/36.
49 Ibid. 77c 1/30.
50 Thomas Thompson, 'Tithes Indefensible', 3rd ed. (York, 1796), p.50.
51 'Political Register', xiii (1808), pp.248-9.
52 See, among many similar examples, the vicar of Ellastone (Staffs.) in 1832, CCF NB20/125. Delabere Pritchett began his lengthy campaign against the parishioners of Cheadle in 1817 with a demand for all tithes in kind, Staffs. RO D239/M4458. Bishop Richard Smallbroke was concerned that his clergy should preserve accurate terriers of their property rights so that new incumbents should inherit an accurate record of what they might legitimately claim, 'Charge to the Diocese of Lichfield and Coventry', 1732-3, WSL Visitation Charges, Eighteenth Century.
53 This was standard practice also. When the vicar of Garstang, John Peddar, claimed potatoes for the first time he demanded the tithe in kind in the first instance. Lancs. RO DDPd 45/10. John Dearle, vicar of Baswich, had pursued a similar course in 1741-2, WSL S.Ms. 429/iii. Rev. George Lee demanded tithe in kind in 1804 from one of his tenants in Water Stratford who had refused to accept revised composition payments. Bucks. RO D/LE/14/31/1, Joseph Parrott to Lee, 8 August 1804. The parishioners of Rev. Thomas Pearse in Westoring nr Ampthill (Beds.) demanded to pay tithe in kind rather than accede to the vicar's new tithe demands, Lancs. RO DDGr (uncatalogued), Pearse to Greene, 18 December 1830.
54 Observations of Edward Sawyer on a tithe bill, 24 July 1830. Bucks. RO D/LE/14/37.
55 S.C. Poor Laws PP(HC) 1834, xxviii, pp.206, 239 and 307.
56 'Quaesitor' in 'Monthly Magazine', v (1798), p.122.
57 Staffs. RO D239/M4616-20.
58 CCF NB20/206.
59 Staffs. RO D593/F/3/7/1-33. Bishton charged 8d in the pound

on the value of the tithes in this compact parish of just over 1,500 acres. For the origins of the Sutherland fortune, see Eric Richards, 'Leviathan of Wealth' (1973), pp.3-18. The Marquis of Stafford became 1st Duke of Sutherland in 1833.
60 Northumb. RO ZDT 7 and ZRI 45/10.
61 Bucks. RO D85/39.
62 Lancs. RO DDPd 45/19, 27 and 30.
63 Durham RO D/EL Box 23. William Marshall calculated that a 'medium' rent for tithe per acre in the 1780s was about 4s to 5s per acre for arable and 2s for grass land. At this time arable land of reasonable quality could be rented for about £1 per acre, 'Rural Economy of the Midland Counties', 2 vols, 2nd ed. (1796), i, p.17. In Hertfordshire tithes were paid at an average rate of 3s 5½d per acre at the turn of the century, and apparently nowhere at more than 5s per acre. Arthur Young, 'A General View of the Agriculture of the County of Hertfordshire' (1804), pp.30-1.
64 PP(HC) 1836, viii pt i, pp.155 and 163.
65 Ibid. 1821, ix, p.142.
66 Staffs. RO D240/E444. Tithe Corn Book, 1814.
67 S.C. Agric. Distress, PP(HC) 1821, ix, p.70.
68 Lancs. RO DDPd 45/59.
69 PRO IR 18/9549.
70 Staffs. RO D593/K/1/3/25. Lewis to Loch, 18 February 1837 and D593/K/1/3/22 (May).
71 LCA Ingilby Records 3007. Sir John Ingilby to Dr Kershaw, 10 November 1759.
72 Jane Austen, 'Pride and Prejudice' (1813, Pan ed. 1967), esp. pp.46-7 and 52.
73 Lancs. RO DDGr (uncat.). Letters of John Thirkins, 19 May 1828 and R.B. Podmore, 19 February 1830.
74 CCF NB20/210 and 9.
75 O.F. Christie, ed., 'The Diary of Rev William Jones, 1777-1821' (1929), p.147.
76 Lancs. RO DDGr (uncat.). Greene to the archbishops and bishops, August 1827.
77 Wheat rose from an average price of 43s per quarter in 1792 to 119s 6d in 1801 and 126s 6d in 1812. It fell to 65s in 1815, 44s 7d in 1822 and 39s 4d in 1835.
78 F.M.L. Thompson, 'English Landed Society in the Nineteenth Century' (1963), pp.217-20. For a more detailed regional study arriving at similar conclusions, see H.G. Hunt, Agricultural rent in south-east England, 'Agric. Hist. Rev.', vii (1959), pp.93-108.
79 S.C. Agric. Distress, PP(HC) 1821, ix, pp.92-3, 213.
80 Staffs. RO D240/E443.
81 Ibid. D260/M/E/10/11.
82 Ibid. D593/F/3/7/1-33 and G/5/11.
83 Northumb. RO ZRI 45/10.
84 Ibid. ZRI 13/5.
85 PP(HC) 1833, v, clause 5957. Evidence of Joseph Lee.
86 W.K. Riland-Bedford, 'Three Hundred Years of a Family Living' (Birmingham, 1889), pp.136-41.

Chapter 2

87 W. Cobbett, 'Rural Rides', 2 vols (Everyman ed., 1966), i, p.120.
88 'Political Register', xii (1808), pp.341-5.
89 Lancs. RO DDGr (uncat.). John Norcross to Greene, 5 February 1828. Joddrell to Greene, 10 September 1828.
90 'British Magazine', iii (1833), p.180-1.
91 Staffs. RO D593/K/1/3/16 (January).
92 'Staffordshire Advertiser', 20 January 1827.
93 Staffs. RO D908/5.
94 'Bibliographica Topographica Britannica Antiquities', 10 vols (1790-4), iv, pp.24-5. I am indebted for this reference to Dr R.W. Malcolmson, Queen's University, Ontario.
95 J. Beresford, ed., 'Diary of a Country Parson', 5 vols (Oxford, 1924), i, p.193.
96 Ibid. ii, pp.46, 59 and 107.
97 Ibid. v, p.413. Letter of Elizabeth Girling, 6 May 1803.
98 WSL M842 (undated, but probably 1830s).
99 Essex RO D/DOP B120/886A and 887.
100 G.F.A. Best, 'Temporal Pillars' (Cambridge, 1964), pp.187-8.
101 Staffs. RO D593/K/1/3/12. Lewis to Loch, 22 May 1824.
102 Ibid. D593/K/1/3/12. William Lewis to Loch, April 1824.
103 Staffs. RO D593/G/3/4/2-67.
104 Ibid. D593/T/2/19.
105 Ibid. D260/M/E/10/11.
106 Lancs. RO DDCa 22/10/2.
107 Thompson, op. cit. pp.232-5. Hunt, loc. cit. p.108, and Joan Thirsk and J. Imray, Suffolk farming in the nineteenth century, 'Suffolk Record Society Publications'; i (1958), pp.96ff.
108 BRL Jewel Baillie MSS 272/22 and 272/18.
109 Staffs. RO D1790(W)/D/3/2.
110 LCA Newby Hall MSS 2992/1.
111 Bucks. RO D/CH/A/417.
112 Lancs. RO DX1643-68. For another attempt to sell tithes, see the interest of the Delaval family in Doddington (Northumberland), Northumb. RO 2DE/14/53/17 and 18.
113 7 and 8 Geo. IV c. 41.
114 'Victoria County History of Staffordshire', viii (1970), pp.186-7.
115 Staffs. RO D593/K/1/3/19. Lewis to Loch, 12 July 1831.
116 Ibid. D593/T/2/18.
117 A complete set of tithe maps and apportionments are held by the PRO listed as IR 29 and 30. Most county record offices have good sets of the documents in the area under their jurisdiction.
118 Eric J. Evans, 'A History of the Tithe System in England, 1690-1850, with special reference to Staffordshire' (unpublished University of Warwick Ph D thesis, 1970), pp.445-60 gives a full list of Staffordshire awards and tithe owners.
119 For which see Margaret James, The political importance of the tithes controversy in the English Revolution, 1640-60, 'History', xxvi (1941), pp.1-18.

CHAPTER 3

TITHE DISPUTES AND LITIGATION

I

If the uncertainties of assessment gave ample reason for generalized discontent with the tithe system, the travails of litigants in tithe causes provided the clearest possible evidence of its specific evils. Tithe law was so confusing and contradictory and the courts so ponderous, that a prospective litigant needed to be young, fit and possessed of ample resources to be sure of seeing the matter through. Many tithe adversaries died locked in the labyrinthine complexities of an action in chancery or exchequer. The results of a successful action could be so rewarding, however, that there was no shortage of litigants. A modus set aside or a valuable crop established as tithable could treble or quadruple tithe income. Equally, a proprietor who could sustain ancient customary payments against attack by a tithe owner would look to his reward in the hard currency of higher rents. It was well known that tenants, who usually paid the tithe directly, would be prepared to agree to higher payments in such a situation. If the hazards of litigation were great, so too were the fruits of success.

Statute and common law was of only limited usefulness in defining tithe rights. The statute of 1549 circumscribed rights particularly to personal tithes, (1) and by Acts passed in 1699 and 1757 three new crops deemed important for the national economy could not be levied at a higher rate than 5s per acre. (2) Common law merely allowed a tithe to be taken of all yearly increase of the produce of the soil, with many exceptions and deference always to the custom of the parish. By the middle of the seventeenth century, a protracted and bitter struggle by the church for its tenth of minerals such as coal, iron and tin had been largely lost. (3) Tithes of minerals and fish had to be justified by special custom. (4) Here the normal practice of tithe being assumed payable unless a contrary custom could be shown was reversed.

Common right to tithes, of course, was nothing more than an aggregate of customary practice. It stood only when local practices did not countermand it. Plowden believed that 'such has been the extent of interference by the legislature, or deviation from the original payment of tithes ... that few parishes are to be found in England which pay their tithes in every particular according to the common law principles, usage and practice of tithing'. (5) Distinctions were often very finely drawn. Bees, for example, were regarded as 'ferae naturae' and tithe free. Most tithe honey, however, was tithable since when collected into hives bees were considered someone's property and no longer 'ferae naturae'. (6) Various suits attempted to establish precedents in such doubtful cases. The rector of Simonburn (Northumberland), Dr John Scott, began a case in the bishop's court at Durham in 1779 to establish rights to tithe honey from Sir Lancelot Allgood. (7)

Tithe suits were heard in a variety of courts. Ecclesiastical jurisdiction was by means of episcopal consistory courts, sitting usually in the cathedral city of the diocese. These were frequently the courts of first resort, particularly for the clergy; but their competence to determine cases was limited particularly after the triumph of Sir Edward Coke in the early seventeenth century. (8) The church courts could not decide suits involving modus claims, since these were a matter of temporal, not spiritual, right. The same proscription applied to claims involving allegedly tithe-free land, and claims which derived from customary usage rather than common right. A defendant cited to appear before an ecclesiastical court could, on application to a common law court, obtain a Writ of Prohibition to suspend proceedings in the church court and have them transferred to common law. Prohibitions had to be applied for, and since some defendants calculated that the transfer of jurisdiction would only increase costs, the emasculation of the church courts was not total. Certainly, these courts continued to hear many cases in which a Prohibition would without doubt have been granted if it had been sought, and many modus issues were still tried in church courts in the second half of the eighteenth century. (9) The historian is surprised rather at the continued vitality of these courts in the eighteenth century than at their lack of power or relevance. (10) In the diocese of Lichfield and Coventry, for example, no fewer than 559 tithe suits were begun in the diocesan court between 1700 and 1836, (11) and although the number instituted had declined considerably by 1800, the influence of the church courts should not be underestimated. (12) Appeals from the consistory courts were to the Court of Arches or High Court of Delegates, half of whose members were laymen. (13) Prohibited cases were decided in common law courts, usually before a jury at assizes, empanelled to determine the facts relating to a dispute. The Prohibition, in Burn's view, manifested the 'superintendency of the courts of common law' over ecclesiastical jurisdiction. (14) If a case were determined in a church court and the tithe owner were successful the court would make an order for double value of the tithes to be paid to the plaintiff. Costs were also usually granted. (15)

At the end of the seventeenth century, the principle of summary jurisdiction was introduced in tithe disputes, probably as part of a Whig reaction against the pretensions of the church

courts. Complaints had constantly been heard that procedures for
the recovery of tithes were unnecessarily cumbersome and, because
costs mounted with time, too punitive. By an Act of 1696 owners
of tithes claiming arrears of not more than £2 were enabled to
apply to two Justices of the Peace who would summon the defaulter
and order payment on pain of distraint of goods. By special
dispensation, cases involving Quakers could be so determined up to
a maximum tithe value of £10. (16) Recourse to this legislation
was entirely optional. Tithe owners could subject their adversaries to the full rigours of the law if they chose to do so.
The breach in the dyke, therefore, was a small one. Even given
goodwill on both sides the legislation was of limited usefulness
since the sums involved were so small.

Temporal determination of tithe disputes was largely the
prerogative of the equity courts of chancery and exchequer.
These courts were not hampered by restraints on right or value.
Thus, most of the great 'causes célèbres', quoted with such relish
by opponents of the tithe system in the 1820s and 1830s, came
before the Barons of the exchequer or Lord High Chancellor after
a stately and measured progress through the preliminary stages of
bill of complaint, demurrer, cross-bill and replication.
Evidence was either heard in London or taken by sworn commission
in the locality of the protagonists. If a modus was at issue,
judgment was usually reserved by the Barons or Chancellor until
a trial by jury had been held at the local assizes. When this
verdict was known, the court proceeded to final judgment unless
the parties had come to a prior agreement, as not infrequently
happened. Appeals from the judgment of an equity court were
heard only in the House of Lords. (17)

II

Tithe disputes were endemic in British society, and litigation
was instituted by all manner of tithe owners. J.A. Venn is misleading when he implies that most tithe cases were brought by
vicars anxious to define their right to contentious small
tithes. (18) His view derives from consulting 'all the reports
of legal cases concerning tithes from the fourteenth century up
to the nineteenth'. Such a view reflects only the concern of
tithe experts with new principles which could swell the already
mountainous case law on the subject. Because of the great variety
of small tithes there were far more cases which could later be
cited as precedents about whether parsley, onions or turnips
were tithable, whether hot-house plants could be collected, what
rules should apply to agistment tithe when animals were wintered
in a neighbouring parish, and whether saffron and wood were
great or small tithes. The history of tithe disputes cannot be
written from the law books, because these deliberately selected
exceptional cases which served to amplify the law on the subject.
(19) A more reliable guide is obtained from working through
tithe causes in the respective courts. It is clear from this
evidence that while laymen and clerics used both temporal and
spiritual courts, there was a natural tendency for more cases to be

instigated by clerics in their own court, and for laymen to predominate in the equity courts. There was a popular belief that the clergy were more easily satisfied with their tithe income, and hence less likely to go to law. Lena Tadman expressed the usual view in asserting that impropriators 'tease and vex us more by half than the clergy'. (20) The clergy, however, by no means eschewed recourse to law. Of 550 cases in the Lichfield diocesan court in which it has been possible to distinguish the protagonists with certainty, 322 were begun by the clergy between 1690 and 1830 and 228 by impropriators. Of 130 Staffordshire tithe causes in the exchequer, 75 were brought by laymen and 55 by the clergy. (21) Of these 75, 28 were brought by impropriators in their own right and 47 by lessees, thus lending some weight to the conclusion that lessees were most concerned of all to maximize returns on what for them was a business transaction.

What were the issues over which so many parishes were plunged into tithe strife? A correspondent involved in litigation at Guiseley (Yorks.) had no doubt. He wrote that 'A design, which has been long concerting, is now (1747) putting into Execution, to break thro' the Ancient Moduses and Compositions for Tythes, established in divers parts of the Nation, Time Immemorial.' (22) His particular concern was with tithe owners' growing interest in establishing claims for agistment of cows and colts for which small modus payments of one or two pence had traditionally been made. A 'member of the Church of England' wrote to the Dean of Lincoln in 1792, complaining that the church had been 'suffered to stir dormant claims, so antiquated, that all memory and evidence of the original transaction are gone'. (23) An apologist for the Church nevertheless remarked in 1782 that in the previous thirty years the clergy 'have been more attentive and better informed and have therefore made a considerable progress in augmenting their composition for tithes'. (24) This meant that they had become successful litigants. There was a concerted attack on moduses in the second half of the eighteenth century. As agricultural profits began at last to rise, tithe owners demanded their share of the improved yields. The main obstacle in their way was the modus. It frequently amounted to little more than a tithe of a tithe, and its evil influence could only be removed by recourse to law. Farmers and landowners guarded it jealously, and by 1800 with new crops introduced ever more quickly and lucratively and scientific farming making more profitable use of old ones, the modus was the obvious standard around which tithe battles raged.

Hay and agistment tithes, in particular, were more strictly collected in this period. Cases concerning these products abound and it would be redundant to provide an extensive catalogue. A few examples must indicate the general trend. In 1752, Elisha Millichamp, vicar of Coleshill (Warwickshire) brought John Barton, a substantial farmer, into court for non-payment of tithes from a very substantial flock of sheep, some of which had been kept within the parish all year, but many of which had not. (25) Evidence was called establishing that no wool tithes had previously been claimed for sheep sold out of the parish before shearing time. At Worfield (Salop) there were many disputes in the 1750s and 1760s about tithes due 'for unprofitable Cattle & Sheep not sheer'd within the Parish & fed in the Parish'. The parishioners argued that no tithe was payable on cattle fed on after-mowings and stubble. (26) Tithe owners were particularly interested in obtaining their full tenth of the value gained by farmers keeping sheep from shearing time until slaughter and on cows not yielding milk from weaning to calving. Thomas Bateman, vicar of Whaplode (Lincs.), was able to reverse previous decisions with a successful action in 1774 for agistment tithe from land which had in the same year produced a hay crop. He wrote a prolix pamphlet proclaiming his triumphs and urging others to try their luck in a similar way. (27) The inhabitants at Kirdford (Sussex) took legal advice about new claims by their vicar to tithes of young cattle, sheep fed on turnips, vegetables consumed in the family, fresh-water fish, mill profits and cattle depastured on the common. (28) At Brewood (Staffs.) the lessee of the prebend brought an exchequer suit in 1782 claiming tithes of hay and clover which the proprietors alleged to be covered by moduses. Thomas Plimley, who occupied 152 acres there, had never paid more for tithe hay than two customary payments of 2s 6d and 5s 11d. (29) Richard Goodwin of Cheadle claimed that his 175 acre farm was exempted from claims for hay tithe by a modus of 3d. (30) Joseph Delves, vicar of Abbots Bromley brought various suits between 1779 and 1785 in consistory and exchequer courts to establish claims for hay and agistment tithes neglected by his predecessors. (31)

The pattern is clear. Tithe owners were determined to assert their rights. Many cases turned on the tithability of crops which before about the middle of the century had either not been grown in many parts of the country, or grown in such small quantities as to be of no interest. The most important of these 'new' crops was undoubtedly potatoes. In market garden areas, the potato crop even displaced wheat as the most valuable product of the soil. While many tithe owners would deliberately overlook small allotments sown with potatoes for domestic consumption, they were hardly likely to forgo their rights when the crop was produced for the market. Rev. Henry Heathcote, rector of Walton nr Liverpool, made it clear when he began suits for potato tithes in 1787 that he was activated by a need to preserve the profits of his living in a much-changed agricultural situation: (32)

> I am therefore call'd upon by every duty I owe to the Church, the patron, my successors & my own family to look after those other tithes which the alterations in husbandry give rise to & to which we are justly intitled. I wish not to raise up claims where prescriptive rights are well grounded but the articles I am pursuing at present are such as did not exist to any degree of consequence a very few years ago. Viz. Agistment and pasturage of unprofitable cattle that is of horses not kept for the plough or agisted or taken in to graze at so much per week or for the season, of sheep from their last shearing, of Butcher's cattle & of cows that are agisted for hire & not milk'd in the parish & of course do not pay the Vicar's tithe of milk. 2. New

Gardens or ground laid down in Gardening of which there are
many acres & likely to be many more for the supplying
Liverpool Market. 3. Potatoes.

Heathcote wished a speedy settlement in amity, but if this were
not forthcoming he would not eschew 'any redress which the Court
of Exchequer will afford'. Heathcote's attitude was a common one.
The vicar of Eastham (Cheshire), Rev. George Travis, obtained an
exchequer decree in 1770, entitling him to tithe of potatoes which
had recently become much more valuable. (33) At Gosforth
(Cumberland), the rector, Rev. Charles Cobbe Church had to take
his claim for potatoes to trial by jury in 1802. The potatoes
in question were grown in the open fields and supplied to the
Whitehaven market. (34) The important tithe cause at Hornchurch
(Essex), which meandered its way through consistory court, assizes,
court of Arches and high court of Delegates in the first half of
the nineteenth century, poisoning relations in the process, concerned potatoes grown for the London market. (35) Rev. Thomas
Blundell finally established his right to potato tithes at
Halsall (Lancs.) in 1810 after a long struggle which had defeated
the efforts of his predecessor. (36) George Peake's demands for
agistment, potato and turnip tithes in Aston in the 1820s caused
great acrimony and resentment. (37) In Cheadle, Rev. Delabere
Pritchett attempted to establish his rights to turnips and potatoes
when he was first appointed to the living in 1814. His
parishioners, never having been faced with such a claim before,
considered them tithe-free. Pritchett found that parochial
relations virtually broke down as he instituted suit after suit
to compel payment. He noted in his Diary: 'Long afterwards Women
& Children cried out after the Rector as he passed along the
streets: "Tatoes, Potatoes, Turnips & Potatoes, Potatoe-Guts".
The same words were written on the walls & doors in chalk with
caricatured figures of the Rector'. (38)

Most tithe suits revolved around attempts to break moduses, or
assumed exemptions from tithe. There were, however, many examples
of unusual or eccentric claims which had considerable economic
significance in particular areas. Prime among these were claims
to tithe of wood. Statute law exempted wood of more than twenty
years growth from demands for tithe, but there were - as ever -
many variations in local practice. At Swinnerton and Weeford
(Staffs.) there was a long dispute in the exchequer about claims
by the rector for tithe of wood. (39) At Woolford (Warwickshire)
a dispute about wood tithes arose following the presentation of
Rev. T.H. Pye to the vicarage in 1794. The Earl of Northampton,
the largest landowner in the parish, had paid an annual sum of
£10 plus two loads of oak faggots in lieu of tithe underwood to
Pye's predecessor. Pye demanded an increased composition, and
when this was refused insisted on payment in kind. The Earl
considered this vexatious and in 1796 took counsel's opinion,
though with little expectation of success. He was advised that
tithe of wood was due in kind, unless a specific custom to the
contrary could be proved. 'Lord Northampton or his Tenant after
the wood is cut, ought to set out for Tythe the full tenth part
in a convenient Manner, "giving Notice" to Mr Pye of the time
when they are about to set it out and permitting him or his agent

to be present at the time - And if they do not set out fairly &
bona fide a tenth part they will be liable to an action at the
suit of Mr. Pye.' (40) A solicitor advised the inhabitants of
Mildenhall (Wiltshire) that an amicable settlement would be much
preferable to a suit over wood: (41)

> I fear there will be more perplexity in this business than
> you apprehend. The few enquiries I have made and casting my
> eyes over the cases reported in Burn's Ecclesiastical Law on
> the subject of Tythe wood, induce me to think neither the
> Facts nor the Law on them very clear. What is usually done
> may not prove an ancient uninterrupted, reasonable Custom
> wch the Courts will take cognizance of.

The courts usually upheld claims for 'new' tithes. It was not
a good defence to assert that no tithe had been requested or paid
hitherto. A defendant had to show good cause why no tithes were
payable, or sustain a valid modus. Most pleaded valid moduses,
but it was common also for a defendant to attempt to prove that
his land had been monastic land before the Reformation, since
no tithe was payable on monastic property. Some also tried to
suggest that the tithes claimed were not within the jurisdiction of the claimant. An interesting case exercised legal
opinion in the 1790s when the rector of Holy Trinity, Chester,
claimed corn tithes from lands which had been drained fifty
years before and which now produced a valuable crop. The River
Dee Company believed that the tithes were due rather to the
rectory of Hawarden across the Welsh border. While the rectors
haggled about the precise limits of the boundary of England and
Wales, the Company enjoyed effectively tithe-free land. (42)

Tithe disputes involving new claims or modus disputes were
especially prone to occur soon after a change of incumbency,
or when a new tithe lease was taken out. Clerics were often
urged by their bishops or the dean and chapter to take particular
care of their tithe interests when first entering a new living.
(43) They were urged to assert their claims irrespective of
personal preference, since they were at best only life-tenants
of the benefice, and failure to attend to their tithes could
harm their successors' interests. These arguments were reinforced
in the early nineteenth century when clergymen could see a new
prosperity among the farming community. When the living of
Llanwarne fell vacant in 1807 James Woodhouse bemoaned the fact
that the previous incumbent had made only £116 a year from
it. (44)

> I think it may be advanced to £250 a yr. or more as it is a
> very large Parish, but Mr Thomas never advanced any one of
> them 1/- and he has had the living about 30 Years. I
> believe no advance was made for 20 or 30 Yrs before, which is
> the only Parish in this County that has not been doubled &
> trebled in that time.

Thus many new vicars and rectors commissioned fresh valuations
and surveys of their tithe rights. If the new claims which
followed such valuations were disputed, legal action was the
obvious course. Perhaps the most celebrated instance occurred
in Halifax in 1827 when Charles Musgrave succeeded Dr Coulthurst
as vicar. Coulthurst seems to have received about £750 a year

in small tithe compositions from his vast and increasingly
populous parish, but Musgrave was confident that the living was
worth more than double this. When the inhabitants of the various
townships in the parish collectively rejected Musgrave's propo-
sitions to augment his tithe income to £1,500, the vicar demanded
tithe in kind, and prepared to go to law to secure his rights.
Agreement was finally reached but not before the various townships had signed a Bond of Association to defend their rights
at joint expense against 'a string of enormous new fangled
claims'. (45) A campaign of vilification was mounted against
the vicar. Richard Oastler, whose first essay in public affairs
this was, became a leading figure in the opposition to the
vicar's claims. As representative of Fixby township, he was
particularly alarmed that certain clergymen should fly in the
face of mounting opposition to the church establishment by
promoting provocatively large claims. What Oastler feared most
of all was 'the alienation of the People from the Clergy and
the Church', and his argument was that Musgrave's action was the
perfect instrument for effecting this separation. (46)

III

When a tithe action was under way, the collection and production
of accurate documentary and verbal evidence assumed paramount
importance. Courts could only be guided on the validity or
otherwise of a modus by the strength of the evidence which could
be mounted. When the vicar of Garstang was trying to set aside
certain moduses, the tenants were advised as to the best means
of defence: (47)

> before any correct opinion can be formed the constitution
> of the Parish with regard to Tithes, the Endowment of the
> Vicarage if there be any such in existence, the old Terriers
> relating to the Parish, the Table or List of Dues under which
> the Tithes were collected and the Ecclesiastical Surveys
> kept in the public Offices with the Evidence of Old persons
> as to the payment of Tithes within Claughton should be seen,
> but this cannot be done without some expense and as it is
> a matter relating to the Township in general all the Land-
> owners are interested in the question and should come to some
> understanding on the subject.

The collection of evidence was an arduous and expensive
business. Moreover, tithe owners held important initial advantages
since they were likely to be in possession of most of the relevant
evidence, or have more convenient access to it. Ecclesiastical
terriers, recognized by most judges as reliable guides to the
tithing customs of a parish, (48) were usually deposited in
the parish chest and if not, copies could be obtained from the
diocesan office on payment of the appropriate search and copy
fees. (49) Tithe account books in the possession of impropriator
or incumbent were also accepted as valuable evidence. The case
of Armistead v. Bleasdale in Sandbach (Cheshire) turned on the
ability of the vicar to produce a continuous run of account books
from 1641 to 1736. (50) Rev. W.J. Hadow, rector of Haseley

(Warwickshire) who was anxious to improve the tithe revenues of his new living on presentation in 1827, went to enormous trouble to discover his parish's tithe history. He employed clerks and assistants to search records in the Tower of London and the British Museum for histories of the leading families who opposed his new claims and also for previous tithe contents which he could cite as precedents. (51) Tithe owners, however, had relatively easy access to many important documents. Landowners and tenants would probably have to ferret them out. A combination of leading inhabitants from the parish of Aston requested a local solicitor in 1825 to 'procure copies of all Terriers and the Endowment of the Vicarage (if any) and obtain evidence as to the existence of Moduses in the Parish and for all other purposes connected with the investigation of the Vicar's rights'. (52) The expenses of such a search would be met jointly by the defendants.

Documentary evidence was regarded by the courts as the more weighty, but the testimony of the oldest inhabitants could also be called to establish customs 'in the time whereof the memory of man is not to the contrary'. After all, a search for a fourteenth-century endowment might be fruitless, but a few septuagenarians or even octogenarians could usually be found to testify to the state of things in their youth. If they happened to have been the sons of tithe collectors or a member of the rector's tithe collecting army at harvest time, their evidence was the more valuable. Some disputes were so protracted, however, that many an old man was called to his maker before he got his opportunity to be called to the bar of the exchequer to tell his tale. (53)

The production of relevant evidence was only one of many financial burdens imposed on tithe litigants; but it was the one which separated the sheep from the goats. Many litigants could not afford the enormous costs involved in voluminous searches, transcriptions of ancient documents or in the payment of witnesses' expenses, particularly if they had to travel long distances to present their evidence. The expenses contingent on the collection of evidence bulked large in most final statements of account. In the Cheadle case, Pritchett v. Honeybourne, which lasted from 1817 to 1836, the total cost to the defendants of the production, examination and expenses of witnesses amounted to just over £305. In addition, the cost of drawing up defence statements based very largely on the witnesses' evidence was £346. Together, these charges easily outweighed the £325 charged by learned counsel. They form, indeed, the bulk of the £1,507 expended by the defence. (54)

The total cost of tithe suits could be prohibitive. A litigant determined to pursue his claims through the entire gamut of legal options could count on expenses running into thousands of pounds by the early nineteenth century. The Kendal tithe case, lasting over ten years and requiring a private Act of Parliament to settle finally, cost the defendants alone in the region of £11,000. (55) This was exceptional, but costs running to £3,000 or £4,000 for each party were much more common. There is no doubt that many tithe disputes could

only be sustained by affluent protagonists. It followed that
when the contest was between litigants of unequal financial
strength, the chances were that it would be accommodated before
a final decision, on terms favouring the richer party. Out-of-
court settlement was an extremely common feature of tithe cases.
The 'Gentleman's Magazine' remarked on the problems of new
incumbents 'coming strangers to a parish, of procuring Evidence
to contest pretended Exemptions, the want of Money or Spirit
to enter into a Just Law Suit with a powerful Adversary'. (56)
Randall Darwall, rector of Haughton from 1726 to 1777 found
himself unable to sustain a struggle for new tithe claims
against a combination of inhabitants whose powers of prevarication,
litigation and appeal greatly outstripped his own. Unfortunately
for Darwall, in the ranks of those lined against him stood the
Lord of the Manor, Francis Elde, who was a Master in Chancery
with a keen interest in tithe matters. Darwall's frustration
found vent in the normally sober parchment of a glebe terrier.
In 1766, he noted that his attempts to regain lost tithe rights
had seen him 'expos'd to very injust obloquy' with the
parishioners, including the Master in Chancery 'determined (it
seems) that "Might" shall overcome "Right"'. (57)

Darwall's 'cri de coeur' had a more general validity. It is
clear that the power of the purse was a decisive factor in
determining the outcome of tithe disputes. Just as vicars and
rectors were able to frighten many smaller tenants merely with
the threat of litigation, so all but the most opulently-endowed
incumbents must give way to a combination of the largest landowners, fertile in expedients and possessed of the resources to
bludgeon the tithe owner into submission. A surprisingly small
proportion of tithe cases seem to have been finally settled in
court. Of the 559 cases identified from the diocese of Lichfield
and Coventry, for example, only fourteen have judgments or
sentences attached to them. This is almost certainly an under-
estimate of the total number, since prohibited cases were
determined elsewhere, and since it is clear that some judgments
have been lost. However, the incentives to come to some
arrangement were extremely strong. Many tithe owners were able
to establish their rights merely by issuing a citation from the
court against a defaulter. John Haworth, assistant registrar at
Lichfield, informed George Graysbrook in 1830 that a speedy
outcome might be expected to his claim for Easter dues: (58)

> I beg to state that the mode of proceeding is by citing the
> parties in the first instance and on their giving an
> appearance to give in a short plea stating the Amount of
> the Family and the custom of the Parish in the payment of a
> certain sum per head to the Rector as Easter Dues. In
> these cases the Question seldom arises at a plea - the
> citation generally brings them to their senses, and they
> quietly pay the sum demanded with Costs.

It is not surprising that the threat of legal action and the
prospect of costs of many times the value of the tithes should
deter many from further resistance. The citation was also a
useful device for dealing with parishioners whose truculence led
them to initial refusal. The vicar of Walsall in 1783, for

example, informed his proctor in the ecclesiastical court that a miller in the town had told him 'that he did not pay the Parson any dues in the Parish he came from till he put him in the Court and made him'. (59) Threats were an important weapon. An anonymous author wrote of the alleged rapacious conduct of a new tithe collector for the Manchester Collegiate Church who issued a large number of summonses in the Newton Lane area in the 1790s 'amongst those poverty striken and very wretched class of people ... who had weekly pay from the town, from whom this lay divine by threatening to distrain on their little all had exacted exorbitant Easter dues'. (60)

Threats of legal action often produced a quick, and hence cheap, outcome. This could also be achieved by application to two magistrates under the 1696 statute where the sums involved were sufficiently small. The costs of such an application were usually very light. In 1770, for example, the vicar of Garstang brought an action against 22 occupiers for non-payment of small sums ranging from 6d to 1s 4d. The magistrates made an order for payment on pain of distraint of chattels almost immediately. (61) Costs of 3s were awarded. This avenue was, of course, a restricted one since for the most part only small tithes and Easter offerings could be claimed before magistrates who could hear cases up to a maximum of £2.

If a claim were resisted, ecclesiastical tithe owners would find a ready source of help on legal technicalities in the diocesan registrar. The surviving letter books of the diocesan registrar of Lichfield and Coventry - sadly only from the late 1820s and 1830s - give a fascinating glimpse into what amounted to an unofficial legal aid service. The registrar informed incumbents of their rights, and their chances of success in any litigation they might contemplate. He also attempted to settle matters early by threatening defaulters with dire penalties likely to accrue from continued, and by implication futile, resistance. This tactic could be very successful against individual tithe payers in particular. John Mott wrote to a recalcitrant parishioner on behalf of the vicar of Lapley in 1833: (62)

> I am instructed to commence proceedings against you for the recovery of seven pounds due to Rev. M Ward, Vicar of Lapley, for balance of composition for Tithes. Anxious to avoid expensive litigation I have deemed it right to give you this notice that if the above amount is paid to Mr Ward, or remitted to me within ten days, no further steps will be taken, otherwise I shall comply with my instructions.

For Mr Beech of Swinnerton, there was a similar threat: 'I trust you will come over and make some arrangement about the payment of tithes & costs; otherwise you will oblige the plaintiff to plead, the costs of which will fall on your shoulders.' (63)

Not surprisingly, the ample means for compromise which existed at every stage were frequently used. Even in the most intractable disputes, such as those at Kendal or Cheadle, solicitors' letters suggesting agreement to avoid further expense and bitterness were common. In the Aston dispute, the parishioners, worried by discrepancies in the evidence and concerned that these should not be made the excuse for yet further delay by the other

side, offered the vicar a much improved composition of £1,200 a
year or a private Act of Parliament to commute the tithes at an
agreed sum. The vicar rejected the offer. His belief that the
problems over the evidence would work to his advantage proved
justified. When the tithes were eventually commuted, he received
not £1,200 but £1,800. (64)

Many suits in the ecclesiastical court were settled by the
acceptance of a tender made by defendants who calculated that
continued resistance would only increase costs without much
prospect of eventual victory. The tender recognized that the
tithe owner had established this claim, and amounted to a
surrender on less humiliating terms than might otherwise be
extorted. At Dronfield (Derby.) a tender was made to the vicar
in 1747 explicitly 'to avoid disputes or any further Expense to
be made in this Cause'. (65) At Dacre, nr Ripon, agreement was
reached in 1748 to end a dispute over tithes between the Dean
and Chapter of Ripon and the parishioners: (66)

> The Terms are - That the Dean and Chapter are to pay their
> own Costs - Take £30 instead of £60 for their arrears - And
> accept Four Pounds a Year in lieu of all future Tithes....
> The Money and Defendants Costs are to be shortly raised, and
> paid by each Party, according as He and She is rated to the
> Dacre Poor-Cess (Rate) and they are to covenant to pay
> accordingly.

It is clear that plaintiffs with good prospects of success
frequently preferred to end the matter on acceptable terms short
of total victory rather than continue and fail to get either the
full claim or their opponents' costs when these had become huge.
At Sefton (Lancs.) a potato tithe dispute was halted by compromise agreement serving the interests of the poorest members
of the community. The rector, Richard Rothwell, had begun an
exchequer suit to establish his rights. This was suspended when
the parishioners recognized his right to the tithe on condition
that the rector allowed (67)

> to occupiers of every house or cottage within the same parish
> half an acre of land of the measure of eight yards to the Rod
> or Perch for the growth of Potatoes for the use of their
> respective families free from tythe and without any claim of
> tythe in respect thereof.

Arbitration was another possible way out of impasse. At
Worfield (Salop) after the impropriator had claimed tithe of
wood, clover seed, agistment and turnips and the inhabitants had
claimed moduses in lieu, both sides agreed to accept the determination of two arbitrators chosen one from each side, rather
than wait for the ecclesiastical court to grind its way forward.
(68) At Walton, Lord Molyneux was called upon in 1774 to
arbitrate between rector and parishioners. (69)

The longer a case continued, of course, the more important
became the power of the purse. Most lengthy disputes, significantly, were between tithe owner and a combination of defendants,
banded together to share costs. By thus pooling resources,
defendants could use the law's delay to their own advantage.
Well-financed defendants could run the entire course of bills,
cross-bills, delays and appeals with the hope of forcing either

surrender or compromise from the tithe owner. The uncertainty
of the legal situation worked to the advantage of the rich litigant. There was hardly a judgment which did not offer some
grounds for appeal, hardly a custom which could be sustained
against all the devices of the practised tithe-specialist.
Joseph Delves, vicar of Abbots Bromley in the late eighteenth
century, wrote candidly to Lord Bagot to explain his frustrations
when faced with a stronger adversary: (70)

> Your Lordship cannot but be aware that the foundation of my
> claims arises from the uncertainty and consequent illegality
> of the several Moduses set up to exempt your Lordship's
> estate from the small Endowment that I conceive belongs to
> my Poor Vicarage, in so much that I knew not where to look
> either for Moduses, Compositions or Tithes. Why the Vicars
> of this Parish have so long submitted to forego their just
> Rights, I had rather leave to your Lordship's own candour than
> to give any offence by suggesting the true reasons as con-
> ceived by me, which I think are too obvious to escape your
> Lordship's penetration.
>
> The opposition I have me with and the expense I have been
> put to in endeavouring to obtain and establish the just
> Rights of the Church (which I beg leave to assure your
> Lordship has been my chief motive) may, in part, give your
> Lordship an idea why my Predecessors have chosen to forego
> their rights and remain inactive rather than contend with
> Opulence and Power. And perhaps it might have been better to
> have followed their Example.

At the first hint of a tithe dispute, defence associations
were established in many parishes to fight the tithe owner. (71)
It was politic for landowners to join even if their property was
not under direct attack. Tithe owners commonly selected a few
parishioners to bear the first burden of new claims. If
successful, he could extend his claim to other lands by citing
the precedent of the decisions recently made in his favour.
Thus, a parochial modus could be broken much more cheaply than
by formal confrontation throughout the parish. Tithe defendants
quickly realized the dangers of this oblique approach and guarded
themselves in defence associations from the outset. The additional resources provided by association could then be deployed
to prolong an issue to the disadvantage of a tithe owner with
limited means or to provoke a fight on ground less favourable
to him. In doubtful cases it was an advantage to the proprietors
to have an issue tried by a jury. Rev. Ronald Bligh, rector of
Romaldkirk (Yorks., NR) wrote the history of an unsuccessful
attempt to impose payment of wool tithe in 1815. His attempt
to have his case determined by the consistory court at Richmond
was thwarted by a prohibition. The case was transferred to York
assizes, where a jury of landowners and substantial tenant farmers
decided against him. Bligh inveighed bitterly against a system
which permitted juries of tithe payers to decide on the rights
of tithe payment. (72)

'Iota' warned clerical readers of the 'Church of England
Bulwark' in 1828 about the wiles of defendants with sufficient
resources to give them full play: (73)

Often it has been the stigma of Equity Courts, that judgment could not be had before one or both parties were ruined for ever. Hence the old proverb: 'Summa jus, summa injuria'. And this was more particularly to be noted in Tithe Suits: which can not be sufficiently deplored, when we consider how sacred that property is; and that unless Ministers are duly protected from spoliation, the best interests of religion must suffer severely, and the present and eternal welfare of the community at large be set at nought. Let us only picture to ourselves the former characteristics of a Tithe Suit: In the first place, a bill of complaint was filed. After a long interval, an answer put in. The answer not being to the purpose, exceptions are made to it. Next comes a further answer, flatly denying the claim of the complainant. Upon this, a commission is ordered to examine evidence. After another long interval, the evidence is taken and filed in Court: then the cause is set down for hearing; and after a third long interval, it is heard. Then time is taken to consider the judgment. At length, judgment is given, directing an issue to be tried at the County Assizes by a Jury. Of all horrors few can exceed this! It being notorious, that juries, as tithe payers, have a very strong bias against the rights of a tithe-owner.... Indeed, let us only for a moment think how a question relating to the revenue would be adjudicated by persons who detest taxes, and we shall discover that it is the height of absurdity to expect a fair verdict for a tithe-owner from persons who detest tithes. The only remedy for this is, that Equity Judges should not direct issues of tithe causes, but make a decree themselves upon the evidence before them.

The 'Bulwark' mounted a strenuous campaign to protect the rights of the 'inferior clergy'. In the same issue, 'Verax' castigated the enemies of the church who combined to use their position of financial superiority to browbeat poor clergymen. He advocated the establishment of a fund 'to preserve small benefices from spoliation'. Legal costs were rising beyond the means of the clergy to meet them, and in Rainham (Essex) the vicar suffered grievously to sustain his principles. This 'courageous champion of the church would not basely abandon her sacred rights, but resisted even unto death: just previous to which, wonderful to relate, he entirely defeated his adversaries; but, alas, he died in the most deplorable circumstances in consequence of the enormous expenses he had to defray. Thousands of inferior clergy, appalled by such formidable obstacles, seek no redress whatever.' (74)

The moral was crystal clear. Against the weaker sections of the community, clergymen remained strong. Against those stronger than they, if not defenceless, they were at a serious disadvantage, often despite cases strong in law. In this, of course, tithe litigation was not unlike other branches of civil law. The legal system failed to devise a procedure whereby right overcame might. Two examples of tithe disputes may serve to indicate the difficulties of clergy confronted by 'opulence and power'. In 1830, Rev. Thomas Knight, rector of Ford (Northumberland) had the temerity to bring an exchequer suit for non-payment of tithes against the patron of his living, the Marquis of Waterford. (75) Knight wished to tithe the Marquis's 8,000 acre estate, valued at £10,000 or more. Waterford alleged that a modus of £40 covered the entire estate, although he delayed filing any reply at all until 1835, hoping in the meantime to reach a satisfactory accommodation with the rector. The cause was heard between December 1839 and July 1840 and Baron Alderson gave judgment in favour of the plaintiff in January 1841. Waterford, however, refused to concede defeat. He appealed to the House of Lords, and when in desperation Knight brought a suit at common law to establish the very rights which the equity court seemed to have secured, Waterford employed in his defence the solicitor-general, and Sir Thomas Wilde was 'brought down specially at great expense, for the noble defendant'. At length, both the Lords and a special jury at common law reversed the exchequer judgment. Knight sustained a complete defeat, primarily because the Marquis used every device open to a rich man to secure his own way. The law was duly bent to his will.

At Barlaston (Staffs.), the newly appointed perpetual curate William Oliver set about improving what seemed to him a scandalously depressed living worth only £80 to his predecessor. In 1836 he brought an exchequer suit against five of his parishioners to establish his right to hay and all small tithes. (76) The defendants replied that tithe hay was not payable in most of the parish because Barlaston curates had always held two small meadows, Priest's Meadow, and Dusteloe Dole, explicitly in lieu of this tithe. Pressed by the plaintiff, they stated that, if payable, the full tithe would have realized £174 12s 0d, but alleged that no such payment had been made at least since 1731. The defendants sought to form a defence association and approached the solicitor of the Duke of Sutherland, who was a small landowner in the parish, though uninterested in the case at issue. Probably deliberately, Oliver had not included in his bill of complaint any of the Duke's tenants. Sutherland's solicitor, Robert Fenton, therefore replied that no assistance could be given to the defence association since 'his Grace's own rights are not ostensibly at issue'. (77) The Duke's legal resources, therefore, were not placed at the disposal of the defendants, and this may have had a decisive bearing on the result. In 1839, Baron Alderson decreed in the Exchequer that the defendants had not sufficiently proved exemptions from tithe, and must therefore account with the curate for tithe of hay, milk, calves, wool, lamb and geese. (78) The Sutherland interest considered that Oliver had been fortunate. George Lewis wrote to the estate commissioner, James Loch: 'I think that if the case was fairly gone into he should have but little chance of success.' (79) Fenton even suggested that Oliver's own counsel had been surprised at such an apparently complete victory on the case he had presented. (80)

Nevertheless, Oliver's victory so encouraged him that he determined to capitalize on his success by bringing more parishioners into litigation. At the end of December, 1839, he filed a fresh bill in Chancery against 32 new defendants. Amongst these, apparently by oversight, was a Sutherland tenant,

Chapter 3

Mrs Ashcroft. Oliver was soon to regret this move. He was to write later to the Duke that his solicitors 'had scrupulously avoided putting any of your Grace's Tenants in the Bill although they are all seven years in arrear'. (81) Since Oliver had seen fit to involve the Sutherland interest, his advisers now had no qualms about joining, and dominating, the defence organization. The Duke stood to lose rent if Oliver succeeded. Fenton informed Loch in early 1841: (82)

> The questions which are at issue with Mr Oliver are of some magnitude looking to his Grace's interests only. The Duke has 380 Acres in Barlaston the whole of which will be subject to Tithes of Milk and Calves if Mr Oliver succeeds, and about 229 Acres of that quantity would also be subject to hay tithe to him.

Thus it was that the full machinery of the Sutherland legal expertise was put at the disposal of the defendants to Oliver's second suit when it had been denied in the first. Advice, explicitly critical of the defence of the first suit, was readily available:

> It seems that the Deft in that suit did not call in question the plaintiff's right to hay and what are called the small or vicarial tithes of the Parish - but rested their defence on certain alleged Moduses ... which they failed in supporting.

The Duke's advisers believed 'that the facts of the case were not fully before the Court on the hearing of the last cause or the Result would have been different'. (83) At a meeting of tithe payers in Barlaston in November 1840, Fenton made an address and Oliver sourly noted that he urged all payers to put in similar defences to those suggested by the Duke's legal team, (84)

> with the encouraging assurance that he had little doubt but that if every occupier would put in an answer similar to the one he had prepared for Mrs Ann Ashcroft with the assistance of the usual Modes which offered for legal procrastination they might be able to keep me out of my Tithes for some time to come.

Fenton's optimism was securely founded. Vice-Chancellor Bruce took a different view of Oliver's case from Baron Alderson and directed that the vital moduses should be tried before a special jury at a convenient assizes. (85) Oliver, aware of the likely outcome before a jury of tithe payers, tried a desperate gamble by appealing to the Lord Chancellor on the grounds that his deputy had directed wrongly on the evidence before him. His appeal was dismissed and the special jury tried the moduses at Gloucester Assize in July 1844. It upheld their validity at all points. Oliver was forced to admit defeat, and blamed it on the expertise available to his opponents through the intervention of the Duke. The solicitors tidied up the affair during 1845 and here Oliver gained one useful concession to his pocket if not to his pride. Each side was to pay its own costs. The Duke's solicitors could afford a show of magnanimity, and in any case if they held out for costs it was by no means certain that the curate could oblige. They were, therefore, lenient with a man 'whose circumstances cannot be flourishing and who is likely to give preference to other creditors'. Oliver, humiliated as well as beaten, nursed his grievance with his spiritual influence

cruelly diminished. He even talked for a time about giving up
his benefice and exchanging posts with a local schoolmaster. (86)

IV

Among tithe disputants, the Society of Friends stood out as a
special case. Many dissenters argued the injustice of a legal
obligation to support the local representative of the Anglican
communion while they had at least a moral obligation to contribute
to the stipends of ministers of their own sect. The Quaker objection, however, went deeper. Their practice involved a rigid
adherence to Christ's command to his disciples, 'Freely ye
have received; freely give.' (87) When the Friends' Yearly
Meeting found it necessary in 1832 to recapitulate its reasons for
enjoining on all members a refusal to pay tithes, it was only
maintaining a policy which had been consistently upheld since
the inception of the Society in the 1650s: (88)
> the ministry of the Gospel is to be without pecuniary remuneration. As the gift is free, the exercise of it is to be free
> also.... The forced maintenance of the ministers is in our
> view a violation of the great privileges which God, in his
> wisdom and goodness, bestowed on the human race.

No other sect went to such trouble to ensure that its members
withheld tithe. So seriously was the 'crime' of payment considered that a member could be expelled from the Society for
complying. Although there seems to be no evidence that this
extreme sanction was ever enforced, as it clearly was in the case
of Quakers marrying out of the Society, it indicates that Friends
regarded refusal to pay as a cardinal tenet of their faith.

Refusal to pay brought Quakers into conflict with the law. If
punctiliously faithful to the demands of their belief, they were
left with little room for manoeuvre. Rigorous enforcement of the
law would bring them to financial ruin and lengthy imprisonment.
Although after 1696, JPs were empowered summarily to determine
claims for tithe not exceeding £10, use of such proceedings was
entirely optional for plaintiffs. (89) If a Friend refused to
answer a citation from the ecclesiastical court, he was declared
excommunicate and could be handed over to the secular arm for
imprisonment on a writ 'De Excommunicato Capiendo' or
'Significavit'. It is a testimony to the continued vitality
of the church courts that such imprisonments remained common in
the early eighteenth century. Once imprisoned, a Friend's full
tithe and the costs of the prosecution were to be recovered by
distraint upon his goods and chattels. In 1736, when Friends
were mounting their greatest propaganda onslaught in an attempt
to obtain legislation which would require tithe owners to make
use of summary procedures where small sums were involved, they
revealed that between 1696 and 1736 no fewer than 1,180 prosecutions had been undertaken against Friends. Of these, 659
were heard in the exchequer, 367 in ecclesiastical courts and
154 elsewhere, mostly in king's bench. As a result of these
prosecutions, 302 Quakers had been imprisoned and 9 had died
there. (90) These figures were drawn from meticulously prepared

lists of 'Sufferings' sustained by Friends because of their faithful testimony against tithes. Most historians have seen Friends as the chief recipients of harsh legal penalties for non-payment. Gough argued that (91)
> The distresses and prosecutions for ecclesiastical demands were numerous and many of them exorbitant ... the rigorous enforcing of the ecclesiastical laws were rarely or never suppressed.... The number of those who laid down their lives in prison in consequence of these prosecutions is too large to recite particularly.

In recent years, this view has met with increasing scepticism. Norman Hunt argued that prosecutions of Quakers were declining by the 1730s and that easy accommodations were made between tithe owners and Friends to avoid the full rigours of the system. (92) Friends were maximizing sufferings in order to present their case for amendment of the law more persuasively. My own work in Quaker history of the early eighteenth century confirms Hunt's view. (93) There was, of course, no shortage of lurid examples which could be cited to advance the case of persecution; but these were hardly typical even of the period when Quakers came under strongest attack in the courts. The evidence of the Sufferings Books shows clearly that the number of Friends greatly exceeded the number of prosecutions, and that many Quakers did in fact permit tithe owners to enter their fields and take the tenth. If tithe owners ignored the legal nicety of waiting to be informed of a crop's readiness for tithing, the Quaker's pacific beliefs did not permit him to restrain the titheman in his work. A 'modus vivendi' was thus established. When tithe owners chose to apply to the Justices for a distress warrant in lieu of tithe, there seem to have been few abuses such as the abstraction of materials greatly in excess of the value of the crop and costs. The local meeting of Friends recorded the fact of unjust expropriation when it occurred, but this was rarely.

In fact, tithe was frequently taken from Quakers with minimum interference to both sides, if on occasion by unorthodox methods. In Cumberland, where there was a strong Quaker community, local JPs were kept busy in executing summary jurisdiction on defaulters in the 1750s and 1760s. There is no evidence of persecution of Friends in Embleton or Cockermouth, though defendants had to pay costs of either 6s or 10s for each offence. (94) In Cheshire tithe was either taken in kind or by Justices' warrant, and the tithe or distraint taken usually approximated to the value claimed. In 1814, Thomas Stretch of Morley had £2 19s 0d taken in cash from his drawer to meet a tithe claim authenticated by the Justices of £2 9s 0d. Costs were assessed at 10s. Distraint was made on a wide variety of articles, such as meal, corn, hosiery, house furniture, malt and livestock. Only very rarely, as in the cases of James Broster of Bosley and Samuel Stonehewer of Macclesfield in 1817, did the Quarterly Meeting have any reason to suggest that 'great oppression' resulted from tithe demands. (95) The picture was similar in Herefordshire. In the 1750s and 1760s, for example, tithe was taken by distraint of goods. John Cowles of Ross-on-Wye 'had taken from him 84 yrd of Linen Cloth worth £4 12s 0d' and 5s 2d 'in Cash out of his

Money Boxes' to meet a tithe demand of £4 14s 0d in 1754. There was no hint of oppression in such dealings. Indeed, one JP, Thomas Gwillim, was thanked by the Quarterly Meeting in 1755 for saving a Friend from persecution: (96)

> Justice Gwillim understanding That his Neighbour Dow becoming one of our Society, out of a Conscientious Scruple Refus'd to pay Tithe & apprehending the Consequence, being well acquainted with the Law knew the trouble & Expence of an Exchequer Suit, As the Tithes were of Distinct Properties & Different sorts & kinds, the Justice being an honest good natur'd Man, Contriv'd to Divide them into Several Parcels so as that each Sum might come under the Limitation of the late act & be taken by Justices Warrant.

The extent of Quaker grievances, therefore, may easily be exaggerated. Even in the period of greatest trouble, the careful selection of horror stories by Friends contrived to give a misleading impression. When membership figures began to decline in the second half of the eighteenth century, the problem assumed an altogether lesser importance. Fewer and fewer Friends put much of an obstacle in the way of the titheman. The picture of backsliding from the faithful testimony began to alarm the Yearly Meeting of the Society. As early as 1728, the Meeting for Sufferings reprinted pamphlets urging the continuance of the testimony and 'adding such advice from themselves as they may think necessary for the Enforceing the Reasons and Arguments therein contained'. (97) In 1769 the Yearly Meeting was so concerned about tacit compliance with tithe owners in Essex that it appointed a committee of 'solid, judicious and concerned Friends' to visit the county and convince the Quaker community there of the error of their ways. (98)

Quakers also seem to have been aided in avoiding the penalties of non-payment by their neighbours. In some cases, when tithe was taken in kind, a tenth sheaf was removed by a neighbour and given to the tithe collector when his own tithe was paid. Rev. J.C. Atkinson remembered the assistance given to Friends in his Yorkshire parish: (99)

> Dear old William and his co-religionists never paid a penny of the 'cess' (rate) they were liable for. But somehow or other, when the churchwardens went their collecting rounds, a sheaf or two of corn, of approximate value to the sum set down against their names, stood handy to the said churchwardens' hands, and no inquiry was ever made as to the person who had 'conveyed' the Quakers' corn.

There is little evidence here of the rancour and anguish which Friends implied was their lot as a result of the evils of the tithe system.

Punitive prosecution remained an occasional hazard, but it is significant that when it occurred it was the source of much criticism by the parishioners. In 1781, the vicar of Holy Trinity Coventry, Joseph Rann, brought suits in the church court against seven Friends for non-payment of 2d a year which was due from every householder. The case was contested by the defendants and taken to the Court of Arches. Although able to establish his most recent claims, Rann was opposed by the Mayor and

Corporation of Coventry, and local sympathy for the Quakers was such that a fund was established to support them. It realized £70, which was enough to buy the vicar off in 1789. (100) He signed articles of agreement promising not to bring a similar case to law in the future. In view of the opprobrium which this one had visited upon him, this was an easy pledge to keep.

The Society of Friends' efforts to secure legislation to rid them of the risk of exposure to punitive prosecution continued after their great but abortive campaign of 1736. They tried in 1751 to deprive the church courts of the power to have Friends imprisoned for non-payment of tithes. (101) In the 1770s, 1780s and 1790s there were further moves to reduce these powers which were now seldom used, but remained an irritant. (102) Despite their frequent and usually well-informed pressure, however, tangible relief was not given until 1813 when the risks of punitive prosecution were negligible. The Act for the Better Regulation of Ecclesiastical Courts in England (103) took from them the power of excommunication of those who refused to appear to answer consistory court charges. Excommunication was to be restricted to punishment for purely spiritual offences, and the only civil penalty contingent upon it was imprisonment for a term not exceeding six months. More tangible relief for Quakers was provided by a clause in the Act raising the limit for cognizance of Quaker cases before JPs from £10 to £50. It was not until 1835, however, that the most prized remedy for which Friends had striven for over a century was conceded. By the Act for the More Easy Recovery of Tithes (104) it was determined that litigants must have their redress against Friends on goods or other property rather than on the person by imprisonment. The Act was a century too late to possess much relevance to the contemporary situation. It was, in fact, little more than a clearing-up operation preparatory to tithe commutation which would follow in the next year. Parliament had meantime ignored two well-supported Quaker petitions of 1833 and 1834 which called for 'the entire abolition of tithes' and argued that any legal protection for an ecclesiastical rate or levy was 'an unjustifiable interference on the part of the civil power'. (105)

Quaker discontent with the tithe system, therefore, should be put in a proper perspective. In the late seventeenth and early eighteenth centuries there was some persecution by tithe owners determined to impose the full weight of the law on men of tender conscience. Even at its height, however, only a minority of Friends were involved. Much more frequently a rough-and-ready justice was applied either by tithe owners taking dues without permission, or by agreement and compromise between the parties, sometimes with the collusion of other members of the community. In the second half of the eighteenth century as the use of justices' warrants increased, the problem of persecution all but died away. The Yearly Meeting of Friends railed at an increasingly lax observance of the faithful testimony, but the homilies received at best a muted response. Friends suffered less than a casual perusal of their splendidly detailed Sufferings archive might suggest. Clergyman and Quaker frequently found an acceptable position which satisfied the pocket of the former and the conscience of the latter. Tithing obligations were no more than a constant and nagging ulcer of discontent. Most Quakers were no more disadvantaged by the system than were the rest of the community. The 'Faithful Testimony' of Friends against tithes had become an outworn and irrelevant slogan rather than a vital crusading banner.

NOTES

1 See above, chapter 2, sect. I.
2 By 11 & 12 Will. III c.16, hemp and flax, considered 'exceedingly beneficial to agriculture' and 'deserving of great encouragement by reason of the multitude of people that are and would be employed in the manufacture of these two materials' were singled out for this privileged treatment. Madder, 'an ingredient essentially necessary in dying and calico printing and of great consequence to the trade and manufactures of this Kingdom', was protected by a similar Act, 31 Geo. II c.12.
3 This defeat, which proved an important element in the power struggle between ecclesiastical and cmmon law courts, was rationalized by the victors on the argument that minerals formed part of the substance of the ground and were not nourished by it. Nor were they subject to 'yearly increase'. J.E.C. Hill, 'Economic Problems of the Church' (Oxford, 1956), pp.84-5, and J.A. Venn, 'Foundations of Agricultural Economics' (1923), p.105.
4 H. Gwillim, 'A Collection of Acts and Records ... respecting Tithes', 4 vols (1801), ii, p.616; iii, p.937; and iv, p.158. When rectors pleaded customary usage, as they frequently did in fishing villages of Devon and Cornwall, acrimony was acute. See below, chapter 4, sect. III.
5 F. Plowden, 'The Principles and Law of Tithing' (1806), p.117.
6 Ibid. p.121.
7 Northumb. RO ZAL 30/6.
8 For which see Hill, op. cit. pp.124-31.
9 See, for example, Butteris and Marshall v. Alport, 1753-9, Fowler v. Armishaw, 1785-8, Harvey v. Smith, 1799-1802 and Eddowes v. Burgess, 1812 in LJRO B/C/5. In each of these cases defendants pleaded moduses in lieu of the tithe claimed. In Arblaster v. Fairbanks, ibid. 1780, the defendant argued that some of the land from which tithe was claimed was tithe free.
10 The history of the ecclesiastical courts in the eighteenth century is important and remains to be written. They continued to hear not only tithe cases but matrimonial and testamentary ones and issues of personal morality. A rich vein of social history remains largely untapped. For some interesting, but essentially preliminary, observations, see G.V. Bennett, Conflict in the church, in Geoffrey Holmes, ed., 'Britain after the Glorious Revolution, 1689-1714' (1969), pp.156-7. Clearly, Coke's victory was by no means so decisive or complete as some Whig historians believed.

11 LJRO B/C/5 and Additional Series (Misc.).
12 The commissioners studying the jurisdiction of the church courts noted in 1831 that most of the cases still before them related to matrimony and probate. PP(HC) 1831-2, xxiv p.51.
13 Ibid. p.11.
14 R. Burn, 'Ecclesiastical Law', 8th ed. (1824), p.51.
15 W. Easterby, 'The History of the Law of Tithes in England' (Cambridge, 1888), chapter ix, gives more detail on the respective jurisdictions of ecclesiastical and equity courts.
16 7 & 8 Will. III c.6 and 34.
17 Plowden, op. cit. pp.379-92.
18 Venn, op. cit. pp.100-1.
19 This danger is not avoided in Alan Wharam, Tithes in country life, 'History Today', xxii (1972), pp.426-33.
20 'The Pamphleteer', xii (1818), p.505. See also the evidence of John Neve and Charles Osborne weighing the relative harshness of clergymen and impropriators, PP(HC) 1833, v, pp. 259 and 487-8.
21 PRO E112/739-40, 891-2, 1044-5, 1281-4, 1969-76, 2242, 2334.
22 'The General Advertiser', 24 January 1746/7.
23 'Annals of Agriculture', xix (1793), p.67.
24 Anon., 'Observations on a General Commutation of Tithes for Land or a Corn Rent' (1782), p.5.
25 LJRO B/C/5: 1751-2. Millichamp v. Burton.
26 Ibid. Misc. unsorted papers: Worfield.
27 T. Bateman, 'A Treatise on Agistment Tithe', 2nd ed. (1778). His case excited sufficient interest to justify the publication of an 'Appendix' in 1779 which went into even more exhaustive detail.
28 West Sussex RO Par.116/6/2.
29 PRO E112/1972 No. 104.
30 Ibid. E112/2242 No. 16.
31 LJRO B/C/5, 1779 and 1783, Delves v. Holland. PRO E112/1972 Nos. 111 and 114 and E126/33. See also Hutton Wood, 'A Collection of Decrees by the Court of the Exchequer in Tithe Causes', 4 vols (1798-9), iv, pp.294-304.
32 Lancs. RO DDM 11/60.
33 R.J. Pope, 'The Eighteenth Century Church in Wirral' unpublished MA thesis, University of Wales, 1971), pp.126-7.
34 Cumbria RO (Carlisle), D/Ben 833^1-890^1 and D/Ben/Gosforth.
35 'British Magazine', i (1832), p.387.
36 Lancs. RO PR2820/5 and PR284. For a similar lengthy struggle over potato tithes in Garstang see ibid. DDPd 45/10 and 42.
37 BRL Jewell Baillie MSS 254/2 and 77c 1/30. BRL 381701.
38 WSL M57.
39 Hutton Wood, op. cit. ii, pp.249 and 318-20.
40 Warwickshire RO CR 556/288D.
41 Wiltshire RO 9 (uncat.). Tithe wood dispute in Mildenhall. Savernake MSS.
42 Cheshire RO Pl/330-336. For another example of a boundary dispute, see Luxford v. White in the exchequer where the boundary between Hailsham and Oldham was contested, 'British

Magazine', iv (1833), p.330.
43 Eric J. Evans, Some reasons for the growth of English rural anticlericalism , 'Past and Present', 66 (1975), pp.87-8.
44 Herefordshire and Worcestershire RO (Hereford), C99/III/15.
45 R. Oastler, 'Vicarial Tithes, Halifax' (Halifax, 1827), p.140. See also LCA Sutcliffe Estate Records, 411.
46 Oastler, op. cit. p.182. The Halifax affair is only briefly alluded to in C. Driver, 'Tory Radical: The Life of Richard Oastler' (New York, 1946), pp.33-5.
47 Lancs. RO PR2448. William Shawe to Thomas Cole, 24 April 1830.
48 See Lord McDonald's judgment in Miller v. Foster, Warwick Assizes, 1794, Plowden, op. cit. p.328.
49 The letter books of John Mott, diocesan registrar of Lichfield and Coventry in the 1820s and 1830s, are full of requests for searches for ecclesiastical terriers. See for example, LJRO B/A/19. Book C, Haworth to Graysbrook, 22 February 1830 and Book D, Mott to Staplyton, 6 November 1830.
50 'British Magazine', iv (1833), pp.449-51.
51 Warwickshire RO DR118/8/iii.
52 BRL Jewel Baillie MSS 254/5.
53 Note the frequent use of older inhabitants to fill in some of the gaps left by lacunae in the documentary evidence. The records of exchequer cases, PRO E112, are replete with such evidence. See also the evidence taken in the Kirk Ella (Yorks., ER) tithe dispute in 1777, A. Wilson Barkworth, 'A History of Tithes in the East Riding of Yorkshire' (unfinished MS) Hull Public Library, L336.21, the evidence of Robert Chapman, 80, of Styal in the Wilmslow dispute, Cheshire RO DDF/61/19, and of Thomas Johnson, a 76-year-old labourer, when Henry Heathcote tried to collect potato tithes in 1789, Lancs. RO DDM 51/75. Richard Goodwin, a defendant in the Cheadle dispute of 1817-36, summoned nine witnesses to testify from their personal experience to the validity of the moduses he claimed. They included the 75-year-old schoolmaster, a farm labourer of 68 and two farmers well into their 60s. Staffs. RO D239/M4180-9.
54 Staffs. RO D239/M4378.
55 Eric J. Evans, A nineteenth-century tithe dispute and its significance: the case of Kendal, 'Transactions of the Cumberland and Westmorland Antiquarian and Archaeological Society', lxxiv (1974), pp.159-83.
56 'Gentleman's Magazine', i (1731), pp.110-11.
57 LJRO B/V/6, Haughton.
58 Ibid. B/A/19. Letter Book C, Haworth to Graysbrook, 6 February 1830.
59 Ibid. B/C/5 (Add ser.), Darwall to Buckeridge, 24 December 1783.
60 'T.B.', 'A Concise Exposition of the Trades and Arts used in the Collection of Easter Dues' (Manchester, 1800) (copy in Lancs. RO).
61 Lancs. RO DDPd 45/7. For other examples see ibid. PR2863/2/ 42 and LJRO B/A/19. Book B, Mott to Hickings, 12 November 1829.

Chapter 3

62   LJRO B/A/19. Book H, Mott to Brunion, 5 November 1833.
63   Ibid. Book E, Mott to Beech, 28 June 1831.
64   BRL Jewel Baillie MSS 77c/1/28 and PRO IR 18/10547.
65   LJRO B/C/5, 1747-8, Dronfield.
66   LCA Ingilby MSS 2774.
67   Lancs. RO DDM 11/61. For other examples of compromise see the agreement between the incumbent of Gargrave and his parishioners in 1788, LCA Stansfield MSS 865/D/3/2 and the agreement to end a chancery suit in Culcheth, Lancs. RO DX 496.
68   LJRO Misc. unsorted cause papers, Worfield.
69   Lancs. RO DDM 51/75.
70   Staffs. RO D(W) 1721/3/239. Delves to Bagot, 17 March 1785.
71   See for example at Kendal, Evans, loc. cit. p.164, in Aston, BRL Jewel Baillie MSS 254/5, at Wolstanton in 1772 when 56 inhabitants joined the subscription to defend themselves against the vicar, Sneyd MSS, University of Keele, S.97 (uncat.). In Halsall, 237 inhabitants joined together to defend themselves successfully against the claims of Rev. Glover Moore, Lancs. RO PR 284 and DDHu 48/158.
72   Reginald Bligh, 'The History of a Tithe Cause' (1815), p.8 (copy in Northumb. RO ZAN M12/B19).
73   'The Church of England Bulwark & Clergyman's Protector', i (1828), p.332.
74   Ibid. pp.16-18.
75   Northumb. RO ZBM 12.
76   PRO E112/2334 No.22.
77   Staffs. RO D593/K/1/3/25. Fenton to Brandon and Cattlow, 7 September 1832.
78   Ibid. D593/E/7/16b.
79   Ibid. D593/K/3/26. Lewis to Loch, 5 February 1838.
80   Ibid. D593/K/1/3/30. Fenton to Loch, 10 January 1841.
81   PRO C13/1579, Oliver and Latham, and Staffs. RO D593/K/1/5/39, Oliver to Duke of Sutherland, 14 December 1840.
82   Staffs. RO D593/K/1/3/30. Fenton to Loch, 10 January 1841.
83   Ibid. D593/E/7/16b.
84   Ibid. D593/K/1/5/39. Oliver to Duke of Sutherland, 14 December 1840.
85   Ibid. D593/E/7/16b.
86   Ibid. D593/K/1/3/33. Fenton to Loch, 24 February 1844.
87   Matthew, x v.8.
88   A brief statement why the religious Society of Friends object to the payment of tithes, printed in MYM, xxiv (1832), pp.136-52. Quaker sources, unless otherwise stated, are housed in the Library of Friends House, Euston Road, London NW1.
89   By 7 & 8 Will. III c.34.
90   Anon., 'A Brief Account of the Prosecution of Quakers' (London, 1736), Friends House Tracts 145/1. On prosecutions, see A. Braithwaite, Early Quaker tithe prosecutions, 'Journal of the Friends Historical Society', xlix, no. 3 (1960), pp.148-56. A view less sympathetic to the Friends' own claims will be found in Eric J. Evans, 'Our faithful testimony': the Society of Friends and tithe payments,

1690-1730, ibid. lii no. 2 (1969), pp.106-21. On the Quaker Tithe Bill campaign of 1736 see N.C. Hunt, 'Two Early Political Associations' (Oxford, 1961), pp.62-112. For a more detailed survey of the Friends' attitudes to tithe, see Eric J. Evans, 'A History of the Tithe System in England, 1690-1850, with special reference to Staffordshire' (unpublished PhD thesis University of Warwick, 1970), pp.178-239.
91 J. Gough, 'A History of the People called Quakers', 4 vols (1789-90), ii, pp.414-15.
92 Hunt, op. cit. pp.64-72.
93 Evans, thesis, pp.185-200.
94 Cumberland and Westmorland RO (Carlisle), D/Ben 431^1 and 372.
95 Cheshire RO EFC 1/10/2 and 3.
96 Herefordshire and Worcestershire RO (Hereford), A85/1a.
97 MMS xxiv, pp.221-2.
98 MYM xiii (1769), p.521 and xiv (1770), p.109.
99 J.C. Atkinson, 'Forty Years in a Moorland Parish', 2nd ed. (1891), p.224.
100 LJRO B/C/5 1781-8 (Add.ser.) and MMS xxxiii, pp.160-2.
101 MMS xxix (1751-2), pp.75-8.
102 For further details, see Evans, thesis, pp.217-20.
103 53 Geo. III c.127.
104 5 & 6 Will. IV c.74, clause ii.
105 MYM xxiv, pp.360 and 449-52.

CHAPTER 4

THE MOUNTING PRESSURE FOR REFORM

I

By the end of the eighteenth century, the old tithe system had few friends. Such as they were, their voices were drowned by enemies loquacious in their condemnation. As Geoffrey Best observed, 'Many more books and pamphlets must have been written about tithes than about any other of the conventionally distinguished departments of church affairs.' (1) This writing was concentrated in the period after about 1770 when the twin challenges of tithe-free industrial expansion and increased interest in agricultural improvement brought the system under its harshest scrutiny. Of all the issues raised in pamphlet or periodical none was more important than that stated concisely by Adam Smith. In 'Wealth of Nations', tithe was listed as one of the 'effectual bars' in the chapter on discouragement of agriculture. (2) In 'Political Arithmetic', published two years before the appearance of Smith's great work, Arthur Young argued that tithing in kind dampened all ideas of agricultural improvement. (3) He returned to the same theme in the very first issue of 'Annals of Agriculture' ten years later: (4)

> Tythes are so powerful an obstacle to all spirited husbandry that it can never arise under the extreme burden of their being taken in kind.... It is beyond all the powers of calculation and conjecture what is the amount of annual loss sustained by the community in consequence of this most ill-judged system being continued in such effective force over the kingdom.

It is obviously important to attempt an assessment of the extent to which tithes deterred agricultural improvement. At first glance, given the dramatic increase in agricultural productivity and the apparently inexorable march of the plough up more and more unlikely hillsides, particularly during the French war period (1793-1815), it does not appear that Smith and Young have much of a case. Demonstrably there was vast improvement which was not stifled. The degree of change was such that most writers have argued or assumed that this was the critical period of the agricultural revolution. (5) Chambers and Mingay, in their survey of the period, suggest, though after only a cursory examination, that tithes were 'hardly a real bar to improvement'. (6) Professor Thompson also argues that tithe was a greater psychological than a practical barrier to improvement. (7)

Current opinion flies in the face of most contemporary views which were firmly in the camp authoritatively occupied by Adam Smith and Arthur Young. Their message, and a seductive one during the freak boom of the French war period, was improvement at all costs. More cultivation, and more scientific use of existing farming land, was necessary to feed a rapidly growing population and to maintain self-sufficiency when an ever larger proportion of this population were no longer food producers. Not only was waste land an abomination to the improvers but much pasture should be ploughed up and converted to arable production to swell the national granaries and fortify the country against the French. Some writers took up the cause with such messianic zeal that their sense of perspective was lost. An 'anonymous friend to improvement', believed to be Sir John Sinclair, President of the newly-established Board of Agriculture, resorted to bad verse to drive his point home. Of tithing in kind he exhorted: (8)

> Let us cut off these legal bars
> Which crush the culture of our fruitful Isle
> Were they removed unbounded wealth would flow
> And England soon a second Eden prove.

Rev. James Willis, in an essay which won the Bedfordean Gold Medal for an original contribution to the cause of agricultural improvement, argued that payments in kind had effectively checked 'a due course of husbandry on our whole lands'. 'Our population is lessened also by the neglecting the cultivation of our wastes, the very means we now especially want of raising more supplies, and more people to consume them.' (9) 'Celerius' believed that tithes were primarily responsible for the unproductive condition of 'large tracts of moor, and waste lands capable of much improvement'. (10) A meeting of Devon landowners in Exeter in 1830 declared: (11)

> That the Tythe Laws are most injurious to the interests of agriculture as they are most often an absolute bar to improvement, and are at all times most discouraging to the Farmer, as by their operation he is placed in a worse and different situation than any other speculator, since by embarking his capital in Agricultural pursuits he becomes liable to have the tenth part of his capital taken from him by the Tythe-holder, who, without capital, labour, or risk, frequently derives considerable profit, in instances where the cultivator himself is a loser.

The basic argument rarely varied, though in some writings it was assumed without formal presentation. The great bulk, if not all, the net profit left to the farmer after his heavier initial expenditure in draining, marling and fertilizing was eaten away by the rapacious impropriator or clergyman's tenth. This profit varied according to the quality of the soil. Adam Smith explained: (12)

> The tythe, and every other land-tax of this kind, under the

appearance of perfect equality, are very unequal taxes;
a certain portion of the produce being in different situations,
equivalent to a very different part of the rent.... Upon
the rent of rich lands, the tythe may sometimes be a tax of
no more than one fifth part, or four shillings in the pound;
whereas on that of poorer lands it may sometimes be a tax of
one half, or ten shillings in the pound.

Sir James Sinclair made the similar calculation that a farmer on poorer soils paid effectively twice as much as his more fortunate neighbour. (13) The moral was obvious. In certain situations the whole enterprise of improvement was thwarted by the tithe system.

Examples may be readily cited of farmers neglecting or abandoning improvements and blaming their failure on tithes. John Curwen, a leading protagonist of tithe reform, related the story of a 'gentleman improver' who amazed his farming colleagues by producing a good oat crop from a Cumberland fell, but abandoned the project in the third season because of the burden of tithes and taxes. 'Indeed', Curwen commented, 'the greatest improvers in the country whether landlords or tenants seem to be persuaded that under existing circumstances such improvements are a losing trade; therefore (they) are laying down their lands to grass and allowing those that are unimproved to remain so.' (14) When a tithe cause went against him, a hop farmer in Denbys (Surrey) 'grubbed up his hops, sowed grass-seeds, and made a pasture of his land. Thus was the produce of upwards of thirty pounds an acre reduced to three.' (15) A correspondent to Cobbett's 'Political Register' told how a friend had made great efforts to improve barren land in the Mendips only to be faced with a tithe demand of 10s per acre in the first year. 'The gentleman discontinued any farther improvements in enclosing his waste land, from the rapacity of this man's exorbitant demand. Such vultures, such bloodsuckers are the generality of tithe owners.' (16)

Such examples were of course chosen by their respective contributors and editors precisely because they were extreme. A study of the relevant estate records, however, does tend to confirm that farmers made fairly precise calculations of possible outlay before embarking on large-scale improvement of marginal land. It is not necessary to accept the typicality of the above examples to argue that in many instances the tithe system made an appreciable difference to the course of cultivation. At Alton (Staffs.), James Bull, a ten-acre farmer, converted his meadow into pasture by turning cattle on to his land when faced with what he considered an excessive demand for tithe hay. (17) At Stamfordham (Northumberland) the agent of the Bishop of Durham in the 1790s let the tithes annually to the farmers rather than draw the tithe. He stated that this kept poorer quality land in tillage which would otherwise revert to pasture. In neighbouring townships where part of the land was covered by a modus, that portion was kept in tillage while the rest was largely grass. (18) The valuer of Coppenhall (Cheshire) rectory in 1833 observed that the arable land in the parish was 'generally of a cold and not productive quality' but that it produced lower yields than it should under proper management. Tithe had been drawn in kind for the previous seven years, during which time the arable acreage had declined. The valuer believed that the best solution was to offer all the tithes to the respective landowners, thus at once securing the income of the rectory and providing a base from which improvement could begin. (19) When the Earl of Sefton wished to bring 'several tracts of Heath and uncultivated land' in his parish under the plough in 1781, the agent was careful to negotiate a period of twelve years during which time the rector would take no tithe from the lands thus improved. (20)

It is significant that some of the leading opponents of the hotly contested Needwood Forest enclosure were tithe owners who feared that the farmers would utilize the changes to their detriment. Their main concern was that the enclosure would exonerate tithes over most of the forest, leaving only the old enclosures tithable. (21)

> And the consequence will be that the new allotted Lands will be ploughed and sown with Corn tythe free, while the Former enclosures will be laid down to Grass, and pay little or no Tythe. So that the Rectors of Hamstal Ridware, Rolleston and Scropton will not only receive no Tythe in respects of the new Allotment to each Parish, and the duties consequent upon it, but they will lose the great part of the Tythes which they before possessed.

Also farmers who held modus land as part of their estate were in a favourable position to arrange their crops so as to minimize the burden of tithes. When Charles Bill, impropriator of the Alton tithes, demanded an increased composition from a prominent farmer, Matthew Smith, in 1786 he received the following dusty and revealing reply: (22)

> Hond. Sir,
>
> I recd Youres, and am Sorrey to find you so Obstenate respecting the tithe hay - Donte deny but it may be worth the money you ask if the whether cold (could) be Instrured (entrusted) but Considering the hazard am Unwilling to Pay more than 3/- per Acer, including the Seed Grass, and other Inferior Land. Think it a verry fair Price. If you are determined of so unpresented a Price it will Put Me uppon a footing that I whould not wish to Pershue, as I have it in my Power to Evade myself of paying tithe Corn at all by taking other lands into my hands wher the tith is my one (own) Property and Likewise Mowing the whater meadow wich onely pays a small Modus.
>
> It gives me Concern that a Gentleman of youre Great abillityes should throw cold whater uppon Industarey.

In the corn-growing south, particularly on poorer lands, complaints were heard that tithes in deterring improvement were exacerbating an already acute excess of labour supply. Thus tithes were even blamed for part of the growing poor-rate burden by keeping labourers on the rates when they could have been employed in labour-intensive improvements. Farmers were always anxious to convince the government that excessive taxation was at the root of their troubles, and many took their

Chapter 4

opportunity to tell Select Committees that tithe was an unfair
tax which held them back from investment which would help not
only them but their labourers and the country at large. (23)
Ashurst Majendie, whose task it was to collect evidence for the
Select Committee on the Poor Laws from the 'Swing' counties of
Surrey, Sussex and Kent, reported that when negotiations for
a tithe composition broke down at Northam (Sussex) in 1829,
farmers refrained from improvements and 'the employment of
labourers has been thereby much checked'. At Marden (Kent) the
farmers were determined to 'throw on the lessee of the great
tithes part of the payment of wages: they prefer letting their
land be ill cultivated to the permitting the tithe owner to
profit by a better mode of culture'. At Hawkhurst (Kent) where
tithes were taken in kind by a layman on a lease from Christ
Church (Oxford) the land was in a very bad state. 'As there
exists a low modus on grass-land, some of the proprietors and
occupiers are laying down to pasture land well adopted to the
growth of hops and corn.' From Barton Stacey (Hants),
Captain Pringle reported great pressure on the poor rates since
a leading proprietor deliberately chose to keep his lands out of
cultivation to prevent a heavy tithe burden. From two farms
alone, twenty-four persons were thrown on to the parish. (24)
Mr Stuart explained how tithe disputes could affect the livelihood of labourers in Suffolk:

> When any individual chooses to quarrel with the parson, he
> gratifies his spite by having the tithes rated, and then
> pays off all his labourers who have settlements in the
> parish, and hires men from other parishes for the purpose
> of being revenged by the heavy contribution which will fall
> on the parson, although it is to his own hurt and that of
> all his neighbours.

It was alleged from Hurstmonceux and Pulborough (Sussex) that
'the whole labour has been thrown upon the rates, for the
'avowed' purpose of fighting the person'. (25)

Farmers themselves were ready enough to confirm these stories.
George Webb Hall, who farmed 700 acres near Bristol argued
that it was crucial to his improvement ventures not to have
tithe exceed 3s an acre. 'If the tithe had been taken in kind,
I dare not have cultivated it the way I have done; my tithe
taken at the gross tenth, might have been in some cases more
than the rent; it might have been 40/- an acre on some of my
crops.' (26) John Ellman said that the tithe owner took all
the profit from his improvements, (27) and John Christian Curwen,
MP, told the Select Committee in 1821 that he knew 'of no
situation where the tithe is drawn (i.e. taken in kind) that
the cultivation is not in a very inferior state'. (28)

It is important to get this descriptive evidence in perspective.
Most witnesses gave evidence at times (1821-3 and 1833-6) when
most agricultural historians are agreed the shoe pinched
particularly hard. Farmers wanted government relief and
believed the best way to get it was by a doleful recital of
the burdens under which they laboured. Tithe was only one of
many of these. When the Board of Agriculture sent out a
questionnaire in 1816 asking farmers to itemize the main reasons

for their distress, only 47 of the 326 replies made specific reference to tithe. (29) A catalogue of complaints inevitably distorts. Tithe was not a universal grievance, nor was it so frequently voiced by the agricultural interest as was criticism of the poor laws when rates quadrupled in just over forty years. (30) The problem was, however, that where tithe bit as a grievance, it tended to bite hard. Given the huge disparity of tithing customs over the whole country, it is not surprising that there should have been differential effects. Many farmers could comfortably add tithes to their rent bill in reasonably confident knowledge of total outlay; but no one could be absolutely sure of his ground. A parish in which tithe had been amicably compounded at mutually acceptable rates for a century or more could be plunged into strife and uncertainty by a change of incumbency or the falling in of a lease. Such events were not unusual, and they made nonsense of finely calculated amounts of yield or profit. The uncertainty of the unreformed tithe system was its greatest curse, and it had its effect on land use. Estate records tend to show that improvement was more readily put in train on land which was either tithe free or covered by small moduses, despite the fact that it was invariably subject to a higher rent. Tithe free land which came on to the market was advertised prominently as such, being considered a clear selling point.

Not all the cards were stacked on the tithe owner's side, however. It can be clearly shown that in many instances farmers were able to browbeat tithe owners into accepting much less than their tenth. (31) It is clear also that many clergymen took far less than their due, or allowed compositions to remain undisturbed for years on end while inflation ate into the true value of their livings, in order to buy peace and maintain a viable ministry. Crafty and case-hardened farmers were often more than a match for callow new incumbents and manoeuvered them into a position of weakness. Even lay impropriators, regarded as harsher task masters than their clerical counterparts, were taking less than the true value of their tithes in most cases. So there were factors which could work in favour of would-be improvers, and there is no doubt that many of them grossly overstated their case against tithes, as Chambers and Mingay suggest. Yet a crippling uncertainty about the true nature of the burden remained.

The overall picture on tithe and improvement does not entirely square with Chambers and Mingay's somewhat dismissive view. Tithe was indeed an 'effectual bar' to improvement when taken in kind, and it could be on the less naturally productive soils. Both of these factors were operative in much of the south-east of England, and it is, therefore, not surprising that the bulk of the opposition to tithes comes from this area, and from the extreme north-west where tithe was also commonly taken in kind and soils were for the most part unreceptive. The Board of Agriculture surveys of the 1790s and 1800s further emphasize the differential effect. The Hertfordshire reviewer noted that most tithe owners took moderate compositions which left farmers free to improve, but when a new tithe owner insisted on taking his

produce in kind or refused to renew a lease 'the tenants
immediately cross-crop, and continue that practice till they are
turned out'. Tithe stakes were frequently left rotting in the
fields in rainy seasons for want of adequate collection
facilities when trust and sympathy between tithe owner and
farmer had broken down. (32) The Buckinghamshire reviewer
pointed out the great disparity in the tithe levied 'from the
farmer who goes on the old beaten track of his ancestors ...
compared to the man who aims at improvement'. (33) In
Denbighshire, it was noted that progress in improvement had been
'languid'. Tithe payments which frequently accounted for the
entire profit were blamed: (34)

> Extensive tracts of land are left in England in perpetual
> grass, when it is by no means in a condition for yielding
> the most abundant produce in that state. The quality of
> bread corn is thus necessarily diminished, and with it the
> total amount of food even for beasts is curtailed. Nothing
> can be so ruinous to agriculture.

In Warwickshire the situation was satisfactory (35)

> where lands have been regularly and well cultivated for a
> great length of time ... as in that case it is chiefly a
> tax on the land-owner ... but where much improvement is
> wanted ... almost the whole value of the land depends upon
> personal labour, skill and industry ... & something seems
> necessary to be done to remove so great a bar to the improve-
> ment of such unproductive land.

The Derbyshire reviewer, pointing out that one of the largest
estates in the county was now splendidly productive, thought it
not without significance that there 'the agreeing for the tithes
is left entirely between the clergy and the occupiers of the
land'. (36) Davies's Oxfordshire review was much more sceptical.
He frankly doubted whether tithes were 'such an obstacle to
improvements as sometimes presented'. As few farmers had the
opportunity to work both tithable and non-tithable land the
prospects for profit maximization by selective improvement were
strictly limited. (37)

Those who minimize the disincentives of the tithe system
seem to have over-reacted to the undoubted exaggerations of the
late eighteenth-century writers and proselytizers on agriculture.
It is quite true that many of these isolated this one factor
and used it as a popular target of abuse, thus obscuring the
complexities of the improvement equation. As the Cornish vicar,
Morgan Cove, commented at the time: 'Every shaft which
ingenuity wit or malice could devise hath been levelled against
them insomuch as there is hardly an imaginary or real grievance
with which this country is so pathetically said to be oppressed
which hath not been attributed to the payment of tithes.' (38)
But tithing in kind did survive to remain the dominant form of
collection in some areas. Many lands which were legitimate
targets for improvement even after the great agricultural boom
broke in 1813 required heavy initial capital injections and
these threw into sharp relief the difference between a tenth
of the gross and a tenth of the net produce. Although many
agriculturalists were hopelessly optimistic about the kinds of

soil susceptible to permanent improvement, given the diffusion of contemporary technology, it remains true that tithe was a disincentive to many quite viable improvement schemes. If a simple generalization may be hazarded in this most complex area it is that tithes played a significant part in sharpening the unequal struggle between heavy clays and lighter soils. (39) This battle was particularly ferocious after about 1813 when falling arable prices hit the less productive soils much harder. When tithe in kind was demanded from naturally unproductive land the effect on improvement possibilities was dramatic if not catastrophic.

Tithe, then, was particularly liable to be troublesome on poorer lands, and when heavier than normal initial investment was required. It is perhaps easiest to demonstrate this in the case of hop cultivation which was widespread in Kent, Essex, Suffolk, Worcestershire and Herefordshire. Hops could be extremely profitable, but the crop was something of a speculative investment. It was more liable to sudden failure than most others and it was expensive to cultivate. Arthur Young thought hops 'the gambling of farmers' with promises of rich rewards too often dashed by harsh experience. (40) As a valuable cash crop, it naturally attracted the attention of tithe owners. The Staffordshire agriculturalist William Pitt believed that the 'tythe of hops is more particularly complained of than that of any other article, and considering the very great expense at which they are cultivated, it appears to be with reason'. (41) The Smithite calculations of tithe as a differential tax were perfectly demonstrated here. Compositions for hop tithes were regularly set at £1 per acre or more when the best wheat rarely fetched more than 12s to 14s. After specialist cultivation this represented much more than a tenth of the gross produce and when the crop failed, or even when its yield was moderately disappointing, tithe could be a heavy burden indeed.

The Farnham (Surrey) hop tithe dispute of the 1790s illustrated most of the inherent problems. It began when a new lessee of the Archdeacon of Surrey paid £16,000 for a lease of three lives of the Farnham tithes. (42) Having ascertained that hop tithes had been compounded for at £1 an acre for several years, while prices in general had been rising, the lessee, Henry Halsey, commissioned a new survey as a result of which he determined to raise the compositions to £3 per acre. The only alternative for the farmers was to submit to tithing in kind. A tithe defence association was hastily formed by the proprietors but no modus or exemption could be claimed, and it was decided to obtain sympathy in the face of an unprecedented demand by seeking publicity. Arthur Young was only too pleased to use the pages of the 'Annals of Agriculture' to spread news of a real tithe grievance, and he gave the issue prominent coverage. The farmers argued that the new composition would drive many of them out of business and straight on to the swelling poor rates. With hops less extensively grown, government revenues would suffer. Beer would cost more, and probably taste worse. The blame for this disaster would rest squarely 'with those laws respecting tythes which in the hands

of avaricious and tyrannical men, are the engines of the most
grievous exactions and cry aloud for renovation or repeal'.
Collection of the tithe in kind, they argued, 'would not only
be a very great inconvenience but, from the difficulty of
picking and setting them out, it would frequently be the loss
of half in value to the planter, by the necessary mode of giving
the tenth to the impropriator'. (43)

The publicity afforded by the 'Annals' was designed to shame
the lessee into reducing his 200 per cent increase. When it
failed the only resort was an appeal to Parliament. The legislature had, after all, made special provision for hemp, flax
and madder growers in 1699 and 1757 (44) and hop farmers
contended that they had a similar case for protection. The
crop was a difficult one, but its cultivation directly benefited
the nation, had in recent years become an article of export
and was 'productive of a large Yearly Revenue to Government'.
(45) A petition, bearing fifty-three signatures from Farnham,
was presented to the Commons in 1792. Unusually, the matter
was taken up. In 1793, the petition was referred to an 'ad
hoc' committee which called for relevant evidence. The hop
planters eagerly seized the opportunity for a further presentation of their case. They argued that their work greatly
eased the local poor rate burden by providing employment for
their labourers for a full eight months of the year. Many
argued that they would grub up their plantations rather than pay
tithe in kind. One recalled a recent instance of a 400 acre
field near Canterbury being left uncultivated 'in consequence
of Tythe in Kind having been demanded'. (46)

The Committee in due course presented to the Commons a
report favourable to the planters. The lessee produced a
petition of his own in which he argued that any Bill to regulate
compositions for hop tithes would injure not only himself,
but the archdeacon of Surrey and, by heavy implication, the
interests of the Church of England. (47) Such an appeal
would not go unheeded. By 1793 an ever increasing number of
MPs were fearful of the irreligious and subversive doctrines
which the English Jacobins had imported from France, and it
was deemed necessary to reinforce the traditional structure
of authority by reasserting the importance of the link between
church and state. (48) Edmund Burke, who had seemed a wild
voice crying wolf in 1790 when his 'Reflections on the
Revolution in France' was published, now appeared as the true
prophet whose words all property holders must heed. In a
central passage, Burke had emphasized that established church
and state must stand or fall together. (49)

The Farnham hop planters, therefore, had stirred up issues
deeper than they knew. They had given the conservative interest,
already dominant in Parliament, an opportunity to rehearse
arguments familiar to all historians interested in the struggle
for reform between 1789 and 1832. In this crucial respect,
1793 was not 1699 or 1757. Arguments in favour of a necessary
stimulus for a particular industry were countered by fears of
the interference with the delicate mechanism which bound church
and state together, and thus secured the stability of society.

In the fevered climate of the 1790s, the winner of that argument was never in doubt. Even so, the language employed by the conservative interest seems extreme. The attorney-general, Sir John Scott, (50) called the Bill 'the most violent measure that had ever been attempted to be carried through Parliament'. Sir John Bedford, solicitor-general, believed that it 'militated against every principle on which rested the sacred and inviolable security of private property'. (51) Both men would have plenty of opportunity in the ensuing years to practise their hyperbole on proposals of still more radical intent, but their bludgeons on this occasion were more than enough for the wretched Farnham hop planters. The majority effectively killed the Bill by referring it back to Committee at the very end of the session. (52)

The Farnham case at once showed what a disincentive to improvement tithes could be, and also how long and difficult would be the road to reform. Tithe reform proposals were inextricably bound up with the reform question in general, since the Tories were not slow to hoist yet again the tired banner of 'The Church in Danger'. Overwhelmingly strong cases for reform of particular abuses were to be deflected for more than thirty years by generalized expressions of fear for the established constitution of church and state. It is no accident that tithe reform was delayed until the larger nettle of political reform had been finally grasped by a fearful but beleaguered Parliament and a newly elected Whig government in the 1830s.

II

The agricultural interest, vociferously represented by the arch-priests of improvement, was in the forefront of attacks on the unreformed tithe system. They were most forceful on the issue of disincentives, but this did not exhaust their armoury. Comparability arguments featured almost as prominently. Why should the agriculturalist pay a heavy tax on yield, which increased as efficiency brought more crops, when the new industrialists escaped without penalty? John Payne argued that the iron master or the lawyer would think it outrageous to give a tenth of all he produced and concluded that tithe was not so much a land tax as a tax 'upon capital and labour and no law can give one man a right to the produce of the labour of another without deserving the epithets "odious and oppressive"'. (53) The Hull banker and evangelical MP, Thomas Thompson made the same point more succinctly: 'Is it equitable that, whenever I work for myself, I should be compelled to work for another person also?' (54) Arthur Young drew on the experience of his famous Travels to make harsh comparisons between England and the Continent, (55) and 'Farmers' Magazine' suggested that the absence of tithe in Scotland since the middle of the seventeenth century had contributed towards the fact that public burdens did not hit Scottish tenants much harder than a 1d in the pound rent. (56)

It was argued that tithe slowed down the rate of investment in

agriculture. An 'Old Correspondent' to the 'Bath and West of England Agricultural Society Journal', for example, argued that when £8 or £10 was spent: (57)
> Liming, marling, sub-draining, fallowing and improving land ... taking one tenth of the crop before he is repaid his expenses will turn the balance of the account against him.... He had better lay out his money at interest or in some other way, and live in idleness (as thousands do) to the great injury of the publick.

Political economy added another dimension to the argument when David Ricardo produced his famous 'Principles of Political Economy'. Ricardo sought to combat Adam Smith's argument on tithe by declaring that, far from being an unequal tax, tithe operated in common with all taxes on raw produce by passing the ultimate burden of payment on to the consumer in the form of higher prices for agricultural produce. Tithe was not, therefore, primarily an agricultural burden, but should be the concern of all: (58)
> I have endeavoured to shew that such taxes do not fall with unequal weight on the different classes of farmers or landlords, as they are both compensated by the rise of raw produce, and only contribute to the tax in proportion as they are consumers of raw produce.

Ricardo hoped to instigate general, rather than sectional, resistance to what he called 'this most oppressive and irritating tax'. (59) J.R. McCulloch, on this subject at least a Ricardian, expanded his mentor's thoughts in a long article in the 'Edinburgh Review' in 1820 which must have been singularly tough meat for those used to the simpler language and precepts of the 'Annals of Agriculture'. (60) He warned against the easy assumption that because tithe was ultimately paid by the consumer its abolition would bring lower prices. If it were abolished, the landlord would immediately raise his rents. Because some land was held tithe-free or covered by moduses, some landlords were making extra profit in the form of higher rents while the consumer footed the bill as if all land were equally affected by the burden. McCulloch proposed a solution which would transfer the burden resulting from rent increasing 'proportionally to the gross produce of the soil' by letting it increase 'proportionally to the net produce of the stock employed in its cultivation'. This was to be achieved by establishing a poundage on rents to which estates previously tithe free should contribute an equal amount. Thus, the clergy would receive their due reward and differentials which had provoked much of the criticism of the system would be swept away. McCulloch submitted a draft of his article to Ricardo, and told him that his analysis was constrained by a politic need to appear fair and dispassionate. 'I should like to have handled the clergy more roughly; but the circulation of the Review in England and their very great influence rendered a degree of "management" quite indispensable'. (61)

Ricardo enjoyed McCulloch's exposition but he did draw attention to an obvious drawback to his suggested solution. In a buoyant market for tithe-free land, McCulloch's plan was gravely unjust: (62)

> Many tithe free farms are yearly brought to market, and an additional price is paid for them in consequence of the peculiar advantage they enjoy. It would surely be very unjust to subject such a proprietor to a tax after his paying a valuable contribution to be exempted from it.

It was easy to draw attention to the evils of tithe - far more difficult to suggest practicable and fair solutions. The anti-tithe campaign contained almost as many alternative schemes for commutation as it did denunciations of the existing system. This lack of harmony indicates the intractability of the problem. It had to be solved, however, because tithe was a form of property and property must be safeguarded. Abolition of tithes never came within the realm of practical politics. Writers had to convince tithe owners that they would benefit from reform just as much as would farmers and landowners. Arthur Young in 1784 declared that the clergy were full of 'groundless apprehensions that their interest would suffer' by commutation. (63) Lena Tadman, a Kentish farmer, before beginning an attack on tithes was careful to swear his allegiance to the established church and to pledge his commitment to protect its revenues: (64)

> My opinion is, that unless we keep in view the support of religion, church and clergy, we shall do harm instead of good, by making any alteration in the tithe laws.... Our established church, religion and ministry must be liberally supported, or England herself must fall which God forbid.

Agriculturalists well knew the importance of the search for alternative provision. Various agricultural societies encouraged their correspondents to submit plans. The Bath and West of England Society went so far as to establish a premium for the best essay received on the subject in the hope that 'by agitating the subject, the attention of ingenious men, both in and out of Parliament, may be the more excited to attempt some possible improvement'. (65) The response was steady and numerous articles resulted. It was clear that three possible solutions might be attempted, if the objection of Parliament to any change affecting the church could be overcome. Enclosures furnished numerous examples of the first: commutation of tithe for land. This was the answer recommended by John Bennett who won the Bath and West of England Society's Bedfordean Gold Medal in 1814 for his tithe essay. His objectives were the standard ones - increasing the cultivation of wastes, thus enabling a growing population to be fed, and ending enmity between clergy and their parishioners. Bennett envisaged that tithe owners would lease the lands they received in lieu of tithes, rather than farm them directly. (66)

There were serious objections, however, to extending the scheme adopted in many enclosures. There was a growing belief that the social structure of the parish would be undermined if its clergyman suddenly joined the ranks of the substantial landowners. There would be no obligation on the clergy to lease their lands, and as McCulloch noted, 'It is extremely difficult to reconcile the two characters of a good farmer and a zealous and attentive clergyman'. (67) Many clergy took the same point, and the Bishop of Salisbury, Shute Barrington, warned the incumbents in his diocese that 'the habits of life in which the clergy are educated, and the important office they fill are ill-suited to the occupation of a farmer'. (68)

For these and other reasons, therefore, Bennett's proposals received only lukewarm support in the early nineteenth century. The same was true of the second answer to the problem of satisfactory commutation - a straight cash sum in exoneration. Tithe owners were sufficiently on top of their business to realize that such a solution would have unfortunate results, especially in a period of considerable inflation. They were unwilling to hazard their property in the hope that prices would remain broadly stable in the foreseeable future, or would decline. The experiences of the last decade of the eighteenth century and the first decade of the nineteenth, after all, lent no support to any such assumption. It is not surprising that attention focused increasingly on the third solution. This eliminated the possibility of tithing in kind, but retained the tithe as a perpetual charge on estates previously burdened with it, but now in the form of a money rent tied to the prevailing price of produce. As the price of corn dictated other price movements and as corn tithes were usually the most valuable, discussion eventually centred on a variable corn rent as a legitimate method of commutation. Pryce's 'Essay on the most practicable method of fixing an equitable commutation for Tithes', which won another prize from the Bath and West of England Society, concluded that a fluctuating corn rent was the most acceptable solution, although he argued that the tithe owner should be under no compulsion to alter satisfactory existing arrangements. (69) He visualized a complex series of arrangements to effect commutation, including expert land surveyors, and tithe commissioners chosen by both sides. To ensure that the value of the tithe rent did not fluctuate too wildly, Pryce proposed a decennial adjustment, dictated by price movements over the preceding period. The rent charge would thus reflect the general trend, and would not bear too heavily in an exceptionally bad single year. Pryce took enclosure proceedings as his model for many of the requisite administrative arrangements, but he proposed that Quarter Sessions should regulate the matter for each award, as Parliament was too remote and uninterested in purely local matters.

Pryce's was only one of many plans for tithe commutation which argued along similar lines. (70) The amount of justice given to the complexity of the task ahead naturally varied from writer to writer, but by the 1820s, informed opinion had swung decisively in favour of a variable corn rent as the most elegant solution to the problem. The problem of persuading Parliament that any alteration was necessary or desirable, however, remained a real one.

William Pitt was one of the few politicians prepared to give the matter much serious consideration before the 1830s. In the period before 1792 when he seriously envisaged reforms and took positive steps to implement them, he became convinced that a

variable corn rent offered the best hope of solution. He believed
that tithe as a 'great obstacle to improvement' should be
commuted, and was further persuaded that commutation would
benefit the church, by removing much of the odium which surrounded
it in many quarters. His naturally cautious disposition, however,
led him to believe that measures for commutation would be better
introduced from the episcopal bench. As he wrote in 1786, (71)
> If, therefore, those who are at the head of the clergy will
> look at it soberly and dispassionately, they will see how
> incumbent it is upon them, in every point of view, to promote
> some temperate accommodation and even the appearance of
> concession which might be awkward in Government, could not
> be unbecoming if it originated with them.

In the next few years, Pitt collected evidence from various
sources about the feasibility of commutation, and received memo-
randa from interested parties setting out the difficulties to be
overcome. (72) In 1791, Lord Auckland urged decisive action to
secure a corn rent: (73)
> Perhaps there never was a moment more favourable than the
> present when the Sovereign, Ministers and the Bulk of the
> Nation are equally and jealously disposed to resist all
> Mischievous innovation and to maintain the rights of the
> Church of England and all essential parts of the Constitution:
> in a season less prosperous and still more in times of
> National Ferment and Trouble and Calamity, the same question,
> if not quieted at present, may be stir'd with great disad-
> vantage and hazard.

Pitt, however, remained convinced that the initiative should come
from the clergy. He wrote to the Archbishop of Canterbury in
December 1791, suggesting that the church should take the lead
'in order that they may be enabled to give a proper direction to
the business'. (74) Pitt received no response, and in any
case within a few months the events in France convinced him that
reforms came a poor second to national security. He continued to
examine proposals for commutation and in 1799 informed the
Archbishop of a scheme to vest income from tithe in the funds,
the proceeds to finance clerical incomes. On this occasion,
the plan was discussed by the episcopal bench, but with the
solitary exception of Richard Watson of Llandaff - the leading
practical farmer among the bishops - it received no support. (75)

III

The amount of popular protest against tithes was limited. Despite
the increasing use of potatoes by labourers in small allotments
or gardens, and the disputes which on occasion followed, most
tithe questions were property disputes, and the propertied
preferred litigation to affray. In south-west England, however,
the situation is slightly different. Here opposition was
especially heated. As the vicar of Sithney (Cornwall) noted
in the 1790s, more meetings had been held in the south-west to
discuss commutation than in any other part of the country. (76)
There are three reasons for heightened opposition in this area.

First, the economies of Devon and Cornwall were to a considerable extent dependent on the fishing industry. Although the right to tithe fish was limited after 1549 to places in which it had been the practice continuously for not less than 40 years, (77) the tradition remained firmly established in this area, and was a source of much bitterness. Second, many fishermen were poor, and totally reliant on their catches for their livelihood. The effects of tithe thus reached further down the social scale here than in most other areas. Third, and perhaps more speculatively, there was the well-established tradition of violence and riot, especially in Cornwall, where the tinners had been useful tutors to the rest of the populace. Tithe riots were not unknown in the south-west, and the tradition of violence persisted. In 1729 a local fisherman murdered a justice's officer sent to enforce collection of fish tithes in the parish of Paul (Cornwall). (78) Lt Col. Elford reported to the Duke of Portland an affray in 1800. When the vicar of Lifton (Devon) came to the local inn to collect his compositions, a body of persons assembled outside the window carrying a red flag 'Calling out "Liberty, Equality and No Tythes", declaring they would not pay a farthing - The leader then fired a Gun loaded with Slugs into the Window which fortunately injured no one, but broke Glasses, Bowles etc'. (79) Thus radical, Jacobin slogans had entered into the anti-tithe campaign in the south-west, anticipating by almost thirty years the efforts of the unstamped press.

A few years earlier, Major General Rooke had reported to Portland that an 'unlawful assembly' might develop near Bristol if a tithe collector attempted to collect produce which had never previously been demanded. (80) His fears proved groundless on this occasion, but the home office papers of the 1790s clearly indicate that those responsible for law and order in the south-west considered tithe a real source of grievance which could lead to riot. The same problem was still exercising local magistrates in the 1830s. A Mr Edmonds, addressing the newly formed National Union of the Working Class in 1832, told of a frustrated attempt to tithe fish. His tale was punctuated by loud cheers from the assembled company: (81)

> About two years ago the fishermen of Penzance were pounced upon by the jackalls of the clergy who came to seize every tenth fish, but the women threw the fish at them and drove them off; they then produced pistols which some of the men took from them and threw into the sea. The next day these men were put into gaol, but the tinners and fishermen assembled and told the magistrates that if they were not released they would pull the gaol down, and they were compelled to release them and the tenth fish was not claimed again. In commemoration of this, the fishermen of Penzance have painted over their ships a death's head and marrow-bones with the motto: 'No tithes'.

Tithe conflict played an important part in the Swing riots of 1830-1. (82) It has been recently suggested that the established clergy were coming under increasing pressure in the late eighteenth and early nineteenth centuries. Many were the subject of local odium as harsh magistrates or parsimonious and insulting administrators of poor relief. (83) Many were also unpopular because of their tithe policy. It is noticeable that there appears in many 'Swing' areas an 'ad hoc' alliance between farmers and labourers to bring pressure on the clergy to reduce their tithes. At Goudhurst (Kent) on 15 November 1830, the farmers told their labourers that they could expect increased wages only if they were able to 'stop the tithes'. (84) At Brede (Sussex), tithes were reduced from £715 to £400 a year, and in Robertsbridge the tithe owner was forced to reduce his tithes by 25 per cent, the labourers telling him 'that it should be done to enable the farmers to pay them higher wages'. (85) The curate of West Chiltington (Sussex) accused the farmers in his parish of 'instigating the people to assemble in order to intimidate and compel the clergy to reduce their tithes'. (86) The evidence of collusion between farmers and labourers is even plainer in East Anglia. In Suffolk, Col. Brotherton identified 'collusion ... amounting almost to a case of conspiracy' and Lord Suffield agreed that the farmers 'have in some instances been supposed to incite and encourage the late outrageous proceedings (and) to have suggested the outcry against Tithes and Rents'. (87)

It would be easy, but probably misleading, to assume that the alliance between farmers and labourers was at the dictation of, and purely in the interests of, the former. Farmers were, of course, able to hold a pistol to the heads of their destitute labourers, but their alliance suggests at least a degree of genuine common interest. There is little evidence to suggest that the clergy's relations with the poorer sections of the community were cordial and much circumstantial material relating to the administration of the parish which indicates that the poor were not unwilling conscripts in the farmers' campaign to screw lower tithes. We still await a detailed study of the established church at the beginning of the nineteenth century; but it seems that such a study would reveal widespread social and cultural dislocation. The clergy received more than their share of threatening letters and other clear manifestations of the discontent of the lower orders. (88) If farmers used their labourers, it would be unwise to assume that the lower orders then acted without premeditation on their own account. 'Hodge' was uneducated, but it is imprudent to argue that he was entirely stupid. The clergy were attacked at least in part because it was felt that they no longer discharged their pastoral duties sympathetically in the interests of the community as a whole.

IV

While agriculturalists and political economists anxiously searched for a viable alternative to the old tithe system, and in particular for the means to secure tithe owners' incomes in a more acceptable fashion, the radicals had an altogether shorter way. They rejected commutation in favour of abolition. Attacks on the tithe system formed part of their general pantechnicon of 'Reform'. Tithe was an integral part of Old Corruption and must be swept away with rotten boroughs, tax-eaters, corn laws, Parson Malthus and the rest. Tithes had no foundation in New Testament theology. As the 'Extraordinary Black Book', the most comprehensive critic of the church establishment, put it: 'Christianity contains less authority for tithe than Judaism. Jesus Christ ordained no such burden; and in no part of his history is any compulsory provision for the maintenance of the clergy mentioned.' (89) Further, if tithes had any authenticity as compulsory payments, it had long since been ceded by the perversion of the original uses to which tithes were supposed to have been applied. The arguments about triple and even quadruple divisions of tithe were trotted out to suggest that tithe owners were entitled to no more than a third or a quarter of the total dues collected. (90) 'One thing, however, is certain as regards tithes, namely that in England, in France and probably in all Christian countries they were divided into four portions: one for the bishop, one for the poor, one for the repair of the Church and one for the Priest.' (91)

William Cobbett attempted to draw the lessons which the history of tithes taught him. He was particularly concerned to emphasize that tithe was not a property which could be taken over by the landowner, and that it should in part be applied to relieve the poor. (92) It was public property, rather than church property, and should be disposed of 'as the Parliament shall please' for the public benefit. (93) Cobbett was the most knowledgeable of the radical opponents of tithe. For many others, tithe presented merely a useful stick to beat what the 'Church Examiner' called 'that huge, hideous and lubberly leviathan, the law church'. (94) The main concern of the 'Black Book' was with clerical privilege and the unequal division of church incomes. Tithe formed only a minor part of an attack which concentrated on sinecures and pluralities. Most radicals were outraged by the concept of a church protected by the state and financed by compulsory payments of an odious nature. Perhaps for these reasons, the brunt of the attack was borne by the clergy, although it least a third of all tithes were held by laymen, and were, by general repute, collected by them more harshly and strictly than by the church.

The satirists and cartoonists of the period made much of the stereotype of the fat, bloated and gouty parson stripping poor farmers of their best beasts with singular avarice and lack of charity. (95) The parson clutching his tithe pig symbolized clerical gluttony. Thus Isaac Cruikshank's 'Clerical Anticipation' (1797) has a fat parson with a face suggesting a surfeit of both food and strong drink, leaning over a pig-sty to make his choice of the biggest specimen, (96) while another cartoon has a parson lying flat on his face in a pig-sty whither he had entered to take a fatter animal than the one offered, while a large sow digs her teeth into the clerical rump. The parishioners look on with evident amusement. The cartoon's title is 'Tythe in kind; or the Sow's Revenge'.

By such lampoons as these an indelible image of the clergy was presented which was sufficiently distorted to take on perfect

84 Chapter 4

and luminous reality for those who wished to believe it. Above all, they provided an easy target for town dwellers, unaware of the complexities of the tithe problem, to fasten on to when they included the abolition of tithe as a plank in their radical platform. It must be remembered that most radical writers were town-based and lacked first-hand experience of the operation of the system. In most urban areas, tithe was not a concrete grievance, but this did not hinder the various reform societies, whose activities were given wide coverage in the unstamped press, from supporting motions calling for the abolition of the burden. Edward Edwards tartly criticized the 'weavers of Manchester, the cutlers of Birmingham & the miners of Newcastle' for wishing to put an end to tithes without being aware that in any alternative form of maintenance they might reasonably be expected to make a contribution in taxes which now they were excused. (97)

Certainly, the language used in abolition resolutions was extreme, and the resolutions themselves were clearly dependent on second-hand evidence. The following, from a meeting of the Ashton-under-Lyne Reform Society in 1831, is typical. It calls for the abolition of the Corn Laws, demands wider parliamentary representation, condemns the usurpations of the aristocracy and continues: (98)

> That the tithe system, or revenues of the church, as they are denominated, are unjust as they are tyrannic. They are unjust as they take from the useful and industrious part of society a tenth of the products and improvements of the land to support luxury and idleness. They are tyrannic as they are taken as a substitute for a public robbery committed by a tyrant King, who seized the lands and revenues appropriated for the support of the church and distributed them among an overgrown aristocracy.

Certain radical journals attempted to stimulate greater opposition from the lower orders to tithes than had previously been shown in England. They had, of course, the example of Ireland before them, where opposition from a Catholic majority to paying dues to alien clergymen and impropriators had resulted in violence which exercised the administration to a much greater extent. (99) The 'Church Examiner' stated in August 1832: 'The anti-tithe feeling is certainly not confined to Ireland - it is nearly as strong in England, though at present less obvious. The RESISTANCE, however, is becoming epidemic.' (100) The wish here was father to the thought. Tithe resistance in England was localized and for the most part confined to those who could afford to wage their war in the courts. The contrast between Ireland and England was stark. In Ireland, there was still a largely primitive agrarian, peasant economy in which the great majority of the population, poor as well as rich, paid tithes to heretic priests and alien landlords. England was experiencing an increasingly diversified economy, with rapid industrialization, virtually no peasantry, the towns largely exempt, and in the country Anglican squire or tenant farmer paying to Anglican parson - certainly grudgingly, but with no feeling that he was bolstering an alien regime. In Ireland tithe payments symbolized for many a national disaster which every Catholic was expected to fight. The differential response is hardly surprising.

Nevertheless, the newspapers plugged away, trying to find comparisons between the two countries to light the spark of tithe resistance in England. Hetherington exhorted his readers in 1832: (101)

> Need we cheer you up by the example of those who address you to a similar kind of opposition to TITHE PLUNDER which is equally unjust in this country as in Ireland? Need we exhort you to that resistance so earnestly recommended to you by your fellow sufferers who have already proved its success, not in the resistance of force or violence but of moral, powerful determination not to saction its exertions by voluntary money payments or to countenance its legal recovery by the purchase of articles distrained for its enforcement! Do you in like manner resist tithes and church rates and thereby strengthen the struggle of poor Ireland.

The response was slow, but each instance of communal opposition was rapturously received. In Glossop in 1832, townspeople hindered the vicar's tithe collectors, and when their leaders were brought before two magistrates, they refused to commit them. The 'Church Examiner' commented: 'Thank God! We are at length beginning to see the fruit of our labours, and to the people of Derbyshire, where we know our work is extensively read, belongs the honour of first exhibiting public hostility to the odious tithe impost.' (102) Derbyshire did not, however, rise in tithe revolt. Nor did the rest of England. Such opposition as there was remained isolated and sporadic, a subject of remark rather for its singularity than for indicating a new trend in opposition to tithe payment. The radical press were grateful indeed to the rector of Lockington in the East Riding for attempting to reintroduce the defunct personal tithe on labourers' wages. As a result, one agricultural worker, Jeremiah Dodsworth, was compelled to pay 4d in the pound for tithe on his wages and committed to Beverley house of correction in 1832 for his recalcitrance. The press inveighed against the iniquity of such a burden and tried to make this isolated instance into a crusading cause. Hetherington asked: 'Why should a poor agricultural labourer be taxed a sixtieth of his little wages to the Church while the large increases of a Rothschild in commerce, a Scarlett at the bar or a Halford in Physic are spared the impost?' (103)

A few more instances could be dredged up, but they did not amount to much. When John Pearson, a Rochdale weaver, was arrested in December 1833 for arrears of Easter dues, his property was distrained and to be auctioned to clear the debt. The only bidders, however, were the bailiffs themselves. The sale 'did not last above ten minutes and the proceeds did not amount to ten shillings.' (104) In November 1835, an Oxford auctioneer refused to sell books distrained for non-payment of church rates when he saw the large number of people who were present and voicing their opposition to the sale. (105) It is certain that action on the Irish model was wholly exceptional. Although far more tithe cases were brought in 1833-4 before the

limiting clauses of Lord Tenterden's Act became operative, few
reached the conclusion so eagerly sought by 'Poor Man's Guardian'
and the 'Church Examiner'. (106)

Nevertheless, the radicals had made their point and in
attacking tithes in the 1830s they had certainly caught the tide.
They contributed in no small way to the growing popular antago-
nism against the church. They were widely read. Wade's revised
'Extraordinary Black Book', for example, sold 50,000 copies
between 1831 and 1835. (107) The attitude of most bishops in
opposing the Reform Bill in 1831 fanned the flames of anti-
clericalism, and in attacking the old tithe system, the radicals
were hitting at one of the weakest points in ecclesiastical
defences. More and more, it was being recognized that the
church to survive must accept reform. Reform of tithes came to
be accepted as natural and inevitable after 1832, though it was
clear that the legislature would not be swayed by radical demands
for abolition rather than commutation. When the 'Oxford
Encyclopaedia', which had a strong clerical interest on its
editorial board, published in 1833 an article on tithes, it
included the following comment. 'It is of the utmost importance
to parochial responsibility and even to religion that some just
and reasonable standard of composition should be fixed.' (108)
The radical writers were to have no influence in determining
how this standard of composition should be determined, but
they had played their part in creating a climate of opinion in
which reform was seen as both inevitable and desirable.

V

However strong the onslaught of the agriculturalists, political
economists and radicals against tithes, the defenders of the old
system were not entirely without armoury of their own. Above all,
they were able to suggest to the political establishment that the
existing system was a key link in the vital association between
church and state. In a favourable climate, this alone was enough
to delay reform for a generation. But it proved possible additionally to rebut many of the charges made. The clerical interest
was able to capitalize on the fact that the agriculturalists
had overplayed their hand in giving the impression that only
tithe commutation lay between them and Utopia. As one opponent
of Arthur Young put it in 1791: (109)

> Have not the value and produce of estates gone on improving
> in a wonderful degree, notwithstanding the odious and
> oppressive tax of tythes; notwithstanding this species of
> slavery under which you represent landlords as groaning?
> If we may judge from appearances, it does not appear as if
> it had operated materially to prevent improvements.

A few defenders of the existing system were even prepared
to defend tithing in kind as a natural adjunct to the clergyman's pastoral activities. The personal contact he obtained
from his tithing tour enabled him to preserve the crucial
position he occupied between high and low, ministering to each
and reconciling the one to the other. W.H. Milman argued

in 1833: (110)
> The clergyman of a parish, constructed as the Church now is, stands in a position the most favourable that can be imagined for bracing the upper and lower orders of society together. He has usually the confidence of his people.... His domiciliary visits actually bring him into the closest possible acquaintance with the practical operation of the system upon which an estate is managed.

Many clergy were indeed efficient estate managers, but the general picture presented here was both idealistic and anachronistic by the 1830s, as the clergy themselves recognized. Their main defence of tithes rested squarely on the issue of property. Tithe, as property, deserved as much protection as any piece of land or building. Lord John Russell, who was later to introduce the successful tithe commutation bill in 1836, realized the principles upon which any measure must be based in order to have any chance of success. 'The tythe is part of the gross produce which never belonged to the landowners, but was always the property of another person.' (111) This being so, it could not lightly be tampered with. Indeed, the French Revolution gave the clergy the very opportunity they required to remind their countrymen of the mutual protection of church and state. Even before the Revolution, Lewis Bagot, when Bishop of Norwich, reminded his clergy that the privilege of tithe 'is a right so firmly established, so interwoven in the original texture of our constitution that the hand of power cannot violate it without endangering the rights and liberties of the whole community'. (112)

After the Revolution, this message was hammered home again and again. It was 'No Bishop, No King' revived and refurbished to fit a new danger. Morgan Cove, as usual, had a word on the subject: (113)
> I do not hesitate a moment to assert that if the Civil Constitution of this country should ever fatally suffer from internal foes, it would be preceded by an attack on our Ecclesiastical Establishment.... Our Church and State form but one system: whatever hurts the Church hurts the State: Whatever weakens the credit of the Governors of the Church, takes away from the Civil Power a part of its strength and shakes the whole constitution.

The same tone was found in ministerial speeches when the question of the ecclesiastical establishment was debated in Parliament. The Lord Chancellor, speaking about Queen Anne's Bounty in 1803, accepted that there had been a 'great outcry' against tithes, but believed: (114)
> that no part of the ecclesiastical system as it now stood could be broke in upon without running the risk of utterly destroying every part of the clerical character....
> Tithes were a favourite topic to hold out to alarm the populace and in all the seditious publications from 1793 to 1796 it was selected and held forth as a fit means of degrading the government and putting the subjects out of humour with it.

The French Revolution afforded the best possible example of the

risk taken by those who would venture against established religion. Once the sacred rights of property were violated the floodgates were opened, and reformers and conservatives alike would be swept away by the deluge. A lay titheholder reminded readers of the 'Gentleman's Magazine' in 1816: (115)
> We must once more warn the landowners that when they venture directly or indirectly to attack the right to this species of property, they shaken every other. This was the first great step in the French Revolution; and they know well enough what followed.

Until the spectre of France had receded after 1815, and until the agricultural interest could show evidence of real hardship as a result of excessive taxation, there was little prospect of reform. A reformer noted the fevered climate in 1803: (116)
> only show yourself serious in trying to reform the abuse (of tithes) and the whole body of the clergy is instantly on your top: the hue and cry is forthwith raised that you are going to undermine our well-poised constitution as it is established in Church and State: and you are from that day marked down as a Jacobin and a Democrat. This is the reason why the measure has not been carried into effect.

The climate of opinion changed slowly after 1815. In 1815-16, 1821-3 and, particularly, 1833-6, the agricultural interest was able to present itself to a parliament of landowners as a generally depressed and overburdened sector in the midst of commercial and industrial prosperity. The government began to look afresh at the question of taxes on agriculture. The poor rate issue was opened first, and the tithe question rapidly followed. In the more receptive climate which followed the ending of the French wars, the evidence presented to parliamentary select committees and on the floor of the house pointed incontrovertibly to the need for reform of a system which belonged to an earlier age.

NOTES

1 G.F.A. Best, 'Temporal Pillars' (Cambridge, 1964), p.465.
2 Adam Smith, 'The Wealth of Nations', 2 vols (Everyman ed., 1910), i, p.347.
3 Arthur Young, 'Political Arithmetic' (1774), p.18.
4 'Annals of Agriculture', i (1784), p.73.
5 J.D. Chambers and G.E. Mingay, 'The Agricultural Revolution, 1750-1880' (1966) is the most recent influential guardian of the orthodox tradition. Eric Kerridge attempted to prove, with a veritable lexicon of documentation, that the essential changes took place in the sixteenth and seventeenth centuries, in 'The Agricultural Revolution' (1967).
6 Chambers and Mingay, op. cit. p.46.
7 F.M.L. Thompson, 'Chartered Surveyors, the Growth of a Profession' (1968), pp.101-2.
8 'Farmers Magazine', iv (1803), p.61.
9 Reprinted in 'The Pamphleteer', viii (1808), p.341. The essay was first published in 'Letters and Papers on

Agriculture, Planting etc., Society Instituted at Bath for the Encouragement of Agriculture'', xiii (1813), pp.215-67 (hereafter Bath & West of Eng. Soc.).
10 'Farmers Magazine', v (1804), p.157.
11 Petition collected by Thomas Greene in DDGr MSS uncat., Lancs. RO.
12 Smith, op. cit. i, pp. 318-19.
13 'Farmers Magazine', iv (1803), p.65.
14 Ibid. x (1810), pp.466-8.
15 J. Middleton, 'A General View of the Agriculture of the County of Middlesex' (1795), p.59.
16 Cobbett's 'Political Register', xiii (1808), p.250.
17 Staffs. RO D554/97.
18 Northumb. RO ZBL 76.
19 Cheshire RO P19/8/2, pp.41-3.
20 Lancs. RO DDM 11/54.
21 'The Case of the Petitioners against Parts of the Bill for Inclosing the Forest or Chase of Needwood' (n.d., but probably 1800 or 1801), WSL. Broadsheets 20/6. The rector of Hamstall Ridware petitioned the exchequer in 1806 to the same effect. He feared not only diminishing tithe revenue but that 'the duties of his rectorial office would be greatly increased and his Burthen would be otherwise increased by the additional Roads and additional Parish Rates that would fall upon the Rector', Staffs. RO D1/A/PI 15.
22 Staffs. RO D554/37. Smith to Bill.
23 Recent research has confirmed that, although farmers faced severe problems at various times after 1815, it is wrong to think in terms of blanket depression between then and the repeal of the corn laws. Chambers and Mingay, op. cit. pp.121-33, E.L. Jones, 'The Development of English Agriculture, 1815-1873' (1968), and E.L. Jones, 'Seasons and Prices' (London, 1964), esp. pp.160-8. For a valuable local study, see D.B. Grigg, 'The Agricultural Revolution in South Lincolnshire' (Cambridge, 1966).
24 PP(HC) 1834, xxviii, pp.206, 213, 215, 308.
25 S.G. and E.O.A. Checkland, eds., 'The Poor Law Report of 1834' (1974), pp.194 and 196.
26 S.C. Agric. Distress, PP(HC) 1836, viii pt I, p.254.
27 Ibid. 1821, ix, p.110.
28 Ibid. p.64.
29 Figures quoted in the 'Gentleman's Magazine', lxxvi, pt II (1816), pp.346-7.
30 J.R. Poynter, 'Society and Pauperism' (1969), p.19, and J.D. Marshall, 'The Old Poor Law, 1795-1834' (1968), p.26. Poor rates, which stood at £2,000,000 in 1775 had reached a peak of £8,000,000 in 1818.
31 See above, chapter 2, sect. III.
32 D. Walker, 'A General View of the Agriculture of Hertfordshire' (hereafter referred to purely by name of county) (1795), pp.24 and 74.
33 J. William and W. Malcolm, 'Buckinghamshire' (1794), p.60.
34 G. Kay, 'North Wales' (Edinburgh, 1794), p.23.

35 J. Wedge, 'Warwickshire' (1794), p.39.
36 T. Brown, 'Derbyshire' (1794), p.53.
37 R. Davis, 'Oxfordshire' (1794), p.31.
38 Morgan Cove, 'An Essay on the Revenues of the Church of England', 2nd ed. (1797), p.252.
39 See the general discussion in Jones, 'The Development of English Agriculture', pp.13-17, and local evidence in Grigg, op. cit. pp.110-13 and 175-89, and A. Harris, 'The Rural Landscape of the East Riding of Yorkshire, 1700-1850' (1961), pp.1-13, 41-55, 117-23.
40 Arthur Young, 'A General View of ... Sussex' (1813), p.130.
41 W. Pitt, 'Worcester' (1813), p.133.
42 HCJ, xlviii (1793), p.634.
43 'Annals of Agriculture', xvii (1792), pp.379-82.
44 See above, chapter 3, sect. I.
45 HCJ, xlvii (1792), pp.519-20.
46 Ibid. p.613.
47 Ibid. p.634.
48 The growth of parliamentary opposition to reform is charted in G.S. Veitch, 'The Genesis of Parliamentary Reform' (1913), and P.A. Brown, 'The French Revolution in English History' (1918). See also E.P. Thompson, 'The Making of the English Working Class' (1963), pp.55-185.
49 Edmund Burke, 'Reflections on the Revolution in France' (1790, Everyman ed., 1910), pp.87-102.
50 Later Lord Eldon, leader of the Ultra-Tories.
51 'Parliamentary Register', xxv (1793), pp.632-3. The Bill was discussed on 7 June 1793.
52 HCJ, xlviii (1793), p.874.
53 'Annals of Agriculture', xvii (1792), pp.178-9.
54 T. Thompson, 'Tithes Indefensible', 3rd ed. (York, 1796), p.50.
55 'Annals of Agriculture', xvi (1791), pp.278-83. Young reminded his readers that tithe was virtually abolished in France and Italy and that nowhere in Europe was tithe collected on new objects of culture.
56 'Farmers Magazine', x (1810), p.256.
57 'Bath & West of Eng. Soc.', viii (1796), p.293. See also the similar arguments of Lena Tadman, 'The Pamphleteer', xii (1818), p.503.
58 David Ricardo, 'Principles of Political Economy and Taxation' (Penguin ed., 1971), pp.191-8. This analysis was attacked by the farmers who projected themselves as over-assessed and under-protected by the legislature. See, for example, Con, 'Farmers Magazine', xxii (1821), pp.398-401. Tithes operated 'directly and unequivocally as a deduction from the rent; of which indeed they are a part, and sometimes a very considerable part. To make this quite evident, it is only necessary to reflect that the clergyman does not set fire to his rick-yard or barns after he has safely deposited his tithes in them, but, like the grower himself, carries his corn to market for the general consumption. If the supply therefore be not diminished by this division of it, why should the market

Chapter 4

price be higher on that account.... Tithes operate on prices by restraining cultivation within narrower limits. They have the effect of diminishing the growth of corn, of contracting the supply, and thus the price is raised to the consumer indirectly.'

59 In a letter to J.R. McCulloch, 15 September 1820. P. Sraffa, ed., 'Works of David Ricardo', 10 vols (1951-5), viii, p.381.
60 'Edinburgh Review', xxxiv (1820), pp.61-79.
61 McCulloch to Ricardo, 24 August 1820. Sraffa, ed., op. cit. viii, pp.222-3.
62 Ricardo to McCulloch, ibid. p.381.
63 'Annals of Agriculture', i (1784), p.73.
64 'The Pamphleteer', xii (1818), p.497.
65 'Bath & West of Eng. Soc.', iv (1788). Introduction, pp.xvi-xvii.
66 Printed in 'The Pamphleteer', xi (1815), p.284.
67 'Edinburgh Review', xxxiv (1820) p.77.
68 Quoted in 'Bath & West of Eng. Soc.', iv (1788), p.111.
69 Ibid. pp.109-30.
70 Many of the agricultural magazines devote much space to similar plans. See the essay of Thomas Davis, steward to the Marquis of Bath in 'Bath & West of Eng. Soc.', viii (1796), pp.239ff, and T. Thompson, op. cit. pp.135ff for perhaps the best argued defences of corn rents in lieu of tithe.
71 Pitt to the Duke of Rutland, 7 November 1786. Quoted in Earl Stanhope, 'Life of William Pitt', 4 vols (London, 1861), i, pp.318-19. The letter shows Pitt's general attitude to the tithe question at this time.
72 BM Add MSS 34440 ff 51-81. See in particular the contribution by Dr Sturges, ff 58-63, which explains and attempts to resolve difficulties in the way of accurate valuations, such as when tithes had been slackly collected, giving an unnaturally low average from which to calculate permanent rent charges. He suggested fresh valuations in all cases.
73 Ibid. f 400.
74 Stanhope, op. cit. ii, p.130.
75 Richard Watson, 'Anecdotes', 2 vols (1817), ii, pp.56-8.
76 Cove, op. cit. pp.288-9. This was Arthur Young's opinion also. See Watson, op. cit. ii, p.57. Lord John Russell, who represented south Devon in Parliament, declared in 1834 that farmers in that county were more agitated over tithes than elsewhere, and were frequent petitioners on the subject. 'Hansard' (3rd Ser.), xxi, cols 1038-54.
77 By 2 & 3 Edw. VI c.13.
78 BM Add MSS 36138 ff 228-32.
79 PRO HO 42/49, Elford to Portland, received 22 April 1800. I am indebted to Mr M.J. Thomas of Friends House, London NW1 for this reference.
80 PRO HO 42/34. Rooke to Portland, 15-17 March 1795.
81 Reported in PMG, 14 April 1832. Lord King brought another case of fish tithe agitation to the Lords in April 1833. The new rector of Porlock (Somerset) attempted to take

tithe of herrings for the first time. King suggested that this made 'a little Ireland' of the parish. The tithe proctor was burnt in effigy and the rector himself, unable to enforce his demands, fled the parish. 'Hansard' (3rd Ser.), xv, col. 1134.
82 E.J. Hobsbawm and G.F.E. Rudé, 'Captain Swing' (1969), esp. Appendix III, pp.312-59. They list no fewer than 67 disturbances primarily concerning tithe payment between November 1830 and January 1831.
83 Eric J. Evans, Some reasons for the growth of English rural anti-clericalism, c.1750-c.1830, 'Past and Present', 66 (1975), pp.107-9.
84 M. Dutt, 'The Agricultural Labourers' Revolt of 1830 in Kent, Surrey and Sussex' (unpublished University of London PhD thesis, 1966), p.167. See also Hobsbawm and Rudé, op. cit. p.107.
85 Dutt, op. cit. p.196.
86 Ibid. p.224.
87 Hobsbawm and Rudé, op. cit. p.152.
88 Ibid. pp.112-13, 153-9, 164, and E.P. Thompson, op. cit. p.233. See also A.J. Peacock, 'Bread or Blood' (1965), pp.59-63, 95-106.
89 'The Extraordinary Black Book' (1831), p.9. The point was frequently rehearsed in the radical literature. See, for example, Anon., 'The Claims of the Clergy to Tithes and other Church Revenues Examined' (1830).
90 See above, chapter 2, sect. I.
91 'The Extraordinary Black Book', p.11.
92 See his remarks on the stipendiary curates' Bill, 1805. 'Political Register', vii (1805), pp.789-90. See also his ideas on the origins and subsequent misappropriation of tithe in his influential 'History of the Protestant Reformation in England and Ireland', 2 vols (1829), paras 8ff.
93 W. Cobbett, 'Rural Rides', 2 vols (Everyman ed., 1910), i, p.106.
94 'The Church Examiner and Ecclesiastical Record', 16 June 1832.
95 The best collection of these satires is M.D. George, 'Catalogue of Political and Personal Satires in the British Museum', vols 5-11 (1935-54). See also her commentary in 'English Political Caricature', 2 vols (Oxford, 1959), esp. ii, pp.181-2.
96 George, 'Catalogue', vii, no. 9138, and vi, no. 6737.
97 'Quarterly Review', xlii (1830), p.130.
98 'Voice of the People', 29 January 1831. See also the resolution of the Leeds Radical Political Union in PMG, 4 February 1832 and the Macclesfield Union of the Working Classes, PMG, 16 June 1832 which called for the appropriation of tithes for the support of 'the superannuated, the blind, the lame and the unemployed as a compensation for their birthright'.
99 The Irish situation forms an entirely separate story. See P. O'Donoghue, Causes of the opposition to tithes,

1830-38, 'Studia Hibernica', v (1965), pp.7-28, Opposition to tithe payments in 1830-31, ibid. vi (1966), pp.69-98 and Opposition to tithe payment in 1832-3, xii (1972), pp.77-108. Blow-by-blow accounts of 1834-8 are promised in forthcoming issues.
100 'Church Examiner', 4 August 1832.
101 PMG, 17 March 1832.
102 'Church Examiner', 4 August 1832.
103 PMG, 7 September 1833. Dodsworth was committed to the House of Correction after a distraint warrant had been issued by two magistrates, and nothing had been found to distrain. A suit was brought on behalf of Dodsworth against these magistrates for wrongful exercise of their functions, though without success. It was argued by the defendants that personal tithes were legally due and that the rector had acted entirely properly in referring the case to the JPs, 'British Magazine', iv (1833), pp.451-3.
104 'The Man', 22 December 1833.
105 PMG, 21 November 1835.
106 The proliferation of cases is attacked in 'The Man', 29 September 1833, and PMG, 7 September 1833. See also below, chapter 6, sect. III.
107 O. Chadwick, 'The Victorian Church', 2 vols (1966 and 1970), i, p.33.
108 'Oxford Encyclopaedia' (1833 ed.), vi, p.804.
109 'Annals of Agriculture', xvi (1791), pp.271-8. In an early edition of his 'Political Register', Cobbett claimed that tithes were no impediment to improvement, vi (1804), pp.244-8.
110 'Quarterly Review', xlix (1833), pp.198-211.
111 'Edinburgh Review', xxvi (1816), pp.276-81.
112 L. Bagot, 'Charge to the Clergy of the Diocese of Norwich', 1784. WSL Visitation Charges, Eighteenth Century.
113 Cove, op. cit. pp.19-22.
114 'Political Register', iv (1803), col. 1105.
115 'Gentleman's Magazine', lxxxvi pt II (1816), pp.310-11.
116 'Farmers Magazine', iv (1803), pp.141-7.

CHAPTER 5

TITHES AND THE ENCLOSURE MOVEMENT

I

The parliamentary enclosure movement offered both solutions and precedents for the tithe problem at the very time when the system was coming under its most severe and sustained attack. The solution offered by many enclosure Acts and awards was the commutation of tithe by allotments of land or cash payments. Precedents were provided in that what Parliament could enact piecemeal in thousands of enclosure Acts, it could repeat in more compact and comprehensive form to resolve the problem nationally. The main purpose of most enclosures, of course, was profit, with tithe commutation a useful by-product. Enclosures usually facilitated agricultural improvement, resulting in rents which could be doubled, tripled or even quadrupled within a short space of time. (1) Landowners considered tithes a sufficient vexation, however, to be prepared to rid themselves of the burden when the opportunity offered. Indeed, one of the strongest arguments in support of the thesis that tithes were a disincentive to improvement is that farmers and landowners would concede far more than a tenth of their property in order to exonerate the remainder from the burden in perpetuity. One observer exaggerated when he suggested that 'the hatred and aversion to this system is such that they (the landowners), on almost every enclosure, insist upon commutation of tithes as a preliminary step, a "sine qua non"'; (2) but it was true that the tithe question was considered sufficiently important for consultations to be held at an early stage to discover the tithe owner's views and amenability to commutation.

No tithe owner could be coerced into accepting commutation or exoneration at enclosure. If he calculated that his interests were better served by keeping the enclosed land tithable he so informed the proprietors and the enclosure went ahead without arrangement for tithe. Occasionally, as a result of the tithe owner's decision, the projected enclosure was dropped altogether. A decision not to exonerate was more likely when the enclosure was of commons or waste land. The value of such tithes was much less than from open fields, and it was also more difficult to calculate the possible extent and profitability of productive agriculture after improvement. Although lands deemed naturally waste were exempt from tithes for seven years after improvement, many tithe owners preferred to wait for an eventual share of new produce to which they had contributed nothing in the way of expenditure. On commons and wastes also, tithe was usually less of a burden, so that pressures for commutation from the proprietors were rather less.

It is useful, therefore, to distinguish between the different types of enclosure. Most of the open-field enclosures in this period were concentrated in the English midlands. (3) Enclosures of commons and waste predominated in counties which had experienced earlier enclosure or which had been densely afforested. (4) Open-field enclosure was about twice as common in this period as that of commons and waste. (5) In Warwickshire between 1603 and 1845, 125 open-field enclosure Acts were passed and only 25 exclusively for commons or waste. In Staffordshire, the totals are 24 open-field, and 68 commons or waste. The arrangements made over tithe in these contiguous counties further points the contrast. Of the total acreage of Warwickshire 25 per cent was enclosed by 125 private Acts between 1760 and 1870. Only 2 per cent was covered by Acts enclosing commons and waste. No fewer than 118 of these 125 Acts contained provision for the exoneration of tithe. (6) In Staffordshire, 12½ per cent of the county was enclosed but 75 per cent of the Acts related to commons and waste. Of 101 awards confirmed, only 25 contained provision for tithe. (7) No less than 43 per cent of Oxfordshire was enclosed by Act at this time and all but 3 per cent of this was open-field. Of 47 enclosure Acts between 1777 and 1836, 37 exonerated tithe. (8) In Derbyshire, three-quarters of the 21 per cent enclosed by Act concerned open-field arable. Of 55 enclosure enactments between 1772 and 1832, 39 exonerated tithe. (9)

There is, therefore, a clear correlation between open-field enclosure and the likelihood of tithe exoneration. Professor Ward believes that 70 per cent of enclosure Acts passed between 1757 and 1835 included provision for tithe commutation. (10) It was commuted in one of three ways: by giving the tithe owner allotments of land in lieu, by straight cash payments, or by variable payments, fluctuating with the prevailing price of grain. These last rapidly became known as corn rents. Throughout the period of parliamentary enclosure the first of these alternatives was the most frequently adopted. In the 1760s, of 323 enclosures which included provision for tithe commutation, 298 were exclusively or predominantly by land allotments. In the 1790s, 352 of the 402 exonerations were mainly by land, but the lessons of inflation had taught tithe owners to ask for corn rents rather than cash in the remaining instances. Forty-eight corn rent allotments were made, and only two simple cash payments. There were no money payments in the 1810s, and only eleven corn rents to set against 217 enclosures which allotted land in lieu of tithe. (11)

Land had obvious attractions for both sides as a solution to the tithe problem. It seemed quite definitive. Once allotted,

there was no further need for a yearly audit or for payments of
any kind. There could be no question of debts or arrears. Also
land was seen as the most secure kind of property, the warp and
weft of the social fabric - a worthwhile exchange indeed for
grudging, fluctuating and contested tithe payments, however
assessed. The disadvantages of the exchange were somewhat subtler,
and not fully appreciated until later. By the 1830s, however,
there were few advocates of land allotments as a national solution
to the tithe problem.

Most tithe owners who rejected applications to consider an
arrangement to deal with their property were concerned with basic
economic factors affecting their particular situation. They
might calculate that they would gain more from continuing to
collect in the old way, or they might seek to delay or frustrate
enclosure if they feared that it would prejudice their interests.
This was particularly likely in the case of that minority of
eighteenth-century parliamentary enclosures which were designed
to increase the acreage under pasture at the expense of arable
cultivation. The Bishop of Bath and Wells took his opposition
to a proposed enclosure at Weston Zoyland (Somerset) to the
Lords, where he succeeded in defeating the measure. (12) He
argued that the increase in pasture land after enclosure would
greatly diminish the value of the tithes. It became known as
a consequence that any enclosure which seemed to threaten rather
than enhance the value of a living might expect hot, and
probably successful, opposition from the episcopal bench and
its supporters in the Lords. It was held that the convenience
of the majority of proprietors should not be permitted to over-
ride the interests of an important minority property-holder when
that property-holder was the church. The bishops were, of
course, admirably placed to act as watchdogs of the clerical
interest, and they took more interest in private enclosure
business than did most MPs. Other minority propertied interests -
such as the poor and the smaller proprietors - were noticeably
less well represented where it mattered.

Rev. George White at first opposed the enclosure of Huntspill
(Somerset) because he feared a diminution of corn tithe
revenues. He informed the patrons of the living, Balliol
College, Oxford, in 1799 that Huntspill had been partially
enclosed by agreement for many years and converted to pasture.
Such agreements had already been 'to the no small Detriment of
the Living'. No further agreements could be made without
Act of Parliament since college and glebe land was interspersed
with land belonging to the rest of the proprietors in the open
fields. About 200 acres remained unenclosed, and was tithed in
kind. Eventually, White negotiated what he hoped was an insurance
policy with the remaining proprietors: (13)

> We agreed at length on the following general outlines:
> 1. that after the Inclosure the Lands in Question should
> be tithable as before; i.e. that they should be liable to
> the Tithes of Corn, or Hay in kind. 2. that if any of
> these lands were depastured to prevent any Loss to the
> Rector from this Change in the mode of Husbandry, so much
> an Acre should be paid in Money as would equal to the

> Tithe of Corn and 3. to prevent Frauds, over & above this
> Payment in Money these Lands in this Case should never-
> theless also be subject to the Tithe of Calf, Lamb & Wool....
> I made no Hesitation in preferring Tithes to an Allotment
> of Land, because I would have no more Tithe-free Grounds in
> my Parish having suffered severely from those that were so
> made so on the former Inclosure. They continually serve
> as a Cover to the most Scandalous Frauds, & as a Protection
> to those who commit them. The Diminution of Tithes that
> they occasion is every year very considerable.

Despite these safeguards, the proprietors continued to grow their most productive crops on tithe-free land, and White considered himself 'the Dupe of ... bare-faced Imposture'.

The opposition of the tithe owner was a considerable hindrance to the success of an enclosure. Occasionally, it seems to have halted the enterprise altogether. Pinner common was left unenclosed in the 1790s after the rector had made what the proprietors considered exorbitant demands for his tithe. (14) Rev. John Riland, rector of Sutton Coldfield, effectively postponed the enclosure of his parish for twenty years by his refusal to assent to a bill, not because he was dissatisfied with tithe arrangements, but for the quaint reason that the enclosure would 'prove a considerable and lasting injury to several hundreds' of his parishioners. Riland upheld the interests of the 'bulk of the lower classes of the parish' who had expressed their aversion to enclosure but whose views had been initially overridden by the more substantial landowners. (15)

Only rarely did a clergyman align himself so ostentatiously on the side of the numerical majority against the interests of property when these conflicted. Disagreements over broad policy at enclosure were much less common than haggling over terms. Usually, agreement was ultimately reached but at Fordington (Dorset) and Blore (Staffs.), for example, enclosure went ahead without exoneration of tithe when terms could not be agreed. (16) Tithe differences alone were unlikely to halt an enclosure. The prospects for a tithe owner anticipating improved yields and increased profits after enclosure were hardly bleak whether he commuted his tithes or not.

II

When land was taken in lieu of tithe at enclosure, the crucial question was 'how much should be given?' Superficially, the answer seems simple. If tithe was a tenth of the produce, then a tenth of the land might seem appropriate. But this was to ignore the fact that tithe was a tax on yield. The tithe owner was entitled to a full tenth of a crop at harvest time or of livestock when ready for market. No allowance was made for the farmer's expenses in getting his produce to this state of readiness. It followed that additional compensation must be given to the tithe owner to meet the difference between a tenth of the gross and a tenth of the net produce, if he were to receive a once-for-all settlement of land in lieu of tithe.

Such compensation must take into account the fact that the tithe owner had made no allowance to the farmer for his production costs up to the point of harvesting. The calculation could be put on a more concrete footing by constructing a relationship between the respective values of both tithe and rent which the farmer agreed to pay. Thus, Thomas Thompson explained that no tithe owner would accept a tenth of the arable land as fair exchange 'as he receives a "crop" from the tenth part of the land which, according to the usual mode of calculation is worth more than three times the annual rent of the land; and therefore he receives as much from a tenth of the land, as he would receive if that tenth of the land were his own'. (17) The logic of this argument led inexorably, if unrealistically, to the acceptance of no less than 30 per cent of the land from which the most valuable tithes issued. Less optimistically, a surveyor provided the rector of Hartwell (Bucks.) in 1776 with calculations of the value of crops of wheat, barley and beans growing 'according to the common course of husbandry' in the open fields of his parish, with land lying fallow in the fourth year. The net profit on the crops per acre was £6 14s 3d after deducting expenses, and the tithe amounted to £1 7s 8¼d. Therefore, he concluded, 'you may fairly insist upon 1/5th as an Equivalent or Compensation for the Tythe of the Arable Land. I may venture to submit the above Account to a Jury of Farmers, they may cavill at it, but they cannot disprove it'. (18) Such calculations were based upon the equivalent of a full tenth being taken. As has been argued, this frequently was not the case. (19) However, arrangements at enclosure went by rather different rules. Enclosure was a permanent settlement and a tithe owner who made only moderate demands to keep the goodwill of his parishioners (or because he was unable to get more) would not permit this short-changing to form the basis of definitive tithe calculations of tithe values. The episcopal office was on hand to advise incumbents who were unsure of their rights. The church authorities kept a sharp eye on her patrimony in the second half of the eighteenth century and the enclosure movement offered an opportunity for settlement on favourable terms.

Tithe owners, in fact, were usually in a favourable position at enclosure. The movement fed on profit, and some unwise ventures went ahead at massive expense at the height of the boom during the French wars. (20) In such a climate tithe owners were able to capitalize on their nuisance value. Arthur Young criticized a corn rent of £600, exempt from all poor rates and other parochial assessments, in lieu of tithes at Langton (Leics.). 'Such allowances, and such exemptions, may not be new; but this only proves that tythe is such a horrible oppression that men will give enormous compensations to be rid of it.' (21)

A further consideration strengthened the tithe owner's hand. Writers on enclosure were agreed that the commissioners should take into account the likely improvement in the value of land after the change, and compensate him according to its improved value. (22) Some Acts even incorporated this understanding into the directions given to enclosure commissioners. At Old

Chapter 5

Stratford (1774) and Avon Dassett (1779) instructions were given to allot land in lieu of tithe according to the 'new value' of the land as a whole. (23) When John Sawyer, lord of the manor of Oddington (Oxon.) tried to persuade the rector in 1790 to take existing values as the basis of tithe arrangements, he received the following brusque reply from Trinity College, Oxford, which held the patronage of the living: (24)

> Mr Sawyer's proposal to leave it to the Commissioners to find a fair and just valuation of the Tythes on the Lands as now cultivated and to settle a Corn Rent according to that value is merely to convert the present Tythes into a Money Payment and to onerate the Rector with a part of the Expense of improving the Lands in the parish without a possibility of bettering the Tythes, a proposal which it is needless to say neither the Patrons of the Living nor the Rector can accede to.

It is clear that tithe owners would not accept a mere tenth. The early Acts, of the 1750s and 1760s, give them a considerably better bargain than this, and terms improve as profits rise. Until about the mid-1770s, it was unusual to differentiate between the various types of land to be enclosed. Commissioners were usually instructed to set out a given portion of the land, usually one-eighth or one-seventh. Thereafter, distinctions are made. By the 1790s, allotments in lieu of arable tithes are most frequently one-fifth of the land, though sometimes two-ninths or even more. (25) The less profitable meadow and pasture tithes were commuted at one-eighth, one-ninth or one-tenth. Quite frequently the exact proportions were left to the determination of the commissioners, taking local circumstances into account, but where these were settled by the Act, the most common formula for commutation was in the 1790s one-fifth of the arable, one-eighth of the meadow and one-ninth of the pasture. Some idea of the assumed profitability of enclosure during the boom may be seen in that landowners continued to believe a handsome profit likely even after such losses, and after paying the heavy expenses involved. Twenty enclosure Acts were passed in Warwickshire between 1774 and 1830 in which one-fifth or more of the arable land was given in lieu of tithe. No fewer than eighteen of these were passed in the boom years 1790-1811. (26)

Some tithe owners were even able to determine which lands should be considered arable and which pasture to their own advantage. Certain lands, of course, had been both cropped and grazed in the years before enclosure. At Cropredy (Warwickshire) in 1797 the Act instructed the commissioners to include as arable any land which had borne a crop at any time (however short) in the previous 20 years. At Leek Wootton in 1817 there was a similar injunction, but the relevant period in this instance was ten years. The Washingborough (Lincs.) enclosure Act of 1827 stipulated that the rector should be given as a corn rent the value of one-fifth of the 'lands usually deemed arable or tillage' and two-thirteenths of the remainder. 'For the purpose of ascertaining the value of the tithes ... all the lands which have been pared, ploughed or used in tillage within ten years next before the passing of this Act shall be deemed to be arable land.' (27)

In all, Warwickshire tithe owners received 25,538 acres of land in lieu of tithe. This represented 17.4 per cent of the total land enclosed. Of 43 parliamentary enclosures in Lincolnshire, more than 20 per cent of the land went to tithe owners in 13 instances. In 17 cases between 15 and 20 per cent was given and only in 13 was less than 15 per cent allotted. (28) In Staffordshire by contrast, where most enclosure was of commons and waste, only just over 4,800 acres was given in lieu of tithe. This represented only 5.3 per cent of the total land enclosed. (29)

As experience of parliamentary enclosure grew, the allotments given in lieu of tithe began to approximate to its true value. It was recognized that there was little equity in settling a fixed proportion of a parish irrespective of land use. This procedure in early enclosures had resulted in too much being given by primarily pasture farmers to the benefit of arable producers. The distinctions made in the Acts from the later 1760s and almost universally by the 1790s did something to rectify the situation by giving one proportion in lieu of arable and other, lesser, proportions in lieu of meadow and pasture. Even this refinement, however, could conceal injustice. If tithe was meant to be a tenth of the gross produce, there were difficulties in taking the same proportion of land from a farmer of good quality arable soil as from a farmer who had made poor quality land productive only after heavy investment. The difference between gross and net was obviously much greater in the latter case than in the former, particularly when tithing in kind was practised. Too much should not be made of this, however, for two reasons. First, tithe in kind was relatively rare in areas of heaviest parliamentary enclosure. Second, tithe account books confirm that compositions had not usually shown the fine discrimination between good and poor quality soils which would have been necessary to maintain absolute fairness between farmers. Thus, in practice there was often little change. Proprietors, already beset by heavy enclosure expenses, were reluctant to add to the burden by commissioning detailed surveys which would eliminate possible anomalies. In addition, the administration of enclosure was already complex. Any machinery aimed at taking more land from certain proprietors than from others might well have halted altogether proceedings which were taking five, eight or even ten years to complete as it was.

The choice of the custom-honoured fractions of one-fifth and one-eighth or one-ninth similarly reflected acceptance of Alexander Pope's dictum that 'Whate'er is best administered is best'. They undoubtedly left unsmoothed some very rough edges, but they formed an acceptable compromise. It is noticeable that, even when precise allotments were left to the discretion of the enclosure commissioners, their judgments rarely differed much from the prevailing parameters. The smaller allotments in lieu of meadow and pasture land naturally took into account the smaller expenses necessary for the realization of its produce as well as the usually smaller sums involved per acre. In general, arable farms were more labour-intensive and required heavier injections of capital to keep them profitable. By the 1790s, when farming was booming, credit easy and demands for still greater improvement strident, tithe owners successfully held out for allotments from the arable twice as large as the paper value of the tithe. While this remained less than the full tenth of the gross product calculated by political economists, it represented a very considerable concession by the farming interest, especially when it is remembered that the full tenth was hardly ever collected even by the harshest of lay impropriators. That farmers and proprietors were prepared to concede something near to a full tenth of the assumed improved value of the tithe (itself a gamble) speaks volumes for their anxiety to be rid of the burden and also of their determination to cash in on the boom at almost any cost. Perhaps for the last time, and after a gap of many years, the church was in a position to dictate to the farming community, and it used its advantage to full effect. The enclosure movement reveals the church to have possessed greater business acumen than is usually acknowledged. Some shrewd financial brains stalked the quiet precincts of cathedral closes, and the intelligence service of the deans and chapters ensured that their message penetrated deep into the heart of rural England. Moreover, as will be seen, the benefits which the church enjoyed were not purely financial.

III

The favoured treatment for tithe owners did not end with ample compensation for their property. They enjoyed three further important advantages. They had the right to nominate an enclosure commissioner of their choice to safeguard their interests when detailed arrangements were made. A second benefit derived directly from this. Tithe owners frequently received the land of their choice in prime situations. Finally, the other proprietors paid all of the administrative costs of the enclosure between them. Nearly all Acts specifically stated that the tithe owner was to bear no portion of the cost. Each of these advantages was substantial in its own right. Together they suggest that in many cases the tithe owner was the chief beneficiary of the change.

If enclosure proceeded without tithe commutation it was not unusual for only one commissioner to officiate. This kept costs down. When tithe was commuted, however, the tithe owner invariably insisted on his right to nominate a commissioner. Usually three commissioners were appointed, the remaining two appointed by the lord of the manor and the remaining proprietors. When Rev. W. Bayliffe, rector of Blore (Staffs.), heard of the proprietors' views about enclosure commissioners, he stated his position clearly: (30)

> Tho' it is far from the wish of either Mr Shore or myself to subject the Proprietors to any unnecessary expense, yet after a full and mature consideration of the case, we

conceive it would be highly improper to accede to the
proposal of only 'one' commissioner, as not only the future
general interests of the living but what more immediately
concerns my own Interests from the consequences of the
proposed Exchange are to be considered as now finally
depended, we think it necessary to say decidedly that Two
Commissioners must be appointed.

The clerical appointment was not infrequently a clergyman. Rev. Henry Homer, rector of Birdingbury (Warwickshire) was a prominent commissioner in the 1760s, while Rev. John Horseman officiated in at least nine Oxfordshire enclosures at the end of the century. (31) Certain commissioners also became known as steadfast upholders of the clerical interest, and were much in demand as virtually full-time professionals. (32)

From almost every angle the tithe owners' rights were scrupulously safeguarded. It is perhaps hardly surprising, therefore, that many had the pick of available sites when commissioners came to the ticklish, yet vital, work of apportionment. The siting of allotments was crucial. Badly situated plots, widely dispersed throughout a parish, or at too great a distance from the home farm, were unpopular as they necessitated additional expenditure on new buildings, quite apart from day-to-day inconveniences. Possession of appropriate meadow and pasture land was also a consideration of some importance. Although rare, it was not unheard of for the tithe owner's desiderata as to situation and allocation of tithe plots to be incorporated in the parliamentary Act. At Winterton (Lincs.) in 1769 a clause in the enclosure Act acceded to Lord Mexborough's stipulation that one-third of the lands to be given in lieu of tithes should be laid contiguous to a convenient dwelling house. (33) The Barton-on-Humber enclosure Act of 1793 stated that 900 acres were to be allotted to the impropriator, George Uppleby, in lieu of tithe, the total allotment 'to be lying and being together ... to comprize the whole of the ... Horse pasture, Part of the ... Cow Pasture, and Part of the East Field ... to be bounded on the East by the Lordship of Barrow'. (34) The bursar of Trinity College, Cambridge, impropriators of the rectory of Shillington (Beds.), wrote to the proprietors in 1797 that the college would require the tithe allotment 'to be all laid together & included in the ring fence at the expence (sic) of the other Proprietors'. (35) The college was dissatisfied with the original proposals made by the commissioners appointed under the Act of 1802. 'The particular grievance is the want of proximity to the Homestall whereby an excellent Farm house & proper Outbuildings will be rendered totally useless and this occasioned by an undue preference being given to other proprietors.' (36) The college's grievances were remedied on appeal, and when the much delayed Award was made in 1817 it was clear that no 'undue preference' had been given to anyone ahead of the college. Its land was allocated in convenient blocks at the heart of the parish, convenient to all buildings. (37)

Rev. William Hooper, rector of Carlton, Chellington and Stevington (Beds.) felt his position sufficiently strong when enclosure was mooted in 1804 to insist in a preliminary letter to the proprietors 'that all the Land which may fall to the share of the Rector of Carlton, for Glebe and Tythes, both great and small, be laid contiguous to, and as convenient as can be to the Parsonage House. The same for Chillington Rectory'. (38) Hooper's wishes seem to have been exactly met by the Award of 1807. The impropriator of tithes in Arkesden (Essex), J. Wolfe, wrote to the enclosure commissioners in 1815 requesting favourable situations for his allotments, as tithe owner, landowner and lord of the manor: (39)

> I do request that the lands to be allotted to me in lieu of my Commonfield Lands, Common rights and Manorial Rights, may be set out in Poor street field and Crandsfield, And that the residue of such Lands and the lands to be allotted to me in lieu of my rectorial tithes, may be set out as conveniently as may be to my Homestall in the Occupation of Thomas Dean at Arkesden, giving a preference to such parts of Townfield Church field and Bulbroke field ... as are situate nearest thereto.

The Much Marcle (Herefordshire) enclosure Act (1795) stipulated that twenty acres of the vicar's allotment, properly ring-fenced, should be 'laid adjoining to the Vicarage House of Much Marcle' and that the remainder should be sited 'as near as conveniently may be to the said Vicarage House and the Buildings thereto belonging, in order that the Erection of any additional Buildings for the Occupation of the said Allotment or Allotments may, as far as possible, be rendered unnecessary'. (40)

Since enclosure commissioners' minutes books are usually filled with administrative detail, it is difficult to chart from them the pressures and constraints upon the commissioners themselves. It is clear, however, that Oxford and Cambridge colleges and cathedral deans and chapters were shrewd and practised appraisers of enclosure business and well placed to exert pressure on commissioners in their clients' or their own interests. The presence of a commissioner appointed by tithe owners further guaranteed careful consideration which usually worked to their benefit. The awards show that, more often than not, tithe owners received preferential treatment. The maps which accompany the award do not often reveal badly or awkwardly situated tithe allotments. There is some evidence that enclosure commissioners tended to think first of the interests of those who had been singled out by the Act for special treatment. Of these, the tithe owner and lord of the manor were the most important. In addition, though commissioners usually worked amicably, it remained true that the tithe owners' nominee was representing the interests of only a few individuals - and often only one - while the 'proprietors' commissioner' might hold the same brief for dozens of owners. Finally, it is not necessary to dissent from Gonner's view that 'the work of division and apportionment appears to have been discharged conscientiously and fairly' (41) to maintain that commissioners worked from fixed points of reference, and that one of these was the tithe allocation. Tithe allotments were frequently among the largest made, and however careful the commissioners may have been not to prejudice the interests of smaller proprietors, it was much easier to apportion land in a parish from a base of a few large allotments. (42) Commissioners do not seem to have settled the various claims in promiscuous order, or by means of a pin, and the order they imposed on the situation worked to the advantage of tithe owners. (43)

Tithe owners were spared all of the administrative costs of enclosure. The expenses of application to Parliament, the drafting of the Act, the charges of the enclosure commissioners and, most importantly, the cost of all external fencing and ditching were all borne by the remaining parties in proportion to the size of their respective allotments. This left the tithe owner only with the expenses of internal fencing, the erection of new farm buildings and any improvements to the land after enclosure which he might deem necessary. In themselves, these might be substantial, but to escape the essential administrative charges was a crucial advantage. This became particularly true as enclosures became more expensive during the boom and inflation at the end of the eighteenth century, and when most of the remaining enclosures were more complex operations than those effected during the 1760s and 1770s. In this earlier period, the declared costs of enclosure rarely exceeded £1 per acre. By the 1790s, it was not uncommon to find costs of £3 per acre, with average charges amounting to 34s. (44) Exceptionally, costs rose even higher. Money had to be found not only for solicitors' and commissioners' fees, but for ring-fencing, drains, bridges and new roads. The published cost of the Needwood Forest enclosure in 1805 was £33,390 for 9,630 acres. (45) The total costs were certainly higher, since post-award levies were made on the proprietors for additional road and fencing charges incurred after the award was signed. The Bledlow (Bucks.) cost a horrendous £11 an acre. (46) The 4,632 acres at Barrow-on-Humber (Lincs.) were enclosed in 1803 for £15,176. Interestingly, the fencing of the tithe allotments alone accounted for well over £1,000 of this. (47)

Recent research suggests that the financial burden of enclosure has been underestimated, and it follows that the tithe owner received a thoroughly good bargain by having allotments properly ring-fenced presented to him 'gratis'. Some authorities have even argued that the burden of provision for tithe owners was so heavy that many of the allotments for the smaller proprietors were uneconomic, and the cost of fencing and improving them prohibitive. Accordingly, it is said, they sold up. (48) The story of the decline of peasant proprietorship is a very complex and protracted one, and the tithe problem impinges upon it only marginally. It is true, however, that in real terms the unit costs of fencing and ditching for the smaller allotments were considerably higher than for the larger ones, and that the larger the tithe owner's allotment the greater the pressure on those with the smallest acreages. The uniquely favourable treatment received by tithe owners had at least some repercussions at the bottom of the proprietorial ladder.

IV

It can be shown, therefore, that every accommodation was made to the tithe owner at enclosure. In addition, his yearly income was significantly increased by the change. John Parkinson, who officiated in ten Nottinghamshire enclosures in the early nineteenth century, told Thomas Greene in 1829 that 'in every instance where allotments of Land have been set out for Tithes all parties have been satisfied and very considerable increase of Income has invariably accrued to the Incumbent'. (49) Most incumbents who corresponded with Greene about his tithe reform plans, agreed that they had been substantial gainers by exchanging tithes for land. James Hodgson, rector of Hillington (Norfolk) said that his predecessors had not received more than £200 annually from tithes, though their proper value was nearer £350. After enclosure, the value settled at around £500 'with the advantage besides of receiving my Income without any trouble & vexation by which it was before obtained'. The rector of Clophill (Beds.), W.D. Wetherall said that before enclosure tithes were drawn in kind 'and when let produced with difficulty, and not without much altereation (sic) £192 pr. Ann. but from the year of the enclosure (1808) the value of the Rectory has amounted to £550, Corn Rent £370, Land 70 a(cres) £180'. (50)

Not all improvements were so spectacular, but a steady rise seems to have been normal. The tithes at Ravensthorpe (Northants) were reckoned immediately before the enclosure in 1795 to be worth £108 for the 1,418 acres. At enclosure, the by then normal allotments of one-fifth in lieu of arable and one-ninth in lieu of pasture were made and the new value of the land was calculated to be £225. (51) The tithe owners hoped for still more improvement in rental values once improvements were effected. At Slattenham and Ditchingham (Bucks.), tithes worth £60 before enclosure in 1772 were commuted for land worth £85 immediately afterwards. (52) Joseph Pawsey informed the Marchioness Grey in 1796 that the vicar of Harrold (Beds.) might expect to increase the value of the tithes from £60 to £100 as a result of enclosure developments. (53)

Most of the evidence points in the same direction. When enclosure of open-field arable took place, unless it was undertaken to increase the acreage under pasture, the tithe owner was a very considerable gainer. This seems to have been the case whether the tithe owner accepted commutation or not. Dr Austin in his study of Derbyshire clergy has suggested that those livings which had not received allotments of land in lieu of tithe rose slightly more in value than those which had. (54) In some newly-enclosed parishes, tithe owners immediately leased their holdings for periods of 14 or 21 years, at a fixed rent, and so failed to profit from rising rental values until the leases fell in. Austin's work provides a useful corrective to the over-simple view that acceptance of land was the only way to improved incomes at enclosure; but it is important to stress that the benefits accruing to those who decided to let their tithes go were not only financial. If tithe stayed, so did the old opportunities for disputes and resistance. For many tithe owners

the real benefits of exchanging tithe for land were not to be measured in cash terms. The peace of mind deriving from a secure and honourable source of income was much prized. As Richard Venables wrote from Herefordshire in 1829: (55)
> The Advantages resulting from this measure have been to all parties very great - the income of the Vicar has not only increased considerably but it has been certain & what he can calculate upon independent of the caprice ... of his Parishioners but what is of more importance, harmony & kind feelings have taken the place of squabbling & ill will.

A further advantage derived from taking land. Many incumbents saw their social influence increased by possessing their newly acquired acres. Land remained the 'sine qua non' of advancement in rural society and the proprietor of a secure freehold appeared an altogether better established figure than a man faced with yearly wrangles over a disputed property only grudgingly and partially conceded. As the rector of Launton (Oxon.) bitterly put it: 'Reverence for my office they had none; consideration for me as a gentleman and landlord, and occupant of a large glebe, they had....' (56) The enclosure movement made substantial property holders of many incumbents for the first time. The average increase in glebe from the twenty leading enclosure counties as a result of tithe commutation was nearly 159 acres. (57) Since many of these were vicarages in which the bulk of tithe allotments went to lay impropriators, many rectors were benefiting by far more than this. Country parsons in many parishes could now lease their lands or take up positions as gentleman farmers. The hunting fields would be open to them, and the traditional functions of social leadership, notably those of magistrate, were thrust upon them. It is no accident that whereas at the beginning of George III's reign only one magistrate in ten was a cleric by the end of it one in five was. (58) It is no coincidence either than in counties of heavy enclosure, particularly the midlands, clerical justices were thickest on the ground. By 1830, almost half the magistrates in Lincolnshire, Cambridgeshire and Bedfordshire were parsons. There were other reasons, of course, for the employment of 'squarsons', but the increase in their numbers was greatest where enclosure had made more of them into propertied, if not leisured, gentlemen. The development rarely worked to the advantage of their pastoral concerns. (59)

V

Some clergymen, though probably not enough, were worried about the implications of enclosures for the effectiveness of their ministry. More had practical difficulty in making their new enterprises pay, despite the advantages they had received. The rector of Broughton Hackett (Worcs.) told Thomas Greene that he had leased his allotment to (60)
> three successive tenants who not only impoverished the land and failed in their payment of Rent, but who also put me to

> great trouble and expence (sic) in ejecting them. For
> 5 years afterwards I was compelled at a considerable loss
> to keep the Land in my own Occupation in order to restore its
> condition & subsequently I could find no responsible Tenant,
> till I submitted to a rent much below that Tithe free land in
> other adjoining Parishes produces.

John Keysall, rector of Bredon, received an allotment equivalent to a fifth of the arable and a ninth of the pasture which raised his income by about 25 per cent. (61)

> But from the very great Expenses I have been put to in
> erecting the Buildings necessary for the Occupation of about
> 900 Acres of Land, and the obligation to keep those Buildings
> up, and to be accountable for Dilapidations on the same: I
> do not think upon the whole, that I have derived any material
> Advantage from the Change.

In addition to such charges, dilapidations could be a drain on an incumbent's resources. Dilapidations were sums claimed by the successors to livings on the estate of their predecessors in order to bring the parsonage house and other buildings to a condition of good repair. The claims were vague and variable, but tended to rise considerably as the status of the clergy improved and their dwelling houses were enlarged to fit their new station. Dilapidation fears convinced some clergymen that a corn rent offered a better bargain than land. John Miller of Benefield, an ardent advocate of land in lieu of tithe, believed that the size of dilapidation charges was the 'only considerable objection' to his favoured plan. Edward Jackson, curate of Bolton, believed that a corn rent 'would relieve the clergy from much trouble and uncertainty by bad Tenants etc.: would require no Dilapidations, would easily be proportioned at the Death etc of an Incumbent, would prevent too great and rapid an accumulation of Land to the Church'. (62) The most influential cleric to argue in favour of corn rents was Bishop Pretyman-Tomline of Lincoln. He persuaded his old tutee, William Pitt, of their advantages over land, and this was the preferred solution in Pitt's ill-fated scheme for commutation which was given a brief airing in Parliament in 1791. Like most others of his persuasion, Pretyman-Tomline was most concerned about dilapidation charges and the effects of poor management of land by tenants. (63) It is noticeable, however, that the bishop exercised little persuasion to his Lincolnshire clergy who took land rather than corn rents in roughly the same proportions as elsewhere. (64) The full extent of the problems of taking land were appreciated only in the light of experience, and even after the French wars, land remained much more popular than corn rents.

Corn rents, however, seem to have been received with favour by those who agreed to take them, rather than choosing the more orthodox means of commutation. There were even devices available which saved the tithe owner the trouble of collecting a large number of minor payments. Joseph Pawsey described one such to the Marchioness Grey in the case of the proposed Blunham enclosure: (65)

> If your Ladyship takes the Rectors Allotment of Land at

> Blunham, and pay them a Corn Rent; I beg leave to inform your
> Ladyship that it is customary in all these Cases that to make
> a Corn Rent secure for Time to Come & that the Church may at
> all times be secure in its Income that whoever takes the land,
> suppose 250 Acres, must add to it 250 Acres more of their own
> private property, that the Church may have a very, and over
> & above, good security, in Case of any default in paying the
> Corn Rent for time to Come: This is as it were Locking up
> a part of your own Property to make the Church Secure - ...
> This is what Mr Edwards does at Henlow; and what Mr Thornton
> agrees to do for the Muggerhanger district of Blunham; and
> what your ladyship had better do, ('as the Bishop & Rector
> seem bent on a Corn Rent in Money') for the Blunham districts,
> the Rectors share of Land will be Allotted to your Ladyship
> and will be let with your other Estates at Blunham; I should
> wish the Rectory Barn to be kept standing as it would be
> always Convenient for your Ladyships Tenant of the Tithe
> Allottment (sic) to Lay the Corn in arising from it. But if
> the Tithe Allotment should happen to be at too great a
> distance from the Village, a New Barn etc. must be Built -
> Mrs Campbell will not take any share of the Tithe allotment,
> and as the Living is your Ladyships it had better be taken
> by your Ladyship; But I am sorry to discover such avidity
> in the Bishop and Rector, that they wish to Lay all the
> trouble Hazard and expense on the Shoulders of the Laity;
> if this Living was a 'small one' and the Rector had a
> Large family to support I should think it an Act of Charity
> to be generous to Him; he has now had the Living thirteen
> years, and made very little residence in the Parish, nor
> visited the Sick, nor done much Alms to the Poor; I fear
> these are the reasons that so many go to hear Revd Mr Male,
> the Dissenting Minister.

When enclosure was first mooted in 1792 the absentee rector had
written to the Marchioness, explaining his preference for a corn
rent over land in lieu of tithe: (66)

> I cannot but accord with the Bishop of Lincoln in his
> opinion the same arrangement (i.e. a corn rent) would be
> most advantageous for the preferment throughout the Parish
> should it meet with your Ladyship's opinion, to whom I submit
> the matter with the utmost deference - The Glebe at Blunham
> is more than adequate to the purposes of the resident Rector,
> and Land has in almost every instance been found very
> troublesome and detrimental to the clergy - The Bishop's
> permission to pull down a part of the buildings which are
> very ruinous and a great burden to the Preferment if it
> meets likewise with your consent will render me a most
> essential benefit - If Land was taken in lieu of Tythes
> the barns must be removed, an expence I could very ill
> support after having expended a considerable sum from my
> private property on the House and premises; and it would
> not be possible for a Tenant to live under the same roof
> with myself & family when resident.

The Marchioness acceded to the rector's request, despite her
steward's misgivings and the Award gave him a rent charge of

£306 19s 4d charged entirely on the lands of the impropriator. The device of charging a corn rent on one estate only, thus greatly easing collection problems was also adopted in the Bedfordshire parishes of Caddington, Campton-cum-Shefford, Dunton, Eaton Socon, Henlow, Maulden, Risely, Sandy and Tilbrooke. (67)

Corn rents were an obvious alternative for those who found allotments of land a burdensome prospect, but the evidence strongly suggests that most clergymen adapted to the role of alert and informed landlords, or even practical farmers, after enclosure with surprising ease. The change left them open to obvious attack. Wade's 'Black Book', Wooler's 'Black Dwarf' and Cobbett's 'History of the Protestant Reformation' and 'Rural Rides' all inveighed bitterly against ecclesiastical property and the huge disparities of income which the enclosure movement exacerbated since rectors as a rule received far more substantial estates than vicars or curates. The cartoonists found in the 'bloated clergy' an admirable butt for their satirical shafts. Thus, George Cruikshank's 'Preachee and Flogee Too' (1818) attacks the hypocrisy implicit in the clerical magistrate's dual function. He depicts a parson dispensing sanctimonious homilies to his congregation on Sunday while meting out condign punishments to members of that same congregation for trivial offences during the rest of the week. (68) Frequent reference was also made to the clergy's leisure or farming pursuits, emphasizing their elevated status and increasing distance from their poorer parishioners. They were seen also as the too-willing tools of a repressive state.

In less flamboyant style, the Whig journals pursued the same quarry. Much space was devoted in the 'Edinburgh Review' to a critique of the established church. Attention was drawn to a growing disparity in clerical incomes. Clerical property was argued to be properly public property, and thoroughgoing reform was demanded. Henry Brougham was the most pungent critic. (69) He fastened onto the evils of clerical magistracy which the redistribution of church assets through enclosure had brought into much greater prominence. 'Nothing', he suggested in 1834, 'has a more direct tendency to excite hatred and contempt both towards the men and towards their sacred office.' (70)

The clergyman as landowner was a prime target, but the Church of England in general was the soft underbelly of Toryism in the 1820s and 1830s which could most profitably be probed. On the defensive, Tory statesmen from Sir Robert Peel downwards were forced to place church reform high on their list of legislative priorities if the party were once more to mount an effective electoral challenge after the hegemony of Lord Liverpool had been swept aside. This meant tackling such hardy perennials as pluralism, sincecures, non-residence and the misallocation of resources between town and country as well as the tithe question. (71)

Enclosures helped to draw attention to more than one of these problems. The church found it difficult to defend either professional farming clergymen with too little time for their cures, or absentee landlords drawing large incomes from rents while making the state of a dilapidated parsonage their excuse for non-residence in the parish which provided the bulk of their incomes. Wade's 'Extraordinary Black Book' collected surprisingly accurate data on the extent to which the church's resources were concentrated in too few, pluralistic, hands. Enclosures drew fresh attention to old problems. When national solutions were being applied to the enormous variety of local problems, there developed the general feeling that the enclosure movement had given the tithe owner too much. In addition, some influential clergymen realized that the usual enclosure solution to the tithe problem created more serious long-term problems than had been anticipated. Farmers also became convinced that arrangements to compensate tithe owners by land had been too hurriedly and crudely put into effect. In the rush to enclose in the 1790s, it hardly seemed to matter that a standard fifth of the arable and ninth of meadow and pasture concealed differential treatment depending on the quality of the land enclosed. As the tithe owner was compensated not only for the produce but also for the expense of cultivation and improvement, it followed that an allotment of a fifth of the arable on stiff, poorly drained clays represented a greater loss to the remaining proprietors than the same allotment on light friable loams. The imbalance was only partially corrected by the fact that tithe was less frequently commuted on poorer lands, tithe owners preferring to take a tenth of newly fertile land reclaimed from the waste. The problem was serious, and it rankled especially when falling prices taught imprudent farmers some harsh lessons. It was clear to farmers and political economists alike by the 1820s that some very incautious enclosures had been embarked upon during the war years. Giving a standard allotment in lieu of tithe irrespective of quality was tantamount to suggesting that tithe could be safely calculated as a definite proportion of the rent. As every economist since Adam Smith had been at pains to show the fallacy of this view, it is not surprising that assumptions considered valid during the peak years of enclosure should be decisively rejected twenty or thirty years later. The fall in prices induced a more rational attitude to the viability of improvement, and the tithe owner's bargaining power was reduced as a consequence. Tithe commutation was placed on the sober footing of receipts not expectation, and corn rents rather than land. Opinion had swung decisively against land allotments.

Nevertheless, the enclosure movement had created precedents for the immediate future. Cautious conservatives within the church had been shown that the burden of tithe could be tolerably commuted, and property rights put on a different footing without endangering the constitution. The specific arrangements made at enclosure seemed inappropriate by the 1830s, yet the principle of legislative interference with property rights had been effectively, if not triumphantly, vindicated. The practical tests remained, but the experience of enclosure had removed a great stumbling block in the path of full and effective tithe reform.

Chapter 5

NOTES

1 Contemporary estimates spanned these multiples and recent research has in general accepted them. W.E. Tate, 'The Enclosure Movement and the Village Community' (1967), pp.158-9, and J.D. Chambers and G.E. Mingay, 'The Agricultural Revolution, 1750-1880' (1966), pp.84-5.
2 Anon., letter in 'Farmers Magazine', ii (1801), p.280.
3 In particular the counties of Bedford, Berkshire, Cambridge, Gloucester, Huntingdon, Leicester, Lincoln, Northampton, Warwick and Worcester.
4 This was particularly true in Cheshire, Lancashire, Westmorland and Cumberland, but commons and wastes enclosure was frequent in the south-west (Devon and Cornwall) and the north riding of Yorkshire.
5 Tate, op. cit. p.184. His exact figures are open-field arable enclosures, 1603-1845, 2,792, commons and wastes, 1,393.
6 J.M. Martin, 'Warwickshire and the Parliamentary Enclosure Movement' (unpublished University of Birmingham PhD thesis, 1965). Calculations from Appendix X.
7 Calculations from enclosure Acts and awards in Staffs. RO. The Awards are catalogued Q/RDc. Of the 25 noted, 11 Acts concerned open-field arable.
8 D.M. McClatchey, 'Oxfordshire Clergy, 1777-1869' (Oxford, 1960), p.104. Calculations of percentages covered by parliamentary enclosure appear in E.C.K. Gonner, 'Common Land and Inclosure' (1912), pp.279-81.
9 M.R. Austin, 'The Church of England in the County of Derbyshire, 1772-1832' (unpublished University of London PhD thesis, 1969), pp.180-94.
10 Calculations by W.R. Ward, The tithe question in England in the early nineteenth century, 'Journal of Ecclesiastical History', xvi (1965), p.70. Ward suggests that tithe was commuted in 2,200 of the 3,128 instances of parliamentary enclosure between 1757 and 1835. There must be some doubt about these figures since a parliamentary return of 1836 lists over 3,700 enclosures during this period (PP(HC) 1836, viii, pt II, p.505). In addition, the source which Professor Ward cites purports to be 'A Return from the Inclosure and Other Private Acts in which Provisions are included for the Commutation of Tithes' (PP(HC), 1836, xliv). It is not at all clear from where Ward draws his total number of enclosure Acts. By my calculations the total number of Acts is approximately 3,700, not 3,100, and the proportion of Acts which exonerated tithe is nearer 60 per cent than 70. In any case, it should not be thought that all the available tithe was commuted in Ward's 2,200 cases. In many, important areas (such as old enclosures within the newly-enclosed area) or certain crops were to remain tithable. Sometimes, this left the bulk of the land tithable after enclosure.
11 Calculations from PP(HC) 1836, xliv.
12 J. Billingsley, 'A General View of the Agriculture of the County of Somerset' (1798), p.199.
13 Somerset RO D/P/hun. Case and letters re tithes and

enclosure. George White to Dr Parsons, 24 August 1799.
14 J. Middleton, 'A General View of the Agriculture of the County of Middlesex' (1794), pp.60-1.
15 W.K. Riland-Bedford, 'Three Hundred Years of a Family Living' (Birmingham, 1889), p.132.
16 G.B. Endacott, 'The Progress of Enclosures in Dorset' (unpublished University of Oxford BLitt thesis, 1938), pp.42-3 and Staffs. RO D1851/3/5/1-2.
17 Thomas Thompson, 'Tithes Indefensible', 3rd ed. (York, 1796), pp.46-7.
18 Bucks. RO D/LE 14/26. The surveyor calculated the value of the wheat crop from this specimen acre at £6, the bean crop at £4 4s 0d and barley at £3 13s 6d. From this gross total of £13 17s 6d, £7 3s 3d was deducted for rent, seed, dung and labour. Tithe was calculated by taking a strict tenth of the value of each crop: wheat 12s, beans 8s 4¾d, barley 7s 4d.
19 See above, chapter 2, sect. III.
20 This seems to be confirmed by listing the numbers of enclosure Acts passed in each decade between 1760 and 1830. There is a very close correlation with prevailing profitability. The figures are: 1760s, 375; 1770s, 649; 1780s, 236; 1790s, 479; 1800s, 847; 1810s, 853 (of which 601 were passed between 1810 and 1815); 1820s, 220. PP(HC) 1836, viii, pt ii, p.505.
21 'Annals of Agriculture', xv (1791), p.577.
22 Henry Homer, 'An Essay on the Nature and Method of Ascertaining the Specifick Shares of Proprietors upon the Inclosure of the Common Fields' (Oxford, 1766), and William Marshall, 'On the Appropriation and Inclosure of Commonable and Intermixed Lands' (1801).
23 14 Geo. III c. 31 and 19 Geo. III c.28.
24 McClatchey, op. cit. p.105.
25 PP(HC) 1836, xliv. The largest single allotment seems to have been three-tenths in lieu of arable tithes at Shipton (Hants) in 1792.
26 Martin, op. cit. Appendix X.
27 Copy of the Act in LCA Ingilby MSS 2922.
28 Rex C. Russell, 'Parliamentary Enclosure and Land Awarded in Lieu of Tithes' (unpublished survey of specimen Lincolnshire enclosures, Barton-upon-Humber, 1961).
29 Calculations from Staffs. RO Q/RDc.
30 Staffs. RO D1851/3/5/1-2.
31 Tate, op. cit. pp.86 and 108-9.
32 For the plurality of certain enclosure commissioners see M.W. Beresford, Commissioners of enclosure, 'Econ. Hist. Rev.', xvi (1946), pp.130-40, and W.E. Tate, Parliamentary land enclosures in the county of Nottingham, 'Thoroton Record Series', v (1935), pp. xv-xvii and 153-67. A handful of commissioners seem to have become enclosure centurions. For the younger ones there was a not unimportant link between their early work as enclosure commissioners and their later duties in the 1830s and 1840s as assistant tithe commissioners.

Chapter 5

33 LCA Mexborough Records, 797. R. Parker to Thomas Smith, 2 March 1771.
34 Rex C. Russell, 'The Revolutions in Barton and Hibaldstow' (Barton-upon-Humber, 1961), p.25.
35 Beds. RO HA 731.
36 Ibid. HA 744. The Shellington Enclosure Act is 42 Geo. III c.109.
37 Ibid. A Book L, MA 43.
38 Ibid. GA 1120/14 and A Book M: MA51. The complete text of Hooper's letter may be found in Eric J. Evans, Some reasons for the growth of English rural anti-clericalism, c.1750-c.1830, 'Past and Present', 66 (1975), p.97.
39 Essex RO D/DSs E3.
40 Herefordshire and Worcestershire RO (Hereford), RC/IV/E/247.
41 Gonner, op. cit. p.95.
42 It is not intended here to enter the minefield of the effects of enclosure on the smaller proprietor. For a fair introduction, see Chambers and Mingay, op. cit. pp.85-8. It is, however, tentatively suggested that future research might concentrate rather more on the siting of allotments and the relationship between size of holding and position. Obviously, far more local studies are needed.
43 By the end of the eighteenth century, tithe allotments seem invariably to have been provided 'gratis'. There are very occasional instances of tithe owners bearing their share of the costs a little earlier. The rector in the Ashwood Hay and Wall Heath enclosure (1777) was to ring-fence his allotment of 156¾ acres at his own expense, Staffs. RO Q/RDc 40.
44 These figures are taken from surveys of enclosures in Warwickshire and Buckinghamshire. J.M. Martin The cost of parliamentary enclosure in Warwickshire, 'University of Birmingham Historical Journal', ix (1964), pp.146-56, and M.E. Turner, The cost of parliamentary enclosure in Buckinghamshire, 'Agric. Hist. Rev.', xxi (1973), p.43. For an earlier and somewhat impressionistic assessment, see W.E. Tate, The cost of parliamentary enclosure in England, 'Econ. Hist. Rev.', 2nd ser. v (1952-3), pp.258-65.
45 Staffs. RO Q/RDc 58.
46 Turner, loc. cit. pp.40 and 45.
47 Russell, 'Parliamentary Enclosure ...', p.39.
48 Most importantly, V.M. Lavrovsky, Tithe commutation as a factor in the gradual decrease of landownership by the English peasantry, 'Econ. Hist. Rev.', iv (1933), pp.273-89, and W.G. Hoskins, 'The Midland Peasant' (1957), pp.249-51.
49 Lancs. RO DDGr uncat. MSS. Parkinson to Greene, 21 February 1829. Parkinson's enclosure work is itemized in Tate, 'Parliamentary Land Enclosure in ... Nottingham', p.163.
50 Lancs. RO DDGr. Hodgson to Greene, 22 January 1829 and W.D. Wetherall to Greene, 6 January 1829.
51 Northants RO D2778/34.
52 Bucks. RO D/LE/D 14/55.
53 Beds. RO L30/9/73/25.
54 Austin, op. cit. p.192. Values of rectorial livings increased by 238 per cent between 1772 and 1824 where land

was taken in lieu of tithe, and by 257 per cent where it was not.
55 Lancs. RO DDGr. Venables to Greene, 22 January 1829.
56 McClatchey, op. cit. p.98.
57 Calculations from figures presented in Ward, loc. cit. p.72.
58 PRO C234, Fiats of 1761, and PP(HC) 1831-2, xxv, pp.231-72.
59 For a fuller development of this theme, see Eric J. Evans, Some reasons for the growth of English rural anti-clericalism, c.1750-c.1830, 'Past and Present', 66 (1975), pp.101-4.
60 Lancs. RO DDGr. G. Boraston to Greene, 5 January 1829.
61 Ibid. John Keysall to Greene, 9 January 1829.
62 Ibid. John Miller to Greene, 27 January 1829, and Edward Jackson to Greene, 2 February 1829.
63 BM Add MSS 34, 440 ff 58-63, and Earl Stanhope, 'Life of William Pitt', 2 vols (1861), ii, p.276. John Davies explained Bishop Tomline's preference for corn rents in a letter to Greene, Lancs. RO, DDGr, 6 February 1829. The Bishop of Hereford from 1788 to 1803, John Butler, also inclined towards corn rents. See Edward Wallwyn to the Duke of Norfolk, 21 October 1794, Hereford RO RC/IV/E/24.
64 PP(HC) 1867, liv, pp.36-9.
65 Beds. RO L30/9/73/21. Pawsey to Grey, 3 January 1796.
66 Ibid. L30/9/66, Samuel Lawry to Grey, 21 December 1792.
67 PP(HC) 1867, liv, pp.3-5.
68 M.D. George, ed., 'Catalogue of Political and Personal Satires in the British Museum', 11 vols (1935-54), vii no.13281.
69 See, for example, his attacks on High Tory principles in 'Edinburgh Review', xli (1824), pp.20-30; on church questions, ibid. lvi (1832), pp.203-20; and on religious toleration, ibid. lxvi (1838), pp.461-5.
70 'Edinburgh Review', lviii (1834), p.500.
71 The best guides to the church reform movement are M.L. Mathieson, 'English Church Reform, 1815-1840' (1923); G.F.A. Best, 'Temporal Pillars' (Cambridge, 1964), pp.185-347; Owen Chadwick, 'The Victorian Church', 2 vols (1966-70), i, pp.101-41; and R.M. Soloway, 'Prelates and People' (1969), pp.279-348. On Peel's ecclesiastical policy, see Norman Gash, 'Sir Robert Peel (1972), pp.96-105.

CHAPTER 6

THE TITHE COMMUTATION ACT AND ITS ANTECEDENTS

I

By the 1830s, the battle for tithe reform had been all but won. Philosophical and practical objections had been aired 'in extenso', and every manner of possible reform had been suggested. The long delayed parliamentary Reform Act of 1832 seemed to open the floodgates to change in many spheres. The church and its friends became convinced that a judicious retreat from the last ditch was the only means of preserving the essentials in the face of radical attacks. If the secular arm had adopted a posture of 'reculer pour mieux sauter' in 1832, the spiritual could follow the lead. Indeed the innocuous and innocent Archbishop Howley had introduced a permissive Bill to reform the tithe system by encouraging long leases as early as 1830. The need for reform was urgent and grudgingly recognized. Disestablishment was by no means a remote possibility. In such a climate, the tithe question inevitably loomed large. It gave as much offence as any aspect of church affairs, and as there was room for manoeuvre on this issue, it was placed near the front of the church's reforming shop window, on prominent display. With the Primate of All England prepared to countenance reform, lesser dignitaries could move more easily. Bishop Ryder of Lichfield and Coventry stated in 1832 that he was: (1)

> disposed to view with approbation - not however unhesitating and unqualified - a plan for permanent compulsory composition.... Whatever could relieve the intercourse between the minister and the bulk of his people from occasions of collision, from fuel for discord, and even from dealings of a mere pecuniary description, would ... materially contribute to the maintenance or restoration of a right, pastoral and spiritual feeling between the shepherd and his flock.

In April 1834 an editorial in 'The Times', always a firm friend to the church, asserted that 'All men of all parties express the most anxious desire to see the tithe question set at rest.' (2)

The question was no longer 'whether' but 'how' and precedents during the previous sixty years had shed some light on that matter. Allotments of land in lieu of tithe, so favoured at enclosure, seemed rather less attractive to both sides in the light of experience. When the agricultural boom collapsed after 1815, landowners came to realize that some thoroughly bad tithe exoneration bargains had been struck. The church had been given too much when the imperative to improve seemed overwhelming. Within the church itself, moreover, opinion had begun to move against land, despite its many attractions of security and status. Undoubtedly, Pretyman-Tomline's influence was important in this direction, and it did not cease with the death of his patron, Pitt, in 1806. (3) The problems of vastly increased dilapidation charges and the rooking of inexperienced clerical landlords by unscrupulous tenants were given more point after 1815 when it became necessary to maintain profitability with prices sinking to more realistic levels. Squarsons needed both skill and business acumen, and they also needed to devote more time to their landed enterprises.

The evangelical party, which was gaining strength in this period, looked askance at clerical farmers or landlords. Such activities undermined pastoral effectiveness by seducing a pastor from his primary duties of earnest spiritual endeavour and effective preaching of the gospel. Various factors, which cannot concern us here, conspired to increase the influence of the 'church evangelicals' in the 1820s. As they became stronger they exerted greater pressure on the ecclesiastical hierarchy to seek some less dangerous and diverting means of compensation for tithes. (4) Since the church's radical opponents were also concentrating their fire on ecclesiastical landowners and pluralists, it was not altogether surprising that it should seek a more defensible position in the 1820s and 1830s.

One obvious alternative - a straight cash settlement - had been ruled out of court by the price fluctuations of the past half-century. Increasingly, therefore, informed opinion moved in favour of substituting variable corn rents in lieu of tithe. This seemed acceptable in that it tied clerical fortunes to those of agriculture with fewer opportunities for rancour than under the prevailing system. There was some experience of corn rent solutions both in a minority of enclosures and also in the small number of cases where tithes had been commuted by private Act of Parliament. (5) Here corn rents, rather than land or cash, had been the invariable mode of commutation.

Effective national legislation had to wait for a reformed parliament, but the subject of tithe was frequently raised in both Houses, particularly in the aftermath of the sudden depression of arable prices and profits after 1813. Many petitions, arguing for reform, were marshalled and used by John Christian Curwen, MP for Carlisle, in a campaign to bring the tithe question to the forefront of political debate. Curwen, who had been a Foxite Whig in the 1790s, and who retained a bucolic interest in reforming causes, was a wealthy mine-owner and practical farmer from Workington with a vigorous, if somewhat unstructured, commitment to agricultural improvement. As the founder-member and leading luminary of the Workington Agricultural Society, he did much to initiate the Cumbrian 'statesmen' and yeomen farmers into the possibilities of scientific farming in one of the most

backward agricultural areas of Britain. (6) His opposition to
tithes was that of the true improver. He argued that nearly all
of the petitions on agricultural distress 'place tithes as one
of the most prominent grievances under which they labour'. (7)
His efforts for tithe reform were rewarded by a select committee
established in 1816 to consider the various petitions against
tithe and 'to report to the House if it be expedient to enable
the Owners of Tithes and Occupiers of Tithable lands and others
to substitute pecuniary payments for Tithes in kind during certain
specified periods'. (8)
   In the ensuing debate Curwen and his supporters, though
emphasizing the disincentive effects of tithe to improvement,
were careful to affirm that they anticipated no decrease in tithe
owners' revenues, and looked only to a fairer method of assessment
and collection. (9) Sir William Scott and Viscount Castlereagh
were concerned lest the committee merely collected evidence
against the church, or seemed to be offering what Scott called
a 'bazaar' to receive all manner of ill-informed complaints.
'The Times' warned against general invasions of clerical property
at a time of general confusion: (10)
      Any scheme which tends to force the clergy to a sacrifice
      of their rights, and to drive them from the solid ground
      of lawful & immemorial possession to an eleemosynary
      dependence on the liberality of the state would be utterly
      inconsistent with the stability of the English constitution.
Placing the horrors of the expropriation of the French clergy after
1789 firmly before its readers' eyes, it concluded 'that no
pretence of paying the clergy a mere stipend without reference to
the extent and produce of the soil, ought to be listened to for
a moment'. 'The Times' was concerned to head off proposals far
more radical than those yet presented to parliament. The select
committee's recommendations were extremely mild. It recommended
a general form of lease to enable standard procedures to be
established. (11) In the next session a Bill was introduced to
enable leases to be made to bind successors to a living, provided
only that the bishop agreed to the arrangement. (12) The
purpose, of course, was to lessen the tithe problems which
frequently followed a change of incumbency. Scott, however,
objected that the proposal 'seemed to strike at a great principle
of law, that a tenant for life should not injure his successor'.
(13) Scott's Oxford University constituents were equally unhappy
with the Bill, arguing that it was objectionable 'in principle
and professions'. The Bill was delayed almost until the end of
the session before being sent up to the Lords at the end of
June 1817. It did not return.
   By this time, Curwen was taking a new, and more far-reaching,
tack. He wished to rationalize proceedings in tithe disputes by
enabling any plaintiff or defendant in such a suit to demand a
trial by jury, and to sue a composition before 1570 without
producing the original deed or agreement. The main test of the
validity of a modus should be the experience of living memory. (14)
Curwen attacked the iniquity of lengthy legal proceedings initiated
by certain tithe claims. He quoted the notorious case of Rev.
Peploe Ward, rector of Cottenham (Cambs.) who had successfully

laid aside a modus which had been paid since 1595, by means of a
chancery suit. The parishioners had been undone by their inability
to produce any ancient deed validating the customary payment.
Curwen claimed that his measure was essential to 'prevent the
church from plundering the community and destroying those
exemptions to which they are justly entitled'. (15)

The pattern of the debate assumed a predictable course. Curwen
drummed up support from his Cumbrian constituents in the form of
a petition complaining about the 'great uncertainty' of the
validity of modus payments, while the University of Cambridge
viewed 'with the greatest anxiety and alarm' any attempt to
'overturn those principles upon which for centuries the wisest
lawyers have founded their decisions with respect to tithes....
The law of tithes is interwoven with the Constitution, no less of
the State than of the Church and has been guaranteed by every
Charter of our Civil Liberties.' (16) Curwen was aided in the
debate by the leading Whigs, Samuel Romilly and Henry Brougham.
William Scott, inevitably leading for the defence, was ably
supported by the young Sir Robert Peel, who confessed himself
alarmed at the slurs being cast on the church's reputation by
half-truths and innuendo. He observed that of the 120 tithe
cases brought to light by Curwen's probings, and on which he
rested much of his argument, only 69 had been brought by the
clergy, and only 35 within the previous three years. This was
no evidence of the 'excessive litigation' which Curwen attacked.
Scott was also concerned about atypical instances exaggerated into
misleading and discreditable generalizations at the church's
expense. Even in a thin house, the Tory majority had no difficulty
in scotching Curwen's radical proposals. The second reading of
his Bill was deferred for six months - an effective death sentence
on it, since the end of the session was bound to intervene. (17)

II

The agricultural depression of 1821-3, though it brought many
criticisms of the tithe system, provoked no new legislative
proposals on the subject. Wheat prices temporarily dipped below
50s a quarter, but as they climbed safely back over the 60s
mark in the middle years of the decade, complaints receded. In
any case, even in the worst years, the extent of depression was
exaggerated, the very real sufferings of arable farmers on the
heavy clays being made to do duty for a misleadingly generalized
picture of distress presented for the benefit of the select
committee. (18)

Until the very end of the 1820s, the tithe problem was
virtually ignored by the legislature. (19) It was revived in
1828 by the efforts of another north-western MP, Thomas Greene
of Lancaster. He had been involved in tithe affrays which had
necessitated private legislation to commute tithes in Lancaster
and nearby Cockerham in 1824 and 1825, and had been impressed by
the smooth solutions which had been found there. Accordingly,
he introduced the first Bill for national tithe commutation.
His aim was to facilitate agreements for commutation by corn

rent. (20) The Bill was permissive only, and the consent of
landowners, tithe owners and the respective bishops had to be
obtained. Commutation was to be entrusted to three commissioners,
at least one of whom was to be a beneficed clergyman. The
commissioners would appoint a valuer to make a survey of the
parish and to estimate the average annual value of the tithe
over the previous seven years. A corn rent would be awarded tied
to the average 'price or value of good marketable English wheat
at the principal market of the City of London'. A tithe award
would set down for all future reference the proportion of the
total sum to be borne by each proprietor. There was provision for
reassessment after a period of years, and a clause enabling
tithe owners to demand a reassessment on any land hitherto waste
but brought into cultivation after commutation.

It was a bold scheme, though it owed much to previous plans
submitted to William Pitt and others over the previous thirty
years. It cut through centuries of traditional practice to
achieve agreed and clear values to form the basis of a permanent
settlement. Greene's scheme was not so very different from the
legislation which was to settle the tithe problem eight years
later. His work perhaps deserves better recognition than it has
received.

It was probably inevitable that the first plan for national
commutation to get as far as a parliamentary Bill should receive
a rebuff from the tithe owning interest. The universities of
Oxford and Cambridge once again led the attack. Both petitioned
the House of Commons against the Bill, on the dual grounds that
a permanent commutation based on the average price of wheat over
a specific period of time was unjust and that, under the plan,
collegiate bodies need not be consulted before incumbents of
livings in their patronage made agreements for commutation. (21)
One of Oxford's MPs, Sir Robert Peel, made the major speech
against Greene's Bill. He well appreciated the strength of
feeling of most of his constituents, and as Home Secretary in
Wellington's ministry he was concerned to defend the interests
of the church and all other property holders. On the motion for
committal, Peel moved that 'it be an instruction to the Committee
that they should have the power to limit the duration of any
bargain or agreement entered into under the provisions of this
measure to twenty one years'. (22) He was worried about the long-
term effects of the proposal and pointed out that if such
legislation had been in force in Norfolk before the improvement
of farms due to extensive turnip and barley cultivation, the
tithe owners' income would by no means have kept pace with agricultural improvement. The debate turned on the old question of
whether a tithe owner should share in the improvement of the
land which the farmer had obtained by heavy investment. The
House approved Peel's instruction to the Committee by 81 votes
to 29. The speeches from the majority side, however, indicate
an important shift of ground. They tacitly acknowledged the need
for change, merely taking exception to the particular measure
before the House. Many from the conservative side would have
been happy enough with temporary conversion from tithe to corn
rent. They stuck only at permanent alienation, while reinforcing

their view – readily accepted only a few years before during the enclosure movement – that tithe owners should share in the profits of improved agriculture. A more tractable attitude than this was not to be found in the unreformed Parliament, though the change in tone here was most marked compared with Sir John Scott's hectoring philippics against the enemies of church and state during the French wars. Greene's Bill was deferred in committee, the radicals having lost all interest in its promotion once Peel's wrecking amendment had been passed.

The proposal, however, was of considerable importance. It re-opened Parliamentary interest in the English tithe question. In 1829 and 1830 the number of petitions to Parliament calling for a change in the tithe system greatly increased. The landowners of Rochester, for example, called for 'an early abolition of the Tithe Tax, a measure which would give more satisfaction to the Country and reflect greater credit upon the Legislature than any enactment that has been carried for centuries past'. (23) The inhabitants of Llanthewy (Monmouth) argued that tithe 'was a cause of the most violent and inveterate disputes' and operated as an absolute bar to improvement, while petitioners from Holt (Norfolk) concentrated on the illegitimacy of a system which was nothing more than a 'Popish abuse'. (24) George Gunning of Frendsbury (Kent) asked Parliament to give consideration to an amendment of the poor laws, while arguing that the tithe system greatly exacerbated the situation: (25)

(It) checks improvement, paralyzes industry, promotes pauperism and tends to destroy the virtuous spirit and meritorious exertion of the labouring poor. The petitioner is firmly persuaded that by fixing a percentage on real rents in lieu of tithes, that it would soon decrease vagrancy, lessen crime and promote the happiness of all classes of society.

The usual fate of such petitions was that after presentation they were formally ordered to lie on the table, and thereafter ignored. The initiative of individuals, however, could rescue at least some from oblivion. Joseph Hume, the radical MP for Aberdeen, and veteran of many reforming jousts, took up some anti-tithe petitions and forced a debate in the Commons in 1830. He attacked tithe as a prop to the church establishment he fought so hard to dismantle. He drew attention to recent well-attended meetings at Rochester and Penenden Heath which passed resolutions calling for the abolition of tithe. This done, Hume was convinced 'that many persons would employ labourers for the purpose of improving their property which under the existing system they could not think of doing'. (26) Abolition would enable poor rates to be reduced, and would conduce to the general well-being of the agricultural interest. Pure religion could only be the gainer from such a transaction. 'It was well known in fact that religion flourished most where political establishment for its support were unknown.' In 1831, Hume took up the case of the parishioners of Havering-atte-Bower (Essex). They were subjected to tithe in kind of milk and potatoes after an attempt to set aside moduses had been resisted by the parishioners. Hume made much of a series of letters from the tithe lessee demanding tithe of eggs, and threatening legal action if they were not produced. A thin House witnessed an acrimonious wrangle between Hume and Sir Robert Inglis, Peel's successor as MP for Oxford, before the debate was concluded. (27)

Hume's counterpart in the Lords was Lord King who drew attention there to the 'prevailing spirit of complaint' against the tithe system. He castigated the impost as a public nuisance which had affected the kind and quality of cultivation of many crops, and contributed to the misery of many unemployed labourers. (28) The Swing Riots, of course, presented radicals with a magnificent opportunity to taunt the establishment with the failure of its policies. King more than once roused members of the episcopal bench to hasty, and sometimes unwise, defence of the tithe system.

Hume was right when he argued in presenting the Rochester petition that 'a very great change has taken place in the minds of men of late years'. The case for reform was presented ever more strongly at a time when the church was weakly placed to resist. The repeal of the Test and Corporations Acts and the 'desertion' of Peel and Wellington over Catholic emancipation in 1829 had demoralized the ecclesiastical establishment, and the weakening of the Ultras' position at the election of 1830 brought reform a measurable step nearer. (29) The rejection of the second parliamentary Reform Bill in October 1831 was blamed by the radical interest on the bishops. Of the 26 bishops 21 voted against the Bill in a Lords opposition majority of 41. The failure of the Bill was followed by massive anti-clerical demonstrations in Nottingham, Derby, Bristol and elsewhere. (30) In the period 1831-4, it seems safe to say, the Church of England stood in more imminent danger of disestablishment than at any time before or since.

The church had its quota of moderate and conscientious bishops, such as Blomfield of London, Sumner of Chester or Ryder of Gloucester, who now saw that the church must offer to reform itself to avert a more radical and drastic change imposed from without. The number of pluralists, the scandalous disparity in clerical incomes, the plight of the poorest curates, and the inadequacy of the church's urban ministry were all issues which called for urgent redress. Even before 1832, Eldonite reaction and resistance to all change was as useless a stance on ecclesiastical as on political questions. Robert Peel's recognition of this fact was a considerable help to reformers within the church preparing to concede change on the best terms it could get. A Tory party committed to considered reforms was the most effective prop which the Anglican church could have. Robert Peel told his Tamworth constituents of his views on church reform in December 1834: (31)

> As to Church Property in this country, no person has expressed a more earnest wish than I have done that the question of tithe, complicated and difficult as I acknowledge it to be, should, if possible, be satisfactorily settled by the means of a commutation, founded upon just principles, and proposed after mature deliberation.

III

The Tithe Commutation Act was prefaced by an attack upon the outworks, which concentrated on the problems implicit in tithe litigation. By an Act of 1832, defendants of a modus had only to prove unvarying and continuous payment for 30 years to have the Courts declare it valid. (32) In 1834 tithe owners were prevented from ferreting out and prosecuting antique claims by an Act which prohibited them from going to law for tithe which had not been collected at any time in the previous sixty years. (33) In 1835, the major loophole to vindicative litigation was belatedly closed when tithe owners making claims of less than £10 in value were enjoined to pursue them only in magistrates' courts. (34)

Ironically, the first of these Acts, which was designed to calm the passions aroused by the tithe system, served only to inflame them. Lord Tenterden's Act, as the 1832 Act was known, incorporated a period of a year during which long-dormant claims could be acted upon for the last time. The result delighted the radicals who felt the momentum of their effort flagging after the Reform Bill crisis had passed. During the year of grace an unprecedentedly large number of tithe suits were begun by men anxious to establish rights before the doors finally closed. In August 1833, William Blamire, MP for East Cumberland, asked the solicitor-general about his plans for dealing with the rash of litigation. Sir John Campbell was forced to admit that the evil of unfettered tithe suits was 'of a tremendous kind' and that the clergy seemed to be infatuated with tithe actions. (35) On the following day, Blamire introduced a Bill to suspend all tithe suits until the end of the next session. (36) He was able to draw attention to 1,500 suits recently begun in one parish - Kendal - alone. (37) The measure rapidly passed the Commons, was held up by the Lords under considerable episcopal pressure, but the Bill for preventing the prosecution of old claims became law in 1834.

The reaction to Tenterden's Act increased the tensions on the church. Inevitably clerical tithe owners were singled out for particular criticism although a large number of the new claims had been brought by impropriators. Anti-tithe slogans again became popular. Henry Handley, the radical MP for South Lincolnshire, evoked a warm response from his audience of Holbeach farmers in December 1834 when he attacked tithe as 'a tax upon the capital, skill and industry of the occupiers of the soil'. (38) Lord Brougham developed his charge into a general attack on the viability of the ecclesiastical establishment: (39)

> Those proceedings (the tithe suits) exasperated the country in an unparalleled degree and ... the general hatred of Tithe and Rate and Pluralists and Political Priests and whatever else is made the ground of an attack upon the Establishment, never reached a higher pitch of exacerbation or spread more widely through the Community than of late.

In such an atmosphere a thorough-going Tithe Bill could not be long delayed. Those who worked to preserve both the Church and its temporalities recognized the fact as they appreciated the

Chapter 6

need for reform in other areas of church life. The Ecclesiastical Commission, the most substantial achievement of the short-lived Peel minority government of 1834-5, was effected by a ministry which was a strong supporter of the established church. With four bishops and the Archbishop of Canterbury among its twelve members it proposed and put into execution a series of reforms which ensured that the Victorian church would be in a much healthier state than the Hanoverian church had been. (40) Tithe reform fitted appropriately into the general pattern. It would serve, it was hoped, to cool anti-clerical tempers and baulk the radicals of their disestablishment prize.

In each of the parliamentary sessions of 1833, 1834, 1835 and 1836 a major tithe commutation Bill was introduced by the government of the day. Three Bills were Whig and one Tory. The issue was debated against a background of sharply falling grain prices and renewed cries of agricultural distress. (41) Parliament was made well aware of the pressures combining to make tithe reform necessary, and there was no lack of radical members anxious to hammer the point home on the floor of the House. In 1833, the Whig chancellor of the exchequer, Lord Althorp, introduced a Bill to commute tithes by a corn rent fixed by tithe valuers on the basis of receipts over the previous seven years. (42) A mechanism was incorporated to permit a 10 per cent increase or decrease in the sum payable if a tithe valuer considered that the average was unfair to either party. In the first year of operation, the consent of tithe owners and a majority of tithe payers would be necessary to effect commutation. Thereafter, it would be carried out compulsorily on demand from one party. Althorp laid particular stress on two benefits he expected to be gained from the measure - better relations between incumbent and parishioners, and improved agricultural investment.

All contributors to the debate which followed expressed their commitment to the principle of commutation, but many were apprehensive about the specific proposals. (43) Peel led the doubters. His main objection was to the compulsory clauses. From the radical camp, Cutlar Fergusson suggested that tithe payers should be given the opportunity to purchase lay tithes outright. Debate got bogged down in detail, and the committee stage of the Bill was not reached until July. More in hope than anticipation, Althorp agreed to drop the compulsory clauses. (44) Many members, however, argued reasonably enough that the government's handling of the measure had betrayed its own lack of confidence in its efficacy, and that it would be better to await maturer reflection in the next session. The committee stage was deferred, and the Bill killed.

Early in the next session, the Commons set up a committee to examine the entire question and in April 1834 resolved (45)

> That it is expedient to effect a Commutation of Tithes and to abolish the collection & payment of Tithes in kind throughout England and Wales and in lieu thereof to substitute an annual payment to the Parties entitled to Tithes, with a power for the redemption of such payments under certain conditions.

Althorp's 1834 Bill dealt with each of these desiderata. It was probably the most radically conceived measure of the four in that

it attempted to settle tithe as a premanently fixed proportion of
the rent of the land from which the tithe fell due. Althorp's
experiences of the previous session had apparently convinced him
that commutation must be firmly rooted in local experience and
knowledge. He proposed a separate valuation of land in each
county. The proportion of tithe to be awarded was to be determined
by the local Quarter Sessions, according to prevailing modes of
cultivation. By establishing recognizably local procedures and
by fixing tithe to rent, Althorp hoped to meet the major
objections that tithe, as a tax on yield, discouraged investment,
and that national solutions inevitably meant local injustices.
In addition, the landowners were to be permitted under certain
circumstances to redeem their tithe at twenty-five years purchase.

Despite the fact that the climate was ready for reform of what
was generally recognized to be 'an irksome and tormenting system'
(46) Althorp's measure proved too novel and too controversial.
It was easy to accept the principle while rejecting the mechanics.
Once again, Peel led the way. He complained about vagueness in
the Bill, and despite Althorp's concern with local interests,
suggested that under these proposals such counties as Devon and
Kent would bear a much heavier burden than the rest of the country.
His advocacy of voluntary commutation won much support in the
House, and it became clear that, although Althorp was again
prepared to consider amendments, his Bill would not receive a
sufficiently wide measure of support. (47) As in 1833, there was
not enough time to work out proper solutions on the floor of the
House. Moreover, it was universally felt that the Irish tithe
question was more pressing. Consequently the English Bill was
sacrificed to permit more time to be given to an abortive Irish
tithe Bill. (48) When the general Irish situation precipitated
the fall of Grey's government in July 1834, the English tithe
proposals were hopelessly stuck.

The responsibility of trying to steer a successful tithe Bill
through Parliament, therefore, devolved on Peel and his minority
Tory government. It was already evident that Peel would not
countenance any scheme which comprehended compulsory commutation.
When he brought forward his measure in March 1835, however, it
proved to be the most skilfully drafted and comprehensive proposal
yet devised. In many particulars it was followed by Lord John
Russell when he introduced his successful Bill in 1836. Peel
argued that the issue of tithe commutation was a vital one,
'Not mere party consideration, but involving considerations of much
general importance, attended by great complexity of details,
and affecting to a considerable extent the interests of the
community at large.' (49) He proposed a corn rent, varying with
the price of wheat, barley and oats, in lieu of tithes. There
was provision for changes in the rent every seven years.
Commutation should be voluntarily accepted by not less than two-
thirds of the tithe owners and two-thirds of the tithe payers by
value. Each agreement should be scrutinized by tithe commissioners
to 'prevent fraud and collusion' between the parties, and to ensure
that the corn rent had been agreed according to the principles
laid down in the proposed legislation. Peel wished to provide
maximum opportunity for the exercise of local knowledge in the

hope that this would ensure 'a sense of common interest, a disposition to remove all difficulties and to get rid of expenses'.

Peel's plan presupposed good will and a desire to co-operate on both sides. Many members believed that he was being too sanguine. Mr Rolfe, MP for Penryn, baldly stated that not one in twenty tithe owners would oblige by agreement to commute. Lord John Russell believed that compulsory provisions would prove to be essential, since the present difficulties even in agreeing to compositions showed the measure of the problem. William Blamire, however, welcomed permissive legislation because he failed to see how compulsory commutation could be fairly effected throughout the country.

Peel's expectations could not be put to the test, since the Irish situation was to drive him from office within a month of introducing his Bill. He had appealed for all-party co-operation on the tithe question, and, to a point, he had been given it in the form of a genuine desire for commutation. There remained one important issue dividing the Tories from the Whigs on the issue. Peel knew well when he surrendered the seals that the incoming Whig administration would introduce proposals for compulsory commutation. Though in many respects Lord John Russell's tithe commutation Bill, introduced in February 1836, duplicated the provisions of Peel's, the compulsory clauses enshrined a principle to which the Tories were unable to give their assent.

The central machinery proposed by Russell was virtually the same as that laid down by Peel. There were to be three tithe commissioners in overall charge of the progress of commutation with powers to appoint assistants to supervise or direct individual commutations. The administrative bureaucracy was clearly modelled on the Poor Law Commission, established in 1834. Commutation was to be effected by taking the average value of the tithes over the previous seven years, and laying out this sum in purchase of equal parts of wheat, barley and oats according to the prevailing price of grains over the same period. This was converted into a money payment known as the tithe rent charge. Such, plus clauses on compulsory commutation, were the bare bones of an extremely complex proposal. It was not a party measure as such. The ensuing debate clearly showed the constructive attitude which both sides were adopting to get the Bill through. Russell himself was well aware that his Bill had faults. He admitted that it could not possibly meet all the objections which might be raised in view of the widely differing tithe customs and practices in operation throughout the country. His objective was 'to produce as little disturbance as possible to existing interests', and he agreed readily that Parliament should have an opportunity of a 'thorough sifting' of the Bill. He would consider with an open mind any amendments which MPs might make. (50)

Russell was certainly as good as his word. He knew that his Government was concerned first and foremost to get commutation on to the statute book, and was not sufficiently on top of the details to insist on every clause as it stood. He was convinced that there must be compulsory commutation, but beyond this he kept a fairly open mind. On first reading, Peel pointed out that the plan for arriving at the rent charge would mean wide discrepancies, depending on the strictness with which tithe had been collected during the years taken as the base for the average. Peel's own proposal, however, had been subject to the same criticism, and it was certainly no fairer to relate tithe to rent. There was criticism also of Russell's plan to standardize a deduction to be made for expenses of collection. Russell had proposed (clause 29) that in cases where the average sum collected for tithe was either less than 60 per cent or more than 75 per cent of the total value of the tithe, the amount considered for rent charge should stand at 60 per cent or 75 per cent respectively. (51) Sir Robert Inglis attacked this arbitrary proceeding as an unwarranted attack on property. 'The Times' believed that the 25 to 40 per cent reduction in the value of the tithe would go straight into the pockets of the landlords. 'We for our parts do not see what the clergy of England have done to merit such a spoliation.' (52) By no means all of the argument was on one side, however, and the MP for south Wiltshire believed that a 25 per cent reduction for expenses was almost invariably too low. (53) Russell fought hard in committee to retain some measure of control over deductions for expenses of collection, but was forced in the end to drop the clause and replace it with one giving the tithe commissioners discretionary power to raise or lower the average value of the tithe by not more than 20 per cent if they believed that, for any reason, the averages did not represent the true value. (54)

Another attempt to fix an additional rent charge of 15s an acre when land was newly cultivated with hops was defeated in committee, and a new clause substituted which introduced the concept of 'ordinary' and 'extraordinary' rent charge on hop grounds and market gardens, and left it to the commissioners to fix precise amounts in each case. (55) The general drift of both discussion and amendments was to loosen the controls imposed by the Bill, and give more discretionary powers to the commissioners. This was the nearest the government got to meeting the charge of differential effects in different regions. Russell eventually accepted the potential dangers of making too many national rules to govern widely disparate local circumstances. The committee's work also explained more precisely the functions of the commissioners, the procedure on making maps and depositing Awards, and guidelines for payment and recovery of commutation expenses. Such revisions largely accounted for the extension of this much-amended Bill from its original 54 clauses to its final 97. (56)

The extent of the changes provoked angry comment from some of the government's own supporters. Many saw the general drift of the amendments as strengthening the tithe owners' position. Thomas Pemberton, MP for Ripon, said that hardly a single clause from the original Bill remained unaltered. 'In fact the measure was so little the same that the supporters of the Government were now called upon to vote for the very measure which the former night they had repudiated.' (57) He was exaggerating, but he also mistook the purpose of the government in promoting the measure. The Whigs wanted all-party support, if possible, and were little fixed on any specific proposal so long as some form of compulsory commutation was effected. It was probably true, as Jasper Parrott (Totnes) and others insisted, that even after much debate in committee and on the floor of the House, the complexities of the subject had not been plumbed, but the government would have no truck with his remedy of a commission to enquire into the state of tithes before legislation were accepted. (58) Russell seemed content that many criticisms of his Bill cancelled each other out. He said that as the Bill had been called both 'A clergyman's Bill' and a 'landlord's Bill', this offered convincing evidence that the government was steering an appropriate middle course. (59) He offered the possibility of amendment in the light of experience if any of the criticisms upon which the government had not acted was proved to be valid, or if other disadvantages manifested themselves. He was able to discount such unsupported claims as those of Parrott that the Bill would raise the level of tithes by 20-30 per cent in Cornwall and would lose the government the support of every Whig in the county. (60)

Russell's Bill passed the Commons in June 1836 and the Lords were not disposed to wreck it. Working parties were set up between the Commons and the Lords to thrash out the remaining differences, most of the Lords' contingent comprising bishops and lay impropriators. (61) They insisted on only two amendments of significance. The bishop of the diocese should see every agreement relating to clerical tithes before its confirmation by the commissioners, and lands not exceeding 20 acres in extent could be given in part exchange for certain tithes if both sides agreed. The bishops were by now convinced that this measure was their best chance of converting tithes into more desirable and securer property without significant loss, and the Lords debates included none of the fundamentalist opposition to tithe reform which killed any chance of effective reform in the 1810s or 1820s. (62) Archbishop Howley, in particular, was much in favour of commutation and did much work in committee to facilitate the passage of the Bill.

The Royal Assent was obtained on 13 August 1836. It was received in almost total silence. In the prominent array of administrative reforms passed in this decade - poor laws, municipal corporations, church rates (which greatly exercised the urban radicals) and even Irish tithes - the English Tithe Act has been overlooked. The work of the tithe commissioners has been virtually ignored in the welter of case studies and analytical discussion of the administrative reform movement of the 1830s and 1840s. (63) Yet the Tithe Act is of first importance. It set in train a national reorganization of a system of local taxation uniquely complex and diverse. The administrative machinery necessary to rationalize and reorganize the old system was major. The work of the tithe commission deserves a place in any 'pattern of government growth'.

Undoubtedly, the very complexity of the measure inhibited informed comment and discussion. It is doubtful if more than a small minority even of the active members of the Commons actually understood it. It was widely regarded as a professionals' measure, upon which it would be unwise for the uninitiated to venture an opinion, however free might have been the criticism of the old system which it replaced. More importantly, the

Tithe Act was politically bipartisan. As on the issue of
Municipal Corporations reform, Peel and the Conservatives restricted
their opposition to points of detail. The Act fitted admirably
Peel's nostrum about constructive opposition, and the need to
restrain from attacking measures which were at least in part
accepted by the Conservatives. (64)

The Act was no triumph of statecraft. It did not bear the
stamp of firm government. Its major triumph was in reaching the
statute book at all, after the failure of its predecessors.
Governmental compromises had removed the cutting edge of opposition from most quarters, and it received lukewarm approval.
Almost everyone had reservations on points of detail, but almost
no one was prepared to push these to the point of further
obstruction of a measure which in principle everyone desired.
This was the more true since Russell and the Whigs had shown
themselves admirably open to persuasion and to amending their
original proposal. Croker's Tory analysis is of interest: (65)

> There are some remarkable and instructive circumstances
> connected with this bill. It is, perhaps, the most
> important passed in this session, yet it has excited
> comparatively little observation. It is assuredly that
> which has been most altered and amended from the first
> conception of the government - yet we hear no complaints
> from the ministers of having been forced to yield their
> own better judgments to the dictates of fashion; nor
> from the followers of the ministers, of their having been
> thus pusillanimously compromised on so important a subject.
> Why this unusual submission to correction? Why? - because
> it was an English bill of deep and real importance, and the
> English gentry, even the few radicals who may be reckoned
> in that class would not permit great and permanent interests
> to be made the plaything of faction - a tub to be tossed and
> lashed about by the tail of the leviathan.

Stripped of its rhetoric and a certain Tory windiness, there was
much sense in this appraisal. Tithe had ceased to be a party
issue, and the radicals who had wished to see tithe abolished
had been shunted into a siding in an exercise which, repeated
on numerous other occasions during the 1830s, ensured that the
'decade of reform' produced remarkably few short-term changes in
the fabric of government or society. It remained to be seen
whether this particular parliamentary hybrid, designed to strengthen
and redefine important property interests, would work in practice.

IV

The measure which the tithe commissioners had to put into effect
during the next fifteen years or so deserves consideration and
analysis. As has been seen, its main purpose was to eliminate
for ever the vagaries of tithing in kind, by substituting easily
verifiable money payments. This payment was to fluctuate in
accordance with price movements of the three main arable crops -
wheat, barley and oats. The Act made provision for two kinds of
commutation: that voluntarily agreed by tithe owners and payers,

and compulsory commutation which was imposed on the parties by the tithe commissioners. Russell had originally envisaged giving parties only six months to reach voluntary agreement, after which the commissioners would make a compulsory award. He was persuaded, however, that such a short space of time was not feasible and lengthened it, firstly to twelve months and finally in the Act (c.36) to just over two years. Compulsory commutation was to begin on 1 October 1838.

The chief executives of commutation were the tithe commissioners. Three were to be appointed, two by the Crown - in practice the Home Secretary - and one by the Archbishop of Canterbury. The tithe commissioners were to report to the Home Secretary on their proceedings and to provide a written report for Parliament every year on the state of commutation. (66) They operated from London, and in the field they relied on the work of the assistants they were empowered to appoint to superintend the mechanics of individual agreements, awards and apportionments. Assistants were permitted to claim a maximum of £3 for every day on which they were engaged on a commutation. The salaries of the tithe commissioners and their assistants were paid out of the Consolidated Fund. Other expenses were to be met by the parties concerned. If witnesses or documentary evidence had to be produced to settle a claim, the general rule (c.73) was that those interested in its production should pay the costs involved. The costs incurred in the employment of tithe valuers and surveyors who did most of the detailed work of each commutation were to be met jointly by landowners and proprietors 'in such Proportion, Time and Manner as the Commissioners or Assistant Commissioners shall direct' (c.74). The cost of the apportionment, which set out how much rent charge each piece of land should bear, was to be met exclusively by the landowners 'in rateable Proportion to the Sum charged on the said Lands in lieu of Tithes by such Apportionment' (c.75). In contrast to enclosure proceedings, therefore, it is noticeable that tithe owners were expected to bear at least some of the cost.

The procedure for setting in motion a voluntary commutation was very similar to that employed in enclosure business. The owners of not less than a quarter of the land or tithes could call a meeting to discuss commutation. At that meeting, if two-thirds of the land and tithe owners by value were able to agree on a sum to be paid annually by way of rent charge, this would bind the remainder of the interested parties (c.18). Thus, as at enclosure, a few substantial property holders could dictate terms to the many whose collective stake was smaller. Usually, of course, the conflict of interest was not between great and small landowners, but when it was eighteenth-century norms of property right still held good. The 'Provisional agreement' negotiated between both sides remained unconfirmed until the bishop of the diocese had seen it, the patron of the living had signified his agreement - if any ecclesiastical tithe was involved - and the tithe commissioners had inspected it to ensure that it represented a fair equivalent. This they normally did after receiving reports from one, or occasionally two, assistant commissioners.

Soon after the confirmation of the agreement, or at any stage prior to this, a meeting of land and tithes owners was held to appoint a valuer to apportion the rent charge on particular pieces of land. This involved the area's being mapped and planeed to show which lands were covered by rent charge and to what extent. The valuer worked from an agreed total, and apportioned on individual plots of land. Provision was made for appeals before an assistant commissioner if anyone felt unfairly burdened by the rent charge he was to be obliged to pay. Disputes about the validity of moduses could likewise be determined by assistant commissioners, but if a modus was accepted by all parties it was enshrined in the award, and remained payable in the same manner and on the same lands as before. The tithe commissioners were thus to collect a complete record of every modus throughout the kingdom, and there should be no further cause for dispute.

If the parties could not agree on commutation, the commissioners were empowered to make compulsory awards after October 1838 (c.36). They were to ascertain for themselves the average value of tithes taken in the seven years from Christmas 1829 to Christmas 1835 (c.37). If the tithe had been taken in kind, 'all just Deductions' should be made for collection expenses. The sums thus obtained were to be converted into rent charge by assuming that they were laid out in the purchase of equal portions of wheat, barley and oats at prices published annually by the Comptroller of Corn Returns in the 'London Gazette' (c.76). In January of each year he would state the average price per imperial bushel of each crop during the previous seven years. The scale was first fixed in December 1836 when £100 of tithe would purchase 94.95 bushels of wheat, 168.42 of barley and 242.42 of oats. These were the calculations upon which valuers throughout the country worked to obtain the initial rent charge, and the magical figures appear regularly on tithe awards with the appropriate calculation for each tithe district.

Initially, it was felt that the averages were artificially depressed by two very low price years (1834 and 1835), and tithe owners confidently expected that prices would pick up, thus raising the rent charges at an early stage. Tithe owners could also look forward to easier redress against defaulters than hitherto. If rent charge were not paid within twenty-one days of falling due, the tithe owner could enter the defaulter's lands and distrain the amount outstanding (c.81). If this proved impossible, the Sheriff was empowered to issue a writ taking possession of the defaulter's property until the debt was discharged (c.82). Ease of recovery was now facilitated because the precise amount of the tithe owner's claim was clearly known.

Three further points should be made. First, the Act provided separate treatment for the valuable but disputatious tithes of hops, fruit, garden produce and coppice wood. Hops and orchard tithes were to be separately valued by assistant commissioners according to local, rather than national, prices over the previous seven years (c.40). A similar procedure for coppice wood was laid down (c.41). Second, not all tithes were commuted by the Act. It excluded fish or personal tithes (c.90), except those traditionally due from mines or mills. Nor were easter offerings, mortuaries or surplice fees to be commuted. These were not

Chapter 6

strictly tithes at all, but had been regarded and computed as such in many parishes. Finally, the burden of tithe payments was transferred from tenants to landowners (c.80). Tenants were empowered to deduct their rent charge payments from their rent to the landlord. This procedure had long been in operation in many cases, and there had always been a rental premium on taking up tithe-free land. The clause was of more than superficial significance, however, in that it was now clear who was responsible for the payment of tithe rent charge. Tenants would no longer be cited in tithe suits.

The 1836 Tithe Commutation Act remained the definitive statement on tithe rent charge for a century. There were amendments on points of detail, however. These amendments introduced a few new points of principle, but were to redefine or explain doubtful cases in the light of experience, and to facilitate the execution of tithe awards. The most important of these was the 1838 Act to facilitate the merger of tithes in land. (67) This enabled those who held the tithes of their own land to merge the two properties and so extinguish the charge altogether. It was clearly an unnecessary expense to value and apportion rent charge on land held by the tithe owner, and although it was not mandatory, many landowners did take the opportunity of signing deeds of merger. By 1851, 13,160 separate mergers of land and tithe had been enrolled by the tithe commissioners. A further Act 'to explain and amend the Acts for the Commutation of Tithes' was passed in 1839. (68) This enabled mergers of tithe with glebe land to be effected, and also enabled agreements to be made to commute Easter offerings and other charges not commutable under the 1836 Act. This Act was not designed to presage later compulsory action, but it did enable comprehensive commutation to be made in those districts where there was no dispute. The 1846 Tithe Amendment Act (69) was passed on the initiative of the tithe commissioners who foresaw difficulties at the end of the commutation process with districts in which nearly all tithes had been previously exonerated at enclosure or by merger. The Act permitted landowners to redeem rent charge values of £15 or less at twenty-four years purchase. Even after apportionment, individual rent charges of £1 or less could be redeemed on the same terms. The commissioners were concerned that commutation would be delayed intolerably because only small rent charges remained to be apportioned, and interested parties would be reluctant to pay for a full award and apportionment. Tithe redemption was a device to save disproportionate expense.

The Tithe Act shows that, while tithe owners were treated with scrupulous fairness, they profited far less than at enclosure. The Act finally took away from them the right so lucratively exercised during the enclosure movement of sharing in the increased produce of the land. Tithe rent charge was not to be a tax on yield, as tithe had been. The agricultural improvers had belatedly won their point. The Act was passed towards the end of a trough in arable prices which had finally killed the concept of the tithe owner as co-producer with the farmer. No longer was he to share the fruits of improvement without bearing any share of the expense.

Furthermore, the basis of computation was to be the average of the past seven years' tithe yield. It is true that there were arrangements for correcting anomalies if, for example, receipts during the years of average were weighed down by invalid modus payments, but rent charge was based on collection. No impropriator or dean and chapter would have countenanced such proceedings at enclosure. In the 1790s, with enclosure eagerly sought, the tithe owner could frequently state his own terms, based on notional improved values for his property. By the 1830s, with the radicals rampant and the most vocal and influential element of the agricultural interest depressed, he had to be content with much less. No livings would be doubled or trebled in value by commutation as some had been by enclosure. Ironically, the solution adopted at commutation largely achieved the principle fought for by so many tithe litigants in the eighteenth century. The value of tithe was securely tied to the fortunes of the agricultural interest - or at least the arable section of it. But the solution came three-quarters of a century too late. Instead of a guaranteed share of a rising income, tithe owners had to contend with static or, from the mid-1870s, sharply falling arable prices. It did not work to the advantage of tithe owners to have their fortunes tied to the most volatile sector of the agrarian economy. There were few supporters of the corn rent principle among tithe owners in the 1890s when prices plummeted below 25s a quarter.

Such disasters were unforeseen in 1836. The commissioners went about their work with a will, and found plenty of customers anxious to commute their tithes as early as the autumn of 1836. To understand the success of commutation, and its importance for the agricultural interest it is necessary to learn how the commissioners and their army of assistants operated. Could they translate complex theory into intelligible and acceptable practice?

NOTES

1 Henry Ryder, 'Charge to the Clergy of the Diocese of Lichfield and Coventry' (1832), pp.12-14. WSL, Visitation Charges.
2 'The Times', 17 April 1834.
3 See above, chapter 5, sect. V.
4 The pressures exerted by the church evangelicals are perhaps best experienced by their publication, the 'Christian Observer', which took an increasing interest in church finances and allied matters in the 1820s. On the contribution of the evangelicals see F.K. Brown, 'Fathers of the Victorians' (Cambridge, 1961) and R. Furneaux, 'William Wilberforce' (1974).
5 See, for example, the Acts to commute tithe in Edgbaston (Warwickshire) 1821 (1 & 2 Geo. IV c.35), Lancaster 1824 (5 Geo. IV c.28), Cockerham (Lancs.) 1825, (6 Geo. IV c.22), Grappenhall (Cheshire) 1826 (7 & 8 Geo. IV c.21) and Kendal, 1834 (4 Will. IV c.18). For the origins of the Kendal

Chapter 6

    Corn Rent Act, see Eric J. Evans, A nineteenth-century tithe dispute and its significance: the case of Kendal, 'Transactions of the Cumberland and Westmorland Antiquarian and Archaeological Society', lxxiv (1974), pp.169-85.
6 Curwen's activities in Workington were closely followed in 'Farmers Magazine', esp. x (1809), pp.78-91; xi (1810), pp.73-99; xiii (1812), p.433; xiv (1813), pp.18-27; xix (1818), p.510. There is a hagiographic portrait of Curwen, much motivated by spleen against the rival Lowther interest in Henry Lonsdale, 'The Worthies of Cumberland' (1867), pp.3-204.
7 'Hansard', xxxiv (1816), pp.365-9. Petitions were particularly numerous from the counties of Devon and Essex. See, for example, one from the freeholders and occupiers of Churstow (Devon) asking for 'relief from the tithe laws' to permit the extension of cultivation and improvement, HCJ, lxxi (1816), p.338.
8 HCJ, lxxi (1816), p.391.
9 'Hansard', xxxiv (1816), pp.685-704.
10 'The Times', 23 May 1816.
11 PP(HC) 1816, iv, pp.511-12.
12 PP(HC) 1817, i, pp.219-39.
13 'Hansard', xxxvi (1817), pp.294-6.
14 PP(HC) 1817, ii, p.205.
15 'Hansard', xxxvi (1817), pp.1070-6.
16 HCJ, lxxiii (1818), pp.120 and 140.
17 'Hansard', xxxvii (1818), pp.545-57 and 1131-42.
18 Prevailing wheat prices may be consulted in Lord Ernle, 'English Farming Past and Present', 6th ed. (1961), p.489. In 1822 they reached their lowest point for 30 years and in only 3 years between 1793 and 1850 were prices lower (1835, 1849 and 1850). The problems of those working heavy lands and buoyed up only by wartime prices were real enough. R.W. Sturgess, The agricultural revolution on the English clays, 'Agric. Hist. Rev.', xiv (1966), pp.104-21.
19 There was a short debate in the Commons on the tithe problems of a London parish. 'Hansard', 2nd ser. xv (1826), pp.562-6 and 721-2. In 1826 also a short Act was passed enabling magistrates from outside a particular county to adjudicate in tithe suits in certain cases, 7 Geo. IV c.15.
20 HCJ, lxxxii, (1828), pp.283-320.
21 HCJ, lxxxiii (1828), 6 and 31 March.
22 'Hansard', 2nd ser. xviii (1828), pp.1151-61.
23 HCJ, lxxxv (1830), 18 May and lxxxiv, 4 June.
24 HCJ, lxxxv (1830), 12 and 5 March.
25 Ibid. 8 February.
26 'Hansard', 2nd ser. xxiv (1830), p.819.
27 Ibid. 3rd ser. ii (1831), p.29-48.
28 In presenting a petition from the inhabitants of Southampton, 'Hansard', 3rd ser. i (1830), pp.1109-15.
29 O. Chadwick, 'The Victorian Church', 2 vols (1966-70), i, pp.1-24, Olive Brose, 'Church and Parliament, 1828-60' (Stanford, Calif., 1959), pp.7-21.
30 John Cannon, 'Parliamentary Reform, 1640-1832' (1973), p.225.

J.R.M. Butler, 'The Passing of the Great Reform Bill' (1914), pp.277-327, and Michael Brock, 'The Great Reform Act' (1973), pp.231-67.
31 Quoted in H.J. Hanham, 'The Nineteenth-Century Constitution' (Cambridge, 1969), p.215.
32 2 & 3 Will. IV c.100.
33 4 & 5 Will. IV c.83.
34 5 & 6 Will. IV c.74.
35 'Hansard', 3rd ser. xx (1833), pp.608-10, 14 August.
36 S.C. Agric. Distress, PP(HC) 1833, iv, p.497.
37 'Hansard', 3rd ser. xx (1833), pp.794-6. Blamire took an active interest in the Kendal disputes, Evans, loc. cit. pp.169-72.
38 R.J. Olney, 'Lincolnshire Politics, 1832-1885' (Oxford, 1973), p.102.
39 'Edinburgh Review', lviii (1834), p.502.
40 G.F.A. Best, 'Temporal Pillars' (Cambridge, 1964), pp.296-306, Brose, op. cit. pp.120-35, Norman Gash, 'Sir Robert Peel' (1972), pp.100-5.
41 Ernle, op. cit. p.489.
42 PP(HC) 1833, iv, p.431.
43 'Hansard', 3rd ser. xvii (1833), pp.273-91.
44 'Hansard', 3rd ser. xix (1833), pp.375-82.
45 HCJ, lxxxix (1834), 18 April.
46 The phrase used by 'The Times' in an article on 17 April 1834.
47 The debate may be found in 'Hansard', 3rd ser. xxii (1834), pp.818-42.
48 For which see E. Halévy, 'The Triumph of Reform, 1830-1841', 3rd ed. (1961), pp.169-74.
49 'Hansard', 3rd ser. xxvii (1835), p.170. The whole debate is on pp.170-202.
50 Ibid. xxxi (1836), pp.185-210.
51 Russell's first Bill is in PP(HC) 1836, iv, pp.125ff.
52 'The Times', 11 February 1836.
53 'Hansard', 3rd ser. xxxi (1836), p.697. Second reading of the Bill.
54 6 & 7 Will. IV c.71, clause 38. Professor Chadwick is in error when he states that the standardized calculation of 60-75 per cent was incorporated in the Act, op. cit. i, p.142. See W.L. Mathieson, 'English Church Reform, 1815-1840' (1923), pp.118-24, for a brief but accurate account of the circumstances surrounding the passage of the English Tithe Bill.
55 Clause 31 in the original Bill, clause 42 in the final Act.
56 S.C. Agric. Distress, PP(HC) 1836, iv, pp.125-399 contains the successive drafts of the Bill, and also the amendments made by the Lords in the summer of 1836.
57 'Hansard', 3rd ser. xxxiii (1836), p.505.
58 Ibid. p.503.
59 Ibid. xxxi (1836), p.721.
60 Ibid. xxxiii (1836), p.503.
61 See Lord Hatherton's Diary, 12 July 1836, for a description of such a meeting in the Lords. Staffs. RO D260/M/F/5/26/13.
62 'Hansard', 3rd ser. xxxiv (1836), pp.1291-309.

Chapter 6

63 D. Bruce, 'Victorian Origins of the Welfare State' (1961) makes no reference to them. For an introduction to the works on offer, see the bibliography of Arthur J. Taylor, 'Laissez-Faire and State Intervention in Nineteenth-century Britain' (1972), pp.65-77.
64 'I believe ... that the present strength of the Conservative party and the present condition of the Government have mainly resulted from our having ... kept aloof from Radical union, and from our having honestly supported the Government whenever we thought the Government right.' Peel to Charles Arbuthnot, 27 May 1834. Quoted in Hanham, op. cit. p.117.
65 'Quarterly Review', lvii (1836), pp.242-3.
66 See the Appendix, for an abstract of their Reports.
67 1 & 2 Vic. c.64.
68 2 & 3 Vic. c.62.
69 9 & 10 Vic. c.73.

CHAPTER 7

TITHE COMMUTATION AND THE AGRICULTURAL INTEREST

I

The successful implementation of the Tithe Commutation Act necessitated the creation of a considerable bureaucratic structure. The tithe commission of the 1840s was, in fact, one of the most striking aspects of the growth of government agencies much remarked by historians. In the first twelve years of its existence the commission cost the taxpayer nearly half a million pounds, at an average annual cost of £40,493. (1) In the period 1835-48 the annual cost of the more celebrated poor law commission was slightly less - £40,299. At the apex of the structure were the commissioners themselves, William Blamire and T. Wentworth Buller appointed by the Home Secretary and Richard Jones, the nominee of the Archbishop of Canterbury. Each received an annual salary of £1,500.

The first commissioner appointed and, on the evidence of the commissioners' subsequent work the most active, was Blamire. He was the nephew of John Christian Curwen, and, like him, a Cumbrian and an ardent tithe reformer. Like Curwen, also, he had taken on and beaten the powerful Lowther Tory interest in the fight for a Cumberland county seat. He followed his uncle yet again in acquiring a reputation as a Whig-radical. In acknowledging his victory over the Lowthers in 1831 he had declared: 'I hope a reform in Parliament is the prelude to a reform in the Church.... I believe tithes to be the most improper, the most iniquitous mode of payment ever devised by the ingenuity of man.' (2) Through his association with the Kendal litigants and with other Cumbrian tithe disputes, Blamire probably knew as much of the practical difficulties over tithe as anyone. His speech attacking certain aspects of Russell's Bill in March 1836 was generally acknowledged to be the ablest contribution made to the debate in Parliament, and did much to put him in line for appointment as commissioner. (3) Peel, forgetting party differences as he was apt to do when recognizing real merit, warmly congratulated Blamire on his intervention and supported his appointment. Blamire was the only commissioner with Parliamentary experience, and had to vacate his seat to take

office. His appointment opened the way to a career of distinguished
public service. His extensive practical knowledge of agriculture made him an obvious candidate for the post of enclosure
commissioner in 1845. (4) He combined both jobs until 1851,
and continued to act on the enclosure commission until 1860.
Considering his early partisan position on the tithe question,
Blamire's ability to convince even the most zealous high
churchman of his scrupulous fairness was remarkable. Although
there were various complaints about the tithe commission, few
were directed at Blamire who combined great administrative
skills with a rare conciliatory manner.

Capt. T. Wentworth Buller, RN owed his appointment to the
patronage of Lord John Russell. He held estates in Northamptonshire and Devon, and was known as a keen agriculturalist and
active worker for the Whig cause in the south-west. His qualifi-
cations for the job were perhaps less impressive than Blamire's,
but he had entered the pamphlet war on the agricultural
protection issue in 1822 with an attack on Ricardo's views. (5)
Rev. Richard Jones was an academic. He had held the chair of
Political Economy at King's College, London, his chief publication
being a none-too-successful attack on the ideas of Ricardo. He
had held two curacies in Kent and Sussex in the 1820s, though
his work for the commission between 1836 and 1851 showed no
greater partiality to the interests of the church than Blamire's
did to the farming interest. Both men worked hard at the doctrine
of the political neutrality of government civil service. Before
commutation, Jones had set out his views on the subject in his
'Few Remarks on the Proposed Commutation of Tithes' (1833) and
'Remarks on the Government Bill for the Commutation of Tithes'
(1836) and these works presumably served to bring him to the
attention of Archbishop Howley as a safe and able nominee to
the commission. (6)

The Secretary to the commission was J.E. Hovendon. He was a
much less dynamic figure than Edwin Chadwick, his counterpart
at the Poor Law Office, and was content to implement the policy
enunciated by his superiors rather than challenge it. His
remuneration was £800. His assistant, E. Bethune, was paid
£400. The Chief Clerk received £300 and the commission was
staffed by a large number of clerks whose salaries at the height
of its work in 1841 totalled £6,439. Supernumerary clerks were
also recruited to deal with temporary pressures and the total
cost of extra hours by clerks, largely for copying documents,
was £3,011. (7) Draughtsmen and tracers were paid £3,072, but
the largest charge on the yearly salary bill was for the large
number of assistant commissioners whose duty it was to represent the commissioners in the localities. They had two main
duties. They had to confirm their approval of voluntary agreements for rent charge made by proprietors and tithe owners. This
involved sending reports to London stating their reasons for
acceptance or, more rarely, rejection of the agreement. Their
more complicated duty was to effect compulsory commutation when
the parties could not agree or refused to meet. Meetings had
to be summoned, relevant evidence marshalled, modus claims
determined and fine decisions on tithe values made. Section 45

of the Commutation Act had empowered assistant commissioners to
determine disputed claims 'in situ', and this put great responsibility on their shoulders. Assistant commissioners had to
settle issues which might have grumbled their way through ecclesiastical or equity courts for centuries on and off. It is a
measure of the parties' determination to make commutation work
that they were usually prepared to accept the commissioner's
decision, and refrained from appeals. Nevertheless, the resolution
of modus and related contests took up much time. All moduses
upheld or confirmed were specified in the preamble to each tithe
award. There was thus preserved a complete record of all customs
in lieu of the full tenth. Not surprisingly, the charge on the
commission of the assistants was heavy. In 1841 their salaries
and travelling expenses amounted to £21,677 - nearly 43 per cent
of the total expenditure of the commission. They were the overworked infantry of the commutation army, who carried the battle
in the field, working under strategic direction from Whitehall.

Assistant commissioners needed resourcefulness, initiative and
considerable professional skill. Most were effectively full-time
appointments. The commissioners wished to recruit a force of
men with wide experience as land agents or valuers who could
develop a corporate professional expertise as the work of the
commission developed. Previous experience as an enclosure
commissioner was ideal, and there were many men who spent the
bulk of their working lives employed first as enclosure and then
tithe commissioners. One such was Joseph Townsend of Wood End,
nr Gt Marlow (Bucks.), who gave up employment as a land agent
and enclosure commissioner realizing between £500 and £600 a
year to become an assistant tithe commissioner in 1837. He
held this post until the virtual termination of the commissioners'
work in 1851. In these fourteen years he supervised some
hundreds of commutations mostly in the south and midlands.
Responding to his letter of application in 1837, Richard Jones
outlined the normal terms of appointment as assistant commissioner:
'I have some reason for wishing to know if in the event of your
being appointed an assistant commissioner you could give up all
your time to the service of the commissioners & whether you could
conveniently reside near London.' (8)

Most of the detailed work on local cases came under the supervision of the assistant commissioners. The commissioners' task
was the formulation, enunciation and explanation of general
policy. Their aim was to ensure parity of treatment; but they
were not concerned to obtain rigid standardization at the cost
of delay. The prevailing attitude was - it is difficult to
avoid an overworked word - utilitarian. They tried to persuade
as many interested parties as possible to accept voluntary
commutations, which were cheaper to produce and easier to execute.
If agreement were reached between the parties, there was no need
to go to the trouble of obtaining tithe receipts during the
seven years 1829-35, provided only that the agreement did not seem
to injure either side in the view of an assistant commissioner.
As Bethune reminded Gen. Dyott of Fulfen nr Lichfield, when an
aspect of commutation was queried: 'Under a Voluntary Agreement
it is of course for the parties to work out the terms of their

own arrangements in their own way, free from control or interference on the part of the Commers.' (9)

The commissioners appreciated the value of expert local knowledge. They preferred their assistants to obtain a thorough knowledge of a particular area of the country and to concentrate their energies where they could build up specialist expertise. This they then combined with a knowledge of the law sufficient to settle the technical problems which arose in the determination of modus disputes and the like. Thus, three assistant commissioners, each described as 'barrister-at-law' officiated in 123 of the 148 compulsory commutations in Staffordshire. They were Charles Pym (who supervised 55 commutations), George Cooke (37) and John Rawlinson (31). After a total rent charge had been agreed or determined, the landowners appointed an apportioner to allocate a separate rent charge to each holding. The costs of such apportionments were borne by the landowners alone, as the tithe owner had no direct say in how the total was divided. Bethune told the proprietors of Ulnes Walton (Lancs.) that only rarely did the commissioners interfere with decisions of apportioners: (10)

> The Commissioners have a strong reluctance to interfere with the mode in which a discretion vested in hands so appointed is exercised, and their reluctance is increased by their conviction that few principles can be laid down by them which will prove of universal application, and that local knowledge and a minute attention to local circumstances will in almost every case be necessary in order to arrive at any fair modification of past payments.

The commissioners were anxious to avoid the posture of a centralized bureaucracy concerned only to impose arbitrary and uniform solutions. One important reason for the commission's success, indeed, was its recognition of, and if possible, deference to, local interests and expertise. It heeded the lessons implicit for any government agency of the harsh reception given to the poor law commissioners in the north of England. (11) The commissioners were sensible enough to realize that as the old tithe system had been a patchwork quilt of diverse custom and precedent, so the new system must appreciate and incorporate the strength of local interests. Whatever its faults, the tithe commission did not suffer from collective 'folie de grandeur'. It appreciated the strength of feeling against centralized bureaucratic structures, and its method was to persuade rather than dictate. With William Blamire, who came from independent Cumbrian yeoman stock, as one of the commissioners, it was not likely that the desire would be to impose solutions from preconceived notions. As their encouragement of voluntary commutations indicates, the commissioners preferred viability to uniformity.

Any ideas the commissioners may have had of imposing uniformity on the 12,000 or so tithe districts were scotched by an early defeat over the question of the provision of accurate maps. The Tithe Act had given the commissioners the responsibility of confirming an award and map of each tithe district once apportionment was complete. The commissioners saw merit in a proposal by assistant commissioner Dawson late in 1836 to use the opportunity to make a general (or cadastral) survey of the entire country which could then be used for various purposes, including tax assessments and the operation of a Register of Real Property. (12) Since much surveying and mapping would in any case be necessary, and since the average cost could be kept down to 9d an acre, it seemed an opportunity not to miss. Parliament, and a large section of the landed interest, saw the matter differently. The commissioners' request for a general survey was rejected. It was argued that those who took advantage of the voluntary provisions of the Tithe Act could make use of existing surveys to avoid unnecessary expense in commissioning a new one. Many of these surveys were known to be grossly inaccurate, but the commissioners were authorized to accept them if the parties concerned did not object. Those who intended to use existing surveys as the basis for apportionment were among the first to complain that the commissioners' proposal for a first-class survey was a grandiose project and the total cost - estimated at £1,500,000 - an unacceptable additional burden on the landed interest. The compromise, which the commissioners reluctantly accepted, was incorporated in amending Acts of 1837 and 1839. (13) Commissioners were able to confirm both voluntary and compulsory commutations even though they were not satisfied with the accuracy of the maps which accompanied them. In effect, they were to acknowledge two classes of award. They affixed their seal to the first class, in which they declared themselves satisfied with the reliability of a purpose-designed map. Such an award could be subsequently cited as a true legal record. The second class, in which old surveys were spatchcocked together to do service as tithe maps, were to remain unsealed by the commissioners, and could not be used as evidence in a court of law. As a result, a very large number of inaccurate maps were submitted in order to save landowners' money. It has been estimated that only one-sixth of all maps deposited with the commissioners received their seal. (14) The records of the tithe commission are seriously flawed as a consequence. The commissioners themselves reported in 1841: 'Unquestionably we believe that the maps to which we have attached our Seal are very much more accurate than they would have been had they not gone through the ordeal of this Office....' (15)

The commissioners attempted to aid the process of commutation by issuing publications on how it could best be effected, and by providing simple forms for the completion of award and apportionment details. (16) A 'Course of Proceeding in Making Awards' was circulated when voluntary compositions could not be settled. Instructions were issued about Forms of Apportionment and Maps. When compulsory proceedings began, the secretary issued a circular asking the parties to give early notification of expected boundary disputes, modus disagreements or requests for variation from the seven-year averages. It seems that this factual bombardment bemused as much as it enlightened, (17) but at least it clarified the position not only for estate stewards and agents but also for ecclesiastical administrators and even some inexperienced assistant commissioners and tithe valuers. The parties could not complain of any lack of literature emerging from Somerset House.

The commissioners submitted an annual report to Parliament between 1837 and 1852 on the progress of commutation. These reports indicated the number of awards pending, and ratified, and distinguished between voluntary and compulsory commutations. (18) They also drew attention to any problems which had been encountered in the prosecution of the work. The country was divided into 12,275 tithe districts upon which tithe was to be commuted. Tithe had been completely exonerated in many areas at enclosure, of course, but in a large number some payments for moduses or tithes on old enclosures remained, and these required separate provision. The natural unit for many voluntary agreements remained the parish, but where compulsory commutation was required, the assistant commissioners preferred to divide the larger or more diffuse parishes into smaller tithe districts. Some parishes were split into fifteen or even twenty tithe districts.

It was expected at the outset that voluntary agreements would be quickly effected and that the bulk of the commission's work would be taken up in arranging compulsory commutation. Russell's original Bill, it will be remembered, had only allowed six months for agreements to be reached, but this period was sensibly extended to two years during the committee stage. (19) In the event, even two years proved too short a time for many who were initially slow off the mark, or who wished to gain experience by watching how commutation worked in neighbouring areas. The commissioners, weighed down by work in 1838 and 1839, were happy to be flexible about deadlines, and many voluntary agreements were made between 1839 and 1841. Only 77 per cent of voluntary agreements had been confirmed by the commission by the end of 1840, and this aspect of the work was still not complete four years later, although 98 per cent of agreements had been accepted by then. (20) In the autumn of 1838, the commissioners stated that they were unable to begin general compulsory commutation, because of pressure of work. Instead they would give priority to areas of particular tension, where litigation was in progress, where tithe was still being taken in kind, where a newly-appointed incumbent requested commutation rather than begin the arduous process of negotiating compositions which could necessarily stand only for a short time, or where both sides requested the commissioners' immediate intervention. (21)

The commissioners' arguments to persuade the parties to come to agreements voluntarily seem to have been persuasive. More voluntary awards were made than Russell and the Whigs, and quite possibly Peel and the Tories who had been passionate advocates of the voluntary principle, could have believed possible. Of 11,395 apportionments confirmed by 1852, 7,147 (62.72 per cent) were of voluntary agreements. Nearly all of the 1,000 or so pending commutations were compulsory, but even so voluntary agreements amounted to almost 58 per cent of the total. Compulsory proceedings, naturally more troublesome since they included most of the districts in which tithes had recently been contested or were uncertain, nevertheless moved quite expeditiously once the commissioners had caught up with the initial backlog of voluntary confirmations. Just over 70 per cent of compulsory awards were confirmed between 1840 and 1846. By the end of 1851, over 93 per cent had been confirmed. The very last apportionments, a mere handful of intractable cases, were not to be out of the way until the 1880s, but the effective work of the commission was complete by the later 1850s. The greatest difficulties were experienced where the tithe to be apportioned was small in amount, and parties were unwilling to go to the expense of apportioning a few pounds. The commissioners reported in 1849 that they were 'much impeded by the disinclination of parties to attend our meetings, or give us any assistance in our enquiries' in such circumstances. In 1851 they cited the case of Great Claybrook (Leics.) where tithe remained unapportioned. There, the only remaining tithes were of pigs (value £1) and a mill (value 5s). 'To establish rent charges of 25/- and to proceed by map and apportionment to finish the commutation would be a harsh and burdensome proceeding'. (22) There were about 100 similar instances, mostly in the north of England. The tidying-up process was further impeded in the 1850s by the failure of some who owned the tithes of their own land to merge them under the provisions of the 1838 Act. The commissioners naturally delayed commutation until the maximum number of mergers had been effected. Most of the huge parish of Leek (Staffs.) was in this position. Over the entire parish of more than 25,000 acres only £5 2s 6d was eventually apportioned as rent charge, but the mergers exonerating the remainder were much delayed. No commutation was effected until 1845, and six of the twelve districts had to wait until 1851-3. In Leek and Lowe district, assistant commissioner Charles Pym waited from 1845 to 1851 for declarations of merger from all 53 landowners to be signed. (23) In some instances owners showed no inclination to merge despite all manner of persuasion. The commissioners tentatively suggested in 1851 that the government might introduce legislation to enforce outstanding mergers. Not surprisingly, nothing came of this projected interference with property rights. The problem anyway was a very small one, deriving more from the tidy-mindedness of the commission than from any pressing need for legislation. Successive administrations were prepared to permit the final rites of the commission to be performed as slowly as might be. By the time the commission was merged with the enclosure commission in 1851 the government knew that, with 11,395 of the 12,275 apportionments complete, the outstanding work was relatively trivial.

The detailed work of commutation was carried out with remarkable smoothness. Initially, the major problem was the lack of qualified surveyors to act as apportioners. Landowners tended to rely on a small number of men, usually locals, who had already given evidence of their competence either during enclosure or in earlier commutations. Such men rapidly built up a large portfolio of commutation interests and, since they worked on several districts simultaneously, delays occurred. In 1839, the commissioners reported that apportionment work created 'at least as much, perhaps more employment than can be proceeded with at once by such Mappers and Apportioners as have the

confidence of this country'. (24) In 1840, while asserting that
'contented acquiescence' was the general reaction of the land-
owning interest to apportionment, they conceded that the process
took far longer 'than the six months originally contemplated by
the legislature'. (25) It was this delay which was the prime
reason for the late start on many compulsory commutations. Most
apportionments were complete within eighteen months to two years
of the award of a total rent charge. This is a rather better rate
than was achieved by the enclosure commissioners. The tithe
commissioners were careful to make it plain that, although the
process of apportionment was the landowners' affair, since they
bore the cost, they would interfere if there was any evidence of
'wilful loitering' by landowners or apportioners. (26)

In the early 1840s, the attention of the commissioners was
concentrated on the problem of outstanding litigation. Lord
Tenterden's Act came in for adverse criticism in every report
between 1844 and 1848. (27) The problem was twofold. In some
instances litigation begun in 1832 or 1833 was still in progress
in the equity courts, and the commissioners had to wait for
decisions there before beginning their own work in a district.
Voluntary agreement in these cases was out of the question. Also,
some parties were unwilling to accept the jurisdiction of the
assistant commissioners and made what the commissioners considered
over-frequent use of clause 46 of the 1836 Act permitting appeals
at equity against their decisions. Such instances were
comparatively rare as a proportion of the total, however much
individual instances may have irritated the commissioners, and
it is significant that Parliament's attention was drawn to the
problem only when the bulk of commutation work was over. By the
second half of the 1840s, the commissioners could look forward
to winding up the commission altogether, and their perspectives
had shifted from the immediate pressures of work to the remaining
obstacles in the way of its completion. Only in this way did
outstanding litigation seem a real problem. Given the extreme
litigiousness of many tithe contestants before 1836, the amount
of litigation generated by commutation was slight. This emphasizes
not only the general competence of the commissioners and their
assistants, but also the considerable degree of goodwill which
commutation evinced. Tithe commutation would probably have been
a complete failure if landowners and tithe owners had continued
their traditional squabbles with the same vigour after 1836.
Instead, one of the great redistributions of English property was
effectively complete within fifteen years. It was a remarkable
transformation and one for which all interested parties deserve
credit.

II

It may be properly objected that an impressionistic picture only
is obtained by studying the tithe commissioners' work at a
national level. A better view comes from looking at this work
of their assistants in the localities. Their working notes are
incorporated in over 12,000 tithe files available in the Public

Record Office. (28) Despite drastic administrative pruning by the Tithe Redemption Commission, they remain an indispensable source for the history of tithe commutation.

The problems of assimilating such a mass of material, however, are immense. In order to make systematic use of them at all, it was decided to make a detailed survey of the process of commutation in one county - Staffordshire. Staffordshire was chosen because it was a county of fairly light parliamentary enclosure, and hence heavy commutation. It also contained in the middle of the nineteenth century a most useful admixture of industrial and agricultural settlements. As James Caird wrote in 1850, 'The state of agriculture in Staffordshire is influenced by such a variety of circumstances that examples of every system pursued in England may be found in this county.' (29)

The initiative for commutation in Staffordshire was usually taken by the more substantial landowners. Two of the earliest voluntary agreements were made in Drayton Bassett and Whittington, where Sir Robert Peel was a dominant landowner. At Drayton Bassett, indeed, he owned about 970 of the 1,250 tithable acres and was able to negotiate terms on his own account to bind the other owners, as proprietor of more than two-thirds of the land. Peel's agents had clearly been instructed to put into practice the arguments their employer had advanced in the Commons about the scope for quick and easy voluntary agreements. Commutation was complete in both places by the middle of 1837 - the quickest arrangements in the county. (30) The larger landowners often acted on their own initiative in proposing commutation. Only rarely do requests for commutation come from a majority of landowners both in value and number. At High Offley, for example, only 14 of the 45 landowners signed the agreement, but they owned between them more than 70 per cent of the land. At Caverswall 42 of the 91 landowners signed, and at Darlaston rather less than a third of the total number. (31) The similarity between enclosure and commutation is striking. Still in the 1830s and 1840s smaller property owners should defer to greater, or perhaps more accurately, should trust the great to act on their behalf for the general good of the community. It was a rosy concept, and although there was usually no great divide of interests between smaller and greater proprietors, the practice of relying on majorities by value only could on occasion have unfortunate consequences.

At Uttoxeter, a thriving market town, although all householders were declared liable to render personal tithes, only the substantial landowners were invited to sign the request for commutation. Before commutation, the vicar had taken no tithes from the 500 or so cottagers, although he knew that he was entitled to small payments from each of them. The commutation agreement involved an increase from £140 to £200 rent charge and the tithe apportioners included the cottagers in their dispositions. The vicar himself, alarmed at this new imposition placed on the poorest members of his parish, appealed against the apportionment in 1844, but was told by assistant commissioner Charles Howard that it had been properly made, and that no alteration could be countenanced unless the larger proprietors would accept an increased assessment on their lands. (32) The landowners declined this proposal and many cottagers were left to make payments for the first time as a result of commutation. They had not been consulted at any stage nor did they have any legal redress against the apportioner's decision since all of the proper forms had been gone through. Had such cases been more common, there would undoubtedly have been a general outcry. Uttoxeter, however, was rare in that personal tithes remained due (though not collected) there until well into the nineteenth century.

Once agreement had been reached between the parties, the assistant commissioner reported to London on the fairness or otherwise of the arrangements made. They were asked to make their own rough estimate of the value of the tithes and to set this against the sum agreed to be paid. In most cases, assistant commissioners had little difficulty in recommending acceptance even if there was a significant disparity between the two estimates. The commissioners took the view that the rate at which tithe had been taken, and an agreement freely entered into by knowledgeable parties were more reliable guides to true value than a necessarily hurried survey by an assistant commissioner, which might overlook local customs. Thus, at Handsworth the commissioners were prepared to confirm an agreement giving the rector £1,391 although assistant commissioner Woolley had valued the tithes at £1,766. At Kingsley, a valuation of £233 was not considered sufficient cause to lay aside an agreement of £200 freely negotiated. (33)

Assistant commissioners were instructed that in scrutinizing agreements they should take particular care that the interests of the Church were safeguarded. Impropriators were considered to be men of business who could be relied upon to make advantageous agreements. Clerics, so the argument ran, might lack the requisite acumen to stand up to shrewd proprietors determined to get the best bargain for themselves. Thomas Sudworth, in accepting the Whittington agreement, realistically noted in his report: 'The great tithes of Whittington being now under Lease to the representatives of the late Mary Woods, I presume that they (not having much land in the Parish) will have made the best bargain they could with the landowners.' (34) At Bilbrooke, George Ashdown recommended confirmation of the agreement for tithes although his own estimate of their value was higher. 'If these tithes were Ecclesiastical rather than lay I should not recommend this agreement to be confirmed until there is a further enquiry....' (35) Jelinger Symons took a similar view at Farewell. The parties, he reported, (36)

> went on the assumption that the Averages (settled a long time ago) ought not to be altered. The Lay Impropriator must, however, have a perfect knowledge of his own interest: but the Rent Charge is decidedly too low. I apprehend that an addition would be acceded to if recommended by the Board; As, however, there is no ecclesiastical interest at stake and the Tithe Owner is quite aware of the value of the land, I don't recommend a compulsory alteration of the agreement.

One of the few Staffordshire examples of an assistant

commissioner advising non-confirmation of an agreement occurred when rectorial tithes were to be stabilized at a low level. Assistant commissioner R.B. Phillipson objecting to using a long-standing composition of £13 12s 10d for the 81 acres which remained tithable after enclosure as the basis for a permanent rent charge: (37)

> I do not consider the agreement a fair one, in the first place because the rates have not been added to the average receipts ... and ... because I do not consider the sum agreed upon as a rent charge will fairly represent the value of the Tithe. It only reaches 3/3 per acre on 76 acres, 5 acres being covered by a modus (of) 10/6 .... Now Thorpe Constantine 4 miles off and very little superior in quality was valued and I think very low at 5/7½ per acre.
>
> The late Rector was an elderly man, and was content to take the old composition, and the present rector told me he was quite ignorant of the value of the Tithes, having left the matter to Mr. Toovey (the apportioner). Had the whole parish been tithable, I have no doubt a much larger proportionate composition would have been paid, but this being so small a thing, and the living being so amply endowed with Lands, the Incumbents had scarcely thought it worth looking after.

After pressure from the commissioners, (38) the rent charge payment was raised to £30 1s 10d, and at this level the commutation was confirmed. (39)

III

Assistant commissioners were the central figures in negotiations for compulsory commutation. In such cases, there were usually long-standing difficulties which had precluded voluntary agreement, and sometimes preliminary negotiations for agreement had been opened only to break down. It was the assistant commissioner's task to resolve such difficulties and settle an appropriate sum as rent charge. Proceedings were kept as clear and open as possible to avoid giving aggrieved parties too many opportunities for appeal.

Many negotiations for voluntary agreement had broken down over the old problem of modus disputes, and the resolution of such disputes occupied much of the assistant commissioners' time. In the Ellastone tithe districts of Ramshorn and Prestwood, for example, modus claims were the main hindrance to a swift settlement. At Ramshorn the vicar claimed £90 as a fair rent charge, but because they claimed moduses over an extensive part of the parish, the proprietors were unwilling to go beyond £50. (40) George Cooke persuaded both sides to accept the judgment of a valuer, who eventually suggested £60. This was reluctantly accepted by the vicar who had to be persuaded that no further increase was possible without disproportionate hazard and expense. In Prestwood, the landowners claimed numerous small moduses which, although they had appeared regularly in the parish glebe terriers for over two hundred years, the vicar wished to contest. (41) Cooke's ploy to get a swift settlement without recourse to law was to suggest that the moduses would be difficult to sustain, and that as the seven-year averages were very low for 413 acres of good quality land, the landowners might prefer to permit the 20 per cent increase allowable under the Act rather than risk a lengthy and expensive suit. The landowners raised their offer from £22 to £30. The vicar stuck at £31 10s 0d and the assistant split the difference. (42)

At Abbots Bromley the assistant commissioner's aid was necessary only because the Bishop of Lichfield's office had refused to sign an agreement to give the vicar £65, believing that it should be increased. This decision proved costly for the vicar. The landowners had been prepared to suggest an increase in the seven-year averages on the grounds that the previous incumbent had not collected turnip tithes which were acknowledged to be payable. Assistant commissioner R.E. Phillipson had urged the vicar to sign the agreement, being unable himself to compute the tithes at more than £49. He reported to London, 'I do not think the vicar could make better terms.' (43) The landowners' liberality to their vicar quickly evaporated when they learned that the episcopal office intended to submit them to more controversy and probable expense to raise an already generous settlement. The landowners' defence was strong. Most of the parish was covered by moduses in lieu of vicarial tithes which had been established at Stafford assizes as recently as 1787. (44) In addition the seven-year averages had amounted to only just over £37. They threatened to test their claims at law once again, and stated that in view of the changed circumstances they would make no more generous gestures. George Cooke awarded £50 as rent charge. The interference of the episcopal office on a weak pretext had led to the loss of more than 20 per cent of the vicar's tithe income from the district.

Assistant commissioners were kept busy in hearing modus disputes under the summary proceeding laid down in section 45 of the Tithe Act. At Swynnerton in 1842, George Cooke upheld moduses in lieu of tithes of milk, calves, colts and garden produce in the face of a challenge from the rector. (45) The evidence summoned was identical to that which the equity courts would take years to chew over. At Clayton and Seabridge assistant commissioner John Mee Matthew finally determined modus disputes which had kept the protagonists at law for the best part of twenty years. He had to decide on an impressive array of documentary and verbal evidence expertly marshalled by litigants well versed in the art. (46) At Barlaston, where William Oliver was trying against his solicitor's advice to recoup some of the ground lost in his recent fight with the landowners, (47) the assistant commissioner had to decide between two mutually contradictory decisions from the two equity courts. He decided to uphold the more recent Chancery verdict as 'of higher authority and entitled to greater weight', and left Oliver in the same position as before, unable to break important moduses in his parish.

Appeals against the assistant commissioners' decisions on moduses were rare. As the Newbury solicitor, R.F. Graham, told the parliamentary Select Committee on the Enclosure and Improvement of Commons in 1844, the tithe commission provided 'a kind of arbitration which I think has been satisfactory to the people generally.... So far as the proceedings of the Tithe Commissioners have hitherto gone, I am surprised at the submission made to their Awards and the way in which disputes have been arranged.' (48) Commissioner Richard Jones naturally endorsed this view. The assistant commissioners brought 'justice to the door'. 'We trust entirely to these gentlemen in collecting the facts.' One assistant commissioner, John Herbert, had by 1844 made 148 decisions in cases of doubtful tithe rights with only 10 appeals against his judgment. (49) The relatively easy resolution of contentious modus issues was perhaps the most striking aspect of the success of the tithe commission.

Assistant commissioners more regularly had to submit to appeals against the total rent charge awarded than against decisions on moduses. In some instances, however, an appeal was quickly withdrawn when the parties understood the criteria on which the commission acted. At Tipton, where Charles Pym had awarded over £287 in lieu of all tithes, the landowners called an appeal meeting in 1846 to try to reduce the sum. When it was explained to them that the commissioner had taken note of the fact that tithable produce had been steadily decreasing during the years of average due to the increase of mining waste and other industrial projects, and that suitable reduction had been made in the rent charge to cover this, the appeal was withdrawn. (50)

Of more importance were appeals against errors in the award which derived from the complexities of tithe ownership in a particular district. In constructing the Lichfield, St Chad, award in 1848 John Rawlinson observed that 'Great difficulties have arisen in distinguishing the sums payable to each Lessee ... and the completion of this my award has been thereby impeded'. (51) As the ownership of tithes was divided between the dean and chapter, the vicar of St Chad and eight prebendaries whose precise rights were ill-defined, this was not surprising. The uncertainty of ownership was the subject of an appeal by the landowners against the award of £600 rent charge to cover the entire parish. As there was considerable intermingling of tithe-free and tithable lands, Rawlinson decided to reduce his award to £570 to take account of uncertainty which might work to the landowners' disadvantage. At Butterton, a moorland parish in the Peak District near the Derbyshire border, Rawlinson awarded £12 in lieu of tithes to the impropriator, Thomas Carr. Carr appealed against the award, but the landowners countered that the award was fair since the land had become progressively less valuable after hard ploughing had resulted in soil exhaustion. Corn could not be grown on more than fifty acres in the entire district which extended over 1,400 acres. Their contention was that the great tithes were worth no more than £6. The assistant commissioner, however, took the view that hard ploughing had now had its worst effect, and that the seven-year averages, on which the award was based, were not unduly high. Carr's appeal was upheld and the rent charge increased to £15. (52)

149   Chapter 7

Such matters as these were generally decided on the judgment of
the assistant commissioner. When factual errors about the limits
of tithe ownership or the extent of a modus were discovered,
they had to be corrected. If the error was not revealed until
after the commutation had been confirmed, it was necessary to
make a supplementary award to correct it. Some mistakes were
trivial, such as the omission of small sums in lieu of tithe at
Caverswall and Mavesyn Ridware, (53) and easily rectified. A
majority of cases coming to supplementary award represented
little more than a tidying-up process. Some others were potentially
more serious. At Fauld, an agreement was made in 1837 to give
the Bishop of Lichfield's lessees £40 rent charge in lieu of
appropriate tithes. (54) The sum apparently assumed the subsequent
conversion of the largest farm in the tithe district from
pasture to arable cultivation. When this did not occur, the
landowners requested a reduction. An assistant commissioner was
called upon to decide the matter, and the bishop's agent was
induced to accept a significantly reduced rent charge of £26 10s 0d
in the supplementary award, although 'extremely vexed and
mortified now at being obliged to content himself with less than
the landowners had been prepared to give'. (55) This was the
only Staffordshire case of rent charge being reduced by a
supplementary award. There was a disinclination to make any
revision of rent charge if it could possibly be avoided, even
if a prima facie case for such adjustment seemed to have been made.
At Bucknall, for example, although it was discovered that the
acreage exempted from tithe by the 1808 Horton enclosure Act was
210 acres rather than the 25 stated in the original award, no
reduction was made in the total rent charge of £530. (56) The
apportioner was instructed merely to redistribute the rent charge
among the remaining proprietors.

IV

The problems facing tithe apportioners were of a different order
of magnitude from those of the assistant commissioners, and their
work was generally subject to much more criticism. Joseph
Bennett of Tutbury, a tithe valuer of forty years' experience
who frequently acted as an apportioner, explained the situation
in 1838: (57)
   The difficulties of effecting agreements between the
   titheowners and tithepayers, are as nothing in comparison
   with the difficulties of fairly and equitably apportioning
   the gross sum among the landowners, to the satisfaction of
   all. The landowners are mostly of one mind while they have
   the titheowner to contend with; but when that question is
   disposed of, they begin to think of their individual
   interests, and are opposed to each other as to the principle
   upon which the rent-charge should be divided.
      The man who has been occupying his estate in a manner to
   produce the greatest value of tithe, contends that he has
   too large a proportion of tillage to form the proper basis of
   adjustment for ever; and on the other hand the man who has

been in the contrary extreme and has occupied his estate so as to yield the titheowner very little, or perhaps nothing, contends that the apportionment should be made on the basis of the existing mode of occupation, and that because he has paid little or nothing for seven years, or for twenty years, or more, and he cannot be charged with what he has not paid.

Others who are affected more or less between the two extremes, adopt that principle of argument best suited to their interest, and all wishing and trying to pay as small a proportion of the general burthen as possible.

With respect to coming to any agreement among themselves as to the principles of apportionment, they are not likely, when the mode which would serve one set of landowners and be acceptable to them, would be contrary to the interest of the other set, and be opposed accordingly.

No instructions are therefore given nor can there be, under such circumstances, and the apportionment must rest with the valuer or valuers, and the commissioners or their assistants.

Tithe apportioners were the butt of much local criticism - some of it ill-informed - and they were frequently not accorded the respect given to assistant commissioners. Appointed by the landowners themselves and not usually employed full-time on apportionments, they were the outsiders of the system. They often lacked professional expertise for the work they were called upon to do, and were less than perfectly acquainted with the ways of the Commission. It was advantageous to appoint men of local experience and knowledge, often in permanent employment as land stewards or surveyors. The aim was to ensure that there were no wide discrepancies between the methods of apportioning rent charge on similar pieces of land in adjacent districts. To ensure parity of treatment apportioners were frequently appointed to work on all the tithe districts in a particular parish. Joseph Bennett of Tutbury in south-east Staffordshire was apportioner in all five districts of the adjoining parish of Burton-on-Trent, and all six in Hanbury. Joseph Naden of Shenstone apportioned all of the Lichfield awards and Liddle Elliot of Newcastle-under-Lyme handled all the Trentham apportionments. As with assistant commissioners, apportioners frequently worked on several districts simultaneously. In all, Joseph Bennett was in charge of 23 Staffordshire apportionments, Samuel Ginders of Ingestre on 18, Thomas Turnor on 17, Robert Thompson of Walton, near Stone, James Wyley of High Onn and James Harding of Rosliston (Derby.) each on 13.

It has already been noted that delays in the apportionment process were a source of concern to the tithe commissioners. The frequent lack of acquiescence in apportioners' decisions was also worrying. There were far more apportionment appeals than appeals against the initial award. There were two main reasons for this: ignorance of the provisions of the Tithe Act and lack of competence by some apportioners. Complaints about apportioners were not confined to aggrieved landowners saddled with larger payments than they had anticipated. The commissioners' concern about inaccuracy and delay was one of the primary reasons why they supported a professional cadastral survey. One assistant commissioner stated baldly in his report on an agreement in 1839. 'I have seen too much of the local valuers of land to place much confidence in their decisions, and I would much sooner trust to the statements of the tenants themselves as to the crops they actually realize and which they are but little likely to exaggerate than to the valuations of local land agents, who, however respectable, are likely to err.' (58) The commissioners in their 1841 report remarked on the frequency of apportioners' errors, most of them unwitting but sometimes 'Maps are ... sent here containing errors of which the mappers are aware and the existence of which they attempt to conceal by tampering and making compensating errors in the field books or original records of admeasurement.' (59)

Apportionment appeal meetings could be stormy affairs, as it was there that landowners were able to appreciate for the first time only when the draft apportionment was complete what their precise burden would be. Remarkably frequently the implications for individual holdings of a higher global rent charge assessment were just not appreciated. Sometimes the complaint was that one group of landowners was more heavily burdened than another. Joseph Bennett came under severe attack for his work on the Tatenhill apportionment in 1839. The landowners complained that their assessments were higher than those in neighbouring Callingwood. (60) The meeting was adjourned, and when it reconvened apportioner and landowners each had expert witnesses to buttress their own case. The landowners complained not that all were now paying more, but that the calculations had been made on a less advantageous principle than that on which the uncontested tithe compositions had been traditionally paid before 1836. Arguing that the district was almost exclusively dairy land, Bennett had rated meadow and pasture tithe rather higher than usual in relation to the arable. As a result, many small owners of grassland near Tatenhill were bearing a larger proportion of the tithe than previously. The previous compositions had fixed only a moderate charge on the smaller owners. There thus developed in Tatenhill one of the rare instances of open conflict between the interests of larger and smaller proprietors. Assistant commissioner Thomas Woolley's attitude was equivocal. He sympathized with the small owners and felt that it would have been more diplomatic to have burdened the larger proprietors rather more heavily. To set aside the apportionment, however, he needed concrete evidence that the valuer had acted unfairly or incompetently, and this he could not find. He confirmed the apportionment while explaining to the small owners that they could appeal to the commissioners against his decision, and promising them every assistance if they decided to do so. The small men, however, seem to have calculated that the risk of greatly increased legal costs in further appeals outweighed the possible benefit which might accrue from them. The apportionment was confirmed with only one trivial amendment made. (61)

The Tatenhill case illustrates a real problem which often worked to the disadvantage of the smaller proprietors. The tithe apportionment was an inflexible instrument. Unless the apportioner had been specifically instructed not to apportion tithe on certain lands, he had to lay the burden proportionately, giving consideration to the method of farming and any tithing customs confirmed by the award. There was no possibility of the flexible and moderate compositions which had obtained in Tatenhill before 1836. While it is not suggested that the larger owners deliberately set out to increase the burden on their less prosperous brethren, the rules of procedure for commutation must have had this effect in certain instances. This was the more unfortunate in that it was not foreseen. For the most part commutation offered an incomparably better-assessed, more certainly known and altogether more efficient system to the country. The very inefficiency and uncertainty of the old system, however, permitted arrangements to be made which benefited the smaller proprietor, either by positive discrimination in assessing compositions or by settling sums so small that it was not worthwhile for the tithe owner first to discover what was due and then go to the trouble of collecting it. After commutation these small sums formed part of a precisely calculated rent charge, fluctuating only in accordance with known and easily verifiable data. There was much less likelihood that small sums would remain uncollected.

Many apportionment appeals, contentious and passionate affairs as they could be, indicated that the tithe payers did not understand the Tithe Act. George Cooke found the inhabitants of Lichfield, St Michael, 'generally discontented with the rent charge and protesting that it was exorbitant'. (62) It was not possible, however, to question the total rent charge at an apportionment appeal meeting. The landowners had accepted a large increase when the award was made in 1846 and no general objection was then raised. Cooke stated, 'Of course, I had no power to enter into the question. Nothing was stated which led me to suppose that any error had occurred in the computations upon which the rent charge was founded although the rent charge is undoubtedly a high equivalent of the tithes.' There was a similar misapprehension at Longnor where the proprietors were unable to effect a reduction in the total rent charge. (63) At Norton-in-the-Moors the rent charge of £550 represented an increase of over £60 on the seven-year averages. The apportioner had been instructed to charge all of the increase on the arable lands in the parish. As the arable was less than a third of the total acreage it represented a steep increase. The proprietors of arable land led the appeal against their assessments. The assistant commissioner reported that, although many objections had been raised, none had mentioned the injustice of the instructions given to the apportioner. 'Had it been so, I should certainly have felt it my duty to have directed the apportionment to be made upon another principle.' (64)

Almost the only appeals which stood any prospect of success were those which suggested inequality between the rates charged on lands of similar quality and use, and those alleging errors in drawing the boundaries or in land use. Benjamin Burnett of Cannock appealed in 1842 against an assessment of £2 1s 0d on land which the apportioner had valued as arable but which had not been ploughed for more than 30 years. When he was able to produce evidence substantiating his argument, the assistant commissioner directed a reduction of almost 25 per cent. At the same meeting another proprietor was able to prove that his land was covered by a valid modus which the apportioner had ignored. His assessment was reduced from 17s 9d to 3d. (65) Proprietors would have little prospect of sustaining invalid claims of this nature. By this stage, the assistant commissioner had no power to alter the total rent charge, and the other proprietors had to bear a higher charge on their own lands if appeals were upheld. They were of course unwilling to subsidize a neighbour who launched an unwarranted appeal.

Boundary disputes and difficulties were a common source of trouble for apportioners, and appeals not infrequently resulted from their decisions. Charles Howard had to direct many corrections to be made to the Darlaston award after appeals in 1842, and numerous adjustments were made to the Gnosall apportionment in 1839. (66) Inevitably, given the complexity of the task, many incorrect apportionments were confirmed. The commissioners themselves had anticipated as much after they lost their campaign to use commutation as an opportunity for a national cadastral survey. In November 1849, four years after the Beech (Stone) award was confirmed, Samuel Bate wrote to Robert Fenton: (67)

The Award is very inaccurate. I have been over to Mr Ford respecting it & arranged for the £40 payable to the Duke (of Sutherland) to be put upon the greater part of Mr Lewis's farm & the £7 payable to Mr Fitzherbert to be put upon one or two of the fields nearest to Swynnerton....

However, the award is made and confirmed & as the church is not interested I presume the Commrs will not care much abt. the accuracy or consistency of the award.

V

Tithe commutation was not intended to improve the financial position of clergy and impropriators to the same degree as many enclosures had done. Within the deliberately modest compass of the 1836 Act, however, it seems that most were able to improve their position, at least in the short term. In many districts, the rent charge awarded exceeded the sums tithe owners would have received had the seven-year averages been accepted without variation. In 151 Staffordshire tithe districts, it has been possible to compare the rent charges awarded with the officially verified receipts of payments from 1829 to 1835, which were to form the basis of calculation in compulsory awards. The results are shown in Table 1.

Thus, while nearly 40 per cent of districts settled a rent charge to within £1 of the averages, 54 per cent show an increase, and only 6 per cent a decrease. Most of the decreases, moreover, were of trivial amounts. Six of the nine show decreases of less than 4 per cent. The reasons for these rare decreases are usually plain. At Aldridge the rector believed that his parishioners were disadvantaged by the averages in that tithes were taken at a high valuation for six of the seven years,

154 Chapter 7

TABLE 1

Rent charges compared with averages	No.	%
At the level	60	39.74
1-10% above	50	33.11
10-20% above	17	11.26
More than 20% above	15	9.93
1-10% below	9	5.96
More than 10% below	0	0

a 10 per cent deduction having been made in 1835 which perhaps more accurately reflected values over the entire period. The rector was happy to accept £1,300 rather than the £1,366 suggested by the averages. (68) At Bromley-in-Eccleshall a small deduction was accepted by the dean and chapter of Lichfield as the averages had been bolstered by 'an excessive and unfair cropping of one of the Farms for some years'. (69) At Wolverhampton, assistant commissioner Rawlinson reduced the rent charge by £58 on the grounds that the averages had included many arrears computed as if paid. He argued that 'the highness of the compositions has been the cause of the loss which has accrued from these arrears' and that 'these arrears are a loss necessarily attendant upon the system of tithing that has been pursued.' (70)

It is perhaps more important to understand why rent charge so frequently reflected an increase on the averages. It will be remembered that the commissioners had been given the power to raise or lower the averages by not more than one-fifth, if they were convinced that the averages did not 'fairly represent the sum which ought to be taken for calculating a permanent commutation of the Great or Small Tithes (1836 Commutation Act, c.38). These powers were extensively used and in almost 10 per cent of cases, the averages were raised by more than the fifth allowable. This fact seemed to pass with little comment. One of the few references was made by Thomas Salt, a banker and lawyer from Shrewsbury, who alleged in evidence to the Select Committee on Enclosure in 1844 that the commissioners had abandoned the averages as a basis for computing rent charge: (71)

> (They) gave private instructions to their Assistants to allow valuations to include a prima facie case in favour of the party producing them, leaving it to the opposite party to show that the valuation is erroneous or that there has been a change in cultivation since the seven years of average.

The result of this, he suggested, was that the commissioners were flouting the law and permitting larger increases than those sanctioned by the 1836 legislation.

Certainly, the tithe commissioners were flouting the spirit of the law, but it is doubtful whether they were breaking its letter. Clause 37 instructed the commissioners to ascertain 'the clear Average Value ... of the Tithes ... according to the Average of Seven Years'. This was not quite the same as taking average receipts as the basis of calculations, for if a tithe owner plausibly argued, as many did, that average receipts did not represent true value, then the assistant commissioner could presumably award a larger increase. The question fell awkwardly into that twilight land between the principles enunciated by the legislature and the practical effect given to them by the executive. In the sphere of administrative reform of the 1840s, it was by no means unique.

Restrictions on raising or lowering rent charge according to the averages, of course, applied to compulsory commutation only. Voluntary agreements could be made for any sum, subject only to confirmation by the commissioners. It was assumed that both sides would be sufficiently aware of their interests not to allow outrageous demands by the other party. In the Staffordshire examples of large increases referred to above, 8 of the 15 were for compulsory awards and 7 resulted from voluntary agreement duly confirmed.

The Staffordshire examples of large increases show that a real distinction was made between the value of the tithe during the years of average, if properly assessed, and the amounts actually received. At Gratwich, the rector's rent charge of £100 3s 0d was over £28 more than the average of his receipts between 1829 and 1835. The discrepancy was explained by the fact that the rector had never considered it worth while to take more than a nominal sum for small tithes. The rent charge included calculations of the full value of the small tithes for the first time in living memory. (72) At Dilhorne, the vicar's rent charge in lieu of small tithes was raised from £40 to £70 with, as assistant commissioner Matthew reported, 'the express concurrence of the Landowners.... The Vicar has always been moderate with the parishioners & has never collected tithe on potatoe crops which he states would amount to £20 per annum.' (73) At Draycott, the rector's rent charge was raised from the average receipt value of £338 to £423 largely because the clover crop was considered tithable for the first time. As a 'new crop', of course, it was not included in the hay moduses which covered most of the parish. (74) The landowners of Biddulph accepted the vicar's claim that his annual valuations had been very low, and included systematic under-assessment of tithe calves. In addition hay tithes had never been collected. As a result, the landowners agreed that the rent charge should be £90 rather than the £48 suggested by the evidence of the averages. (75)

A large increase could also result from having previously-accepted moduses set aside. At Wednesbury the vicar had received £140 from his parish, and had not taken tithe of milk. During the proceedings for compulsory commutation, the validity of the vicar's right to milk tithe was established and his rent charge was raised to £220. (76) At Gayton, various farm moduses were broken by decision of the assistant commissioner. As a result, the general level of rent charge was more than 34 per cent above the seven-year averages. (77)

By various means, therefore, a majority of Staffordshire tithe values were improved by commutation and some were improved very substantially. Given the commissioners' concern to protect the ecclesiastical interest, this is not altogether surprising, but most of the increases seem to have derived from the inclusion at commutation of tithe rights which had previously been uncertain

in incidence, low in value and indifferently collected. The
redefinition of rights which was an integral part of commutation
usually worked to the tithe owners' advantage, and small sums
which had previously been ignored or overlooked were less likely
to be so when written into an official award of rent charge which
had all the force of law behind it when it came to enforcement.
In Staffordshire at least, landowners accepted these developments
with a good enough grace. They largely welcomed open and
clearly-defined tithing obligations as a great improvement on the
old system when a new incumbent or a change in methods of cultivation might provoke a lengthy and expensive tithe dispute.

VI

The cost of commutation to the parties concerned was relatively
modest since the salaries and expenses of the commissioners and
their assistants were met from national taxation. Unlike the
situation at enclosure, however, tithe owners were expected to
pay their share of the expenses. These were in general restricted
to activities before the apportioner began his work. Since
apportionments comprised the heaviest contributory costs of
commutation, the main burden fell on the landowners. At Yoxall,
where a perfectly straightforward voluntary commutation was
effected in 1838, the formal costs amounted to just over £246
for the 3,500 acre parish. Of this, the tithe owner met only
£17 6s 3d - one-half of the £8 8s 0d charged by the valuer to
calculate the respective amounts of arable, meadow and pasture
in the parish, and one-half of the solicitors' bill to the time
of agreement of the total rent charge. The £177 charged by James
Cooke for the apportionment was, of course, paid entirely by the
landowners. At Hamstall Ridware, the same procedure was adopted
and the rector paid only £16 of the total cost of nearly £178
to commute 2,530 acres of tithable land. (78)

Even for the landowners, however, costs were much lower than
at enclosure. There was no private Act to be passed, for the
parties were acting within a precise legal framework. There were
no expenses resulting from physical alterations to the landscape - ring-fencing, road construction and the like. Enclosure
costs could be extremely high, since none were met from exchequer
funds. In contrast to the average cost of £2-£5 per acre or even
more, commutation charges seem derisorily low. The Yoxall award
and apportionment cost no more than 1s 4d an acre. At Hamstall
Ridware, the cost was 2s 4d. Even where commutation presented
problems, charges were modest. At Lichfield St Chad, where
there were great complexities over tithe ownership and where
there had been lengthy disputes, the cost was only 3s 7d per
acre. Even this cost, the assistant commissioner, George Cooke,
found it necessary to justify to his masters: 'These expenses
are heavy but they appear to be justified by the amount of work
done. The Board is aware that the commutation has extended over
many years and has been entangled with many most intricate
questions of law.' (79)

The costs of commutation brought few complaints. Landowners

Chapter 7

and tithe owners alike were receiving a handsome annual subsidy from the taxpayer to put their relations on a more rational footing, and the expertise of practised assistant commissioners contributed to the avoidance of unnecessary expense. In general, the process of commutation was accepted with a minimum of complaint. There might be resentment, even anger, against an incompetent apportioner, or an unpopular summary modus decision by an assistant commissioner, but it remained localized. There was no nationwide opposition to tithe commutation.

There was only one significant regional exception to the national picture. The commissioners themselves noted in 1844 that south Wales did not accept commutation gladly. (80) Tithe had been a source of real grievance in Wales, and experience of commutation there illustrated perhaps the major drawback to the oppration of the Commutation Act. The corn prices from which the commissioners worked in order to ascertain rent charges were national averages as published in the 'London Gazette'. In south Wales, where prices were very low, the effect of a national average was to burden landowners with higher increases than in the rest of the country. Pembrokeshire farmers argued that the assistant commissioners found tithe levels low and frequently used their powers to increase the averages by a full 20 per cent. In some areas net tithe payments went up by between 20 and 50 per cent after commutation. Thus, although as one advocate of the Welsh farmers' case admitted, 'the provisions of the Tithe Act have been carried into execution with very great skill, judgment and accuracy' a considerable source of grievance was created. (81) This resentment merged with other factors particularly acute in Wales - the high proportion of absentee impropriators who took tithes strictly, and the rapid spread of Dissent - to make the tithe question an important factor in the Rebecca Riots of 1842-3. Tithe owners received threatening letters. Mock auctions of tithe agents and collectors were held, and other manifestations of popular resentment, including riotous assembly, were common. (82) 'The Times' attempted to use the trouble in Wales to launch a general attack on the tithe commission as an important agent of that centralized, bureaucratic administrative reform movement which the newspaper so distrusted: (83)

> The Tithe Commutation Act, though it forms only one among thousands of similar instances that might be produced of modern legislation, has involved, among other things, the substitution of a centralized, uniform and negative machinery.... We are convinced that the general practice of converting everything throughout the country into a level and uniform system with a central commission at its head is one which its oppressive and grievous injustice must sooner or later bring into that condemnation which its intrinsic perversity and impolicy so rightly deserve.

Circumstances in Wales were exceptional. Elsewhere the strictures of 'The Times' seem to have fallen on deaf ears. Tithe owners and payers alike had much cause to welcome unreservedly just that 'level and uniform system' which the newspaper condemned.

Tithe had become by the 1830s a monstrous and anachronistic nuisance of which nearly all men wished to be rid. It was hopelessly out of place in an increasingly urbanized and industrializing society. It could be said to discriminate against the primary producer. Its very uncertainty spawned numerous and contentious disputes. It encouraged covetousness, meanness and deceit. The solution to the problem, worked out in over 12,000 districts between 1836 and the early 1850s, was discovered by a mixture of compromise and accident. The old system, replete with contradictions and complexities, was rapidly and iconoclastically dismantled as befitted the new spirit of administrative reform. As a result, in many parishes the landowner knew for certain for the first time what he must pay and the tithe owner what he might expect. Both could henceforward budget accordingly. The state's intervention was constructive both in intent and effect. The bureaucracy of the tithe office was put at the service of local interests. Only rarely did it seem to dictate to them. Hence the muted criticism of the Tithe Act and its administrative apparatus. 'The Times' was expressing very much the minority view. For the rest, the central fact was that the new system worked, and was of use. A primitive system best suited to a barter economy had given way to Victorian viability and respectability.

NOTES

1 The exact cost between 1837 and 1848 was £485,419. PP(HC) 1849, xxx, p.227.
2 H. Lonsdale, 'The Worthies of Cumberland' (1867), pp.264-5. See also the DNB entry on Blamire, ii, pp.654-6.
3 The speech is in 'Hansard', 3rd ser. xxxii (1836), pp.607-15. Peel's response is ibid. pp.619-24.
4 D. Spring, 'The English Landed Estate in the Nineteenth Century' (Baltimore, 1963), pp.137-8, 157 and 165-7.
5 D. and S. Lysons, 'Magna Britannia', 6 vols (1822), vi, pp.553-4.
6 DNB x, p.1045.
7 Tithe Commrs Report, PP(HC) 1842, xxvi, p.775.
8 Bucks. RO D85/33. Richard Jones to Joseph Townsend, 1 July 1837.
9 Staffs. RO D661/8/5/1/2-3. E. Bethune to Gen Dyott, 30 September 1837.
10 Lancs. RO DDH 805. Letter of Bethune, 2 June 1838.
11 For which see N.C. Edsall, 'The Anti-Poor Law Movement, 1834-44' (Manchester, 1971).
12 PP(HC) 1837, xli, pp.384-402 and vi, pp.77-142. See also F.M.L. Thompson, 'Chartered Surveyors: The Growth of a Profession' (1968), pp.104-6.
13 1 Vic. c.69 and 2 & 3 Vic. c.62 clause 22. The later Act extended the power of the commissioners to confirm inaccurate maps which accompanied compulsory awards. Professor Thompson's statement of the case (op. cit. p.105) is, therefore, accurate for the period 1837-9 only.
14 H.C. Prince, The tithe surveys of the mid-nineteenth century, 'Agric. Hist. Rev.', vii (1959), p.23.

15 PP(HC) 1841, xii, pp.141-4.
16 See, among many others, G.H. Whalley, 'The Tithe Act and the Tithe Amendment Act' (1838), G.H. Whalley, 'The Tithe Amendment Act, 2 & 3 Vic. 62, with Notes and Index' (1839), Richard Jones, 'Remarks on the Manner in which Tithe should be Assessed to the Poor's Rate under Existing Law' (1838), Henry Pyne, 'Commutation Tables' (1837), W. Eagle, 'The Acts for the Commutation of Tithes in England and Wales', 3rd ed. (1840).
17 See below, sect. IV for evidence of a lack of comprehension in Staffordshire of the legislation.
18 The Appendix shows the progress of commutation in tabular form.
19 W.L. Mathiesson, 'English Church Reform, 1815-1840' (1923), pp.122-3.
20 See the Appendix.
21 Commissioners' instructions for carrying out compulsory commutation. A copy may be found in Staffs. RO D593/T/10/27.
22 PP(HC) 1849, xxii, pp.549-50, and 1851, xxii, p.549.
23 PRO IR 18/9418.
24 PP(HC) 1839, xvi, pp.335-9.
25 Ibid. 1840, xxviii, pp.139-43.
26 Ibid.
27 Ibid. 1844, xxxi, pp.419-22; 1845, xxvii, pp.499-502; 1846, xxiv, pp.505-8; 1847, xxiii, pp.355-8; 1848, xxvi, p.551.
28 They are filed as PRO IR 18. See E.A. Cox and B.R. Dittmer, The tithe files of the mid-nineteenth century, 'Agric. Hist. Rev.', xiii (1965), pp.1-16 for a survey of the materials from the standpoint of the interests of historical geographers. See also R.J.P. Kain, Tithe surveys and landownership, 'Journal of Historical Geography', i (1975), pp.39-48.
29 J. Caird, 'English Agriculture in 1850-51', 2nd ed. (1968), p.233.
30 PRO IR 18/9545 and 9338; IR 29/32/83.
31 Ibid. IR 18/9455, 9302 and 9333.
32 Ibid. 9528.
33 Ibid. 9379 and 9411.
34 Ibid. 9545.
35 Ibid. 9258.
36 Ibid. 9355.
37 Ibid. 9346.
38 For which see their letter to Thomas Hodgson, 22 June 1840. Staffs. RO D1851/4/7.
39 PRO IR 29/32/88.
40 Ibid. IR 18/9472.
41 Ibid. 9470.
42 Ibid. IR 29/32/177.
43 Ibid. IR 18/9232.
44 Staffs. RO D1721/3/239.
45 PRO IR 18/9511.
46 Ibid. 9487.
47 For which see above, chapter 3, sect. III. The tithe file is no.9249.
48 PP(HC) 1844, v, cl.4282.

49 Ibid. cl.23.
50 PRO IR 18/9520.
51 Ibid. IR 29/32/139 and 18/9303.
52 Ibid. IR 18/9291.
53 Ibid. IR 29/32/57 and 150.
54 Ibid. IR 29/32/94.
55 Rawlinson's report, ibid. IR 18/9357.
56 Ibid. IR 29/32/43.
57 J.B.H. Bennett 'Letters and Observations on the Subject of Tithe Apportionment' (1839), p.5.
58 PRO IR 18/9268 (Bobbington).
59 PP(HC) 1841, xii, pp.141-4.
60 PRO IR 18/9515.
61 One ¼ acre plot was discovered not to be tithable and the rent charge of 3s 9d was transferred to some of the larger proprietors.
62 PRO IR 18/9422.
63 Ibid. 9425.
64 Ibid. 9451.
65 Ibid. 9298.
66 Ibid. 9333 and 9370.
67 Staffs. RO D593/T/10/11.
68 PRO IR 18/9233.
69 Ibid. 9281.
70 Ibid. 9550.
71 S.C. Enclosures, PP(HC) 1844, v, cl.6504.
72 PRO IR 29/32/105 and IR 18/9371. See also the letter of Samuel Giners to Thomas Sudworth, 10 October 1837, explaining the rector's custom. Staffs. RO D240/M/D/VII/3.
73 PRO IR 18/9335.
74 PRO IR 18/9336.
75 Ibid. 9257.
76 Ibid. 9536.
77 Ibid. 9369.
78 Staffs. RO D1851/4/12.
79 PRO IR 18/9303.
80 PP(HC) 1844, xxi, pp.419-22.
81 'The Times', 11 October 1843. See also other letters on the subject of Welsh commutation in the issues of 4-12 October.
82 D. Williams, 'The Rebecca Riots' (Cardiff, 1955), pp.55, 129-36, 234-5 and 239.
83 'The Times', 29 November 1843.

CHAPTER 8

EPILOGUE: FROM COMMUTATION TO EXONERATION, 1850-1936

I

For about half a century it seemed that commutation had finally solved the tithe problem. Commutation progressed smoothly enough. Such amendments as were necessary were quietly and successfully enacted, usually on the initiative of the commissioners. The abnormally low prices of 1834-5 ensured that rent charges would pick up when the averages were revised in accordance with the Tithe Act. Over the 50-year period 1835-85, however, rent charge values remained remarkably stable. Taking the 1835 value as a base of 100, the average for the period was 102.69, with a low point of 89.79 in 1855 and a peak of 112.78 in 1875. (1) There was little cause for complaint here. Of course, the church no longer received its share of the increase of the produce of the land, but this ground had been extensively covered in the commutation debates. The church, relieved to have weathered the disestablishment storm in the 1830s, was not disposed to re-open dangerous wounds by pressing on sensitive lesions. (2) Landowners could not consider themselves heavily burdened. They had gained by poor law reform in 1834 and by tithe commutation in 1836 effective relief from two of the largest taxation encumbrances which beset them. They were supposed to pay rent charge themselves after commutation, but it was well known that tenant farmers still frequently shouldered the burden making an appropriate rental adjustment.

It could be argued that commutation facilitated the adoption of high farming techniques which seemed in the 1850s and 1860s to be the salvation of the landed interest after the corn laws prop had been removed by Peel in 1846. The tithe commissioners lost little opportunity to proclaim the beneficent effects of the measure. Blamire argued that 'a very great stimulus has been applied to the inclosure of Waste Lands by the passing of the Tithe Act, because such lands are now inclosed tithe free'. He stated that much land in Cornwall had been released for cultivation precisely because commutation had been put into effect. (3) Assistant commissioner Thomas Woolley amplified the point. 'The tithes being settled, there is every inducement for the farmers to

improve their lands, especially as the rent-charges are fixed by
price only without reference to the quantity of produce. Whatever increase in the quantity of produce is gained, it will not
affect the payment of tithe.' At Selston (Notts.), a parish
which Woolley as a Nottinghamshire man knew well, productive
enclosure had become possible only after commutation. Previous
overtures had been blocked by the opposition of the tithe owner,
Sir Wolston Dixie. (4)

Undoubtedly, there was much increased investment in agriculture
between c.1840 and 1870. Many millions of pounds were laid out
in extensive drainage schemes, artificial manures and new farm
buildings. The Duke of Bedford had spent only just over £31,000
on permanent improvements to his Bedfordshire estates between
1816 and 1835, but increased this to £194,652 between 1836 and
1855. (5) The Duke of Cleveland laid out £450,000 between 1846
and 1879, while the Duke of Northumberland ploughed back into
improvements over half his income from agricultural rents between
1848 and 1854 - a total of almost £226,000. (6) Such sums
were unprecedented. Many landowners of more modest means were
similarly persuaded that to offset the effects of the repeal
of the corn laws it was necessary to run ever faster and produce
more in order to stand still. The so-called 'Golden Age' of
English farming was underpinned by massive injections of
capital. (7)

Improvement there was, but tithe commutation can fairly claim
only a minor part in fostering it. There were more direct
stimulants, such as the Public Money Drainage Acts of 1846 and
1850, the Private Money Drainage Act of 1849 and the Lands
Improvement Company founded in 1853. There was also the work
of the enclosure commission. (8) There were by the 1840s few
wastes which it was sensible to improve without heavy initial
expenditure on drainage, so the new freedom of previously waste
land from demands for tithe after cultivation was hardly an
adequate incentive of itself, though in conjunction with other
favourable circumstances it played its part. Also, it is now
clear that there was at least as much productive investment in
livestock fattening and mixed farming as in purely arable
enterprises. (9) English landlords by no means worshipped King
Corn to the exclusion of all other idols. Many were well aware
of a shift towards extra profitability in dairying and fattening
long before the last quarter of the century. It is extremely
doubtful if improvement in the non-arable sector had ever been
impeded by tithe. Little livestock tithe had been taken in
kind in the eighteenth century, and the value of tithe from
meadow and pasture was considerably lower than from corn lands.
This point had been recognized in commutation arrangements, by
the establishment of a corn rent rather than an index tied to
a wider range of agricultural products. The commutation awards
and apportionments continue to show corn tithes as the most
heavily assessed. Arable land was usually commuted for a rent
charge varying between 4s and 7s an acre, though on occasion
much higher than this. Only rarely were the most productive
dairy lands rated as highly as 5s an acre, and meadow and pasture
land was frequently commuted at between 1s and 2s 6d. When

the farmers of the south-east complained in the 1890s of the
disproportionately heavy rent charges they had to pay, they were
merely re-emphasizing the highly rated arable south and east
compared with the relatively lightly tithed north and west where
pasture lands predominated. There was certainly no bar to
improvement in livestock production after commutation, but there
had been little enough before it. Customs and moduses abounded
to reduce the value of these tithes and, despite the efforts
of the church, many of these proved unbreakable.

The main advantages of commutation to the improving farmer
werethose of convenience and certainty. It was valuable to
know that tithe rent charge would fluctuate only in accordance
with known variables, and that massive increases could not be won
by new claims backed with the threat of litigation. The practical
farmer could make precise calculations of the effect of rent in
a way which had not been possible before. It is important not
to overlook the psychological effects of commutation, however.
Tithe commutation created a climate of opinion favourable to
reform, though there were other, better publicized, factors
at work in the same direction. Despite the optimism of the tithe
commissioners on the subject, it would be unwise to push the
effect of commutation on improvement further than this.
Agricultural England as viewed by Arthur Young in 1790 and James
Caird in 1850 were very different places. Although Young and
some of his followers overstated their case, it is clear that a
national commutation in, say, 1800 would of itself have stimulated still more improvement on the less naturally fertile arable
lands, particularly where tithe had been paid in kind. After
1836, the situation was more complex, the requirements more
diverse. Far heavier injections of capital were required which
made tithe calculations less crucial to the improvement equation
in Caird's day than in Young's. Also many farmers had burned
their fingers sufficiently in the relative slump after 1813 to
be more cautious about their improvement plans in the 1830s and
1840s. Tithe commutation during the French wars could have been
of decisive importance to land improvement, at least in the short
term while prices and profits remained at a high level. At best
in the 1840s, it was a contributory factor.

II

The collapse of cereal prices in the 1880s dragged tithe back
towards the centre of the political stage. American and Canadian
competition, bolstered by an ever-improving communications
network, undercut the British arable farmer who thus learned the
harsh but long-delayed lessons of corn law repeal. Rent charge,
which was linked to grain prices, suffered equally. By the
later 1880s, it seemed once again that the tithe system satisfied no one. Clergymen and other tithe owners saw their incomes
dragged towards subsistence level in some cases. Thomas Espin,
rector of Wolsingham (Durham), collected data which he presented
to the Church Congress in Birmingham in 1893 showing that 1,586
of the 4,173 benefices worth less than £200 had become thus

impoverished since the recent collapse of arable prices. The dioceses of Bangor and Peterborough had almost twice as many livings below this level in 1891 as in 1879. (10) The rent charge index which had stood (1835=100) at 107.14 in 1881 was down to 87.44 in 1887 and by 1901 had dropped to 66.59. (11) For their part, farmers saw the £4,000,000 rent charge as an impossible additional burden with profits low or non-existent. Though the burden there was less than in south-east England, resistance to rent charge erupted in tithe-sensitive Wales in 1886 with the formation of an Anti-Tithe League at Ruthin. (12) In Wales memories of alleged unfair treatment at commutation had never died away, and when harnessed to a powerful nonconformist interest anxious to embarrass a privileged and alien ecclesiastical establishment, a powerful engine of protest was set in motion. Rent charge payment was refused and the Anti-Tithe League evoked sufficient memories of the Irish tithe war in the 1830s for Parliament to order an enquiry into the disturbances. (13) The 'war' fizzled out long before Welsh tithe was secularized in 1914 and 1919, and converted to educational purposes, (14) but continued discontent led to the passing of a new Tithe Act in 1891. (15) It did not go as far as the Welsh or arable-sector English farmers wanted, but it did finally lay the payment of rent charge firmly on the landowners who, as a class, were likely to be more amenable to the church, and less likely to withhold payment. Also for the first time the device, rejected in the 1830s, of relating rent charge to rental values was introduced. No rent charge which exceeded two-thirds of the land's annual value could be claimed.

These reforms were enough to patch the system up during the worst period of crisis at the turn of the century, but the question could not be considered settled. After fifty years of virtual silence, the anti-tithe complaints would not be stilled by one piece of legislation which hardly met the case. Depression had created the crisis which led to the 1891 Act, yet wartime prosperity for the farming interest stimulated demand for more radical reform in 1918. As profits rose the 1835 parity value was again exceeded, and by 1918 stood at 109.19 with every prospect of its rising still higher. The complaint now, of course, was that the rent charge took a disproportionate part of legitimate farming profits. The government was forced to act to avert further strife. The 1918 Tithe Act (16) altered the principles of commutation in two major ways. First, it held rent charge at 1918 levels for a period of six years. The moving averages had been temporarily deserted to placate the farmers. Thereafter, rent charge was to be ascertained by a moving 15-year average of grain prices. The second alteration was of still greater significance. Encouragement was given to tithe payers to redeem rent charge payments altogether. Before 1918, although some redemption had been possible, it was not widely encouraged. It could be effected only with the consent of the tithe owner and at twenty-five years purchase at the 1835 parity. After 1880, this was an unattractive bargain indeed, and it is hardly surprising that by 1918 only £73,000 of rent charge had been extinguished. (17) After 1918 redemption could come about with the tithe owner's consent and by a terminable annuity over a maximum of fifty years. By redemption, the annual income of the tithe owner, if invested in government stock, should equal the net amount previously secured by rent charge, after appropriate deductions for costs of collection and taxes. Between 1918 and 1925, tithe to the value of £382,000 was redeemed. For those farmers who had been unable to secure redemption, however, the problem was no nearer solution.

The entire problem in the 1920s was greatly complicated by what has been called 'a startling social revolution in the countryside'. (18) Many of the old estates which had dominated English society in the eighteenth and nineteenth centuries were broken up by families hard hit by increasing taxation and death duties. The Bedfords, Baths, Marlboroughs and Beauforts hardly moved into oblivion, nor did they sell up entirely but they did seek securer investments in the City than the land could now offer. In the short but hectic agricultural boom of 1918-21 they found ready purchasers among their own tenantry. The 6-8,000,000 acres which changed hands in what Professor Thompson has called the most 'enormous and rapid transfer of land' since the Civil War strengthened the yeoman-farming interest. (19) In 1914, only 11 per cent of agricultural land in England and Wales was owner-occupied. By 1927, the proportion had risen dramatically to 36 per cent.

This alteration had serious implications for the tithe question. These new smaller proprietors were much less well equipped to weather the storms of agricultural fortunes than their predecessors had been, and they had bought, usually heavily-mortgaged, at the height of the land market. Naturally, they were seriously alarmed at the fall in both prices and rents after 1921. Rent charge was regarded throughout southern England as a hefty encumbrance. The formation of Tithe-Payers' Associations from the early 1920s persuaded the government that any attempt to impose the new 15-year averages inflated as they would be by wartime prices would be met with stiff, and probably violent, reaction. Putting the 1918 legislation on averages into effect would have saddled landowners with a rent charge index which had risen from 109.19 to 131.57 at a time when prices were falling sharply. Baldwin's response to the crisis was a further large step in the direction of tithe redemption. By the Tithe Act of 1925, (20) moving averages were dropped altogether. Rent charge was fixed at 105 for all tithe, but a sinking fund was established to redeem all rent charges owned by the church. To this fund landowners contributed $4\frac{1}{2}$ per cent of par value, so that lay tithes were stabilized at 105 and ecclesiastical tithes at 109.5 with the promise of ultimate extinction by 2012.

Such a settlement would have placated farmers if prices had begun to pick up in the later 1920s. Even so, it is surprising that the church was prepared to accede to a bargain which offered no compensation whatsoever for all fall in the value of money. In the short term, of course, the boot was to be placed firmly on the other foot by the world depression of 1929-31. In the context of depression prices at the beginning of the 1930s, tithe seemed to have been stabilized at a grossly inflated level. The

Tithe-Payers' Associations revived, and an English 'tithe-war' broke out in parts of south and east England which had always been the most heavily burdened areas. (21) The charge fell proportionately most heavily on the smallest proprietors, and to them payments by the 1930s seemed impossibly severe. Many had seen the value of their land drop by a half since they took it into ownership just after the First World War. The tragi-comedy of refusals to pay, summonses, bailiffs and boycotts of distraint sales was acted out in eastern England in the early 1930s just as it had been in Ireland a century and Wales half a century earlier. The situation was ripe for theatrical exploitation, however, and among the genuine distress caused there was some playing to the gallery from the better-off farmers who could ride out the storm, which was faithfully recorded by improved cinematic techniques and preserved for the delectation of future generations. (22) The whole spectacle seemed ludicrously anachronistic, particularly to those MPs, from both rural and urban constituencies, who demanded, and in 1934 obtained, a royal commission to report on the whole issue and settle it.

Ironically, by the time the commission made its findings known the agricultural scene had brightened considerably, particularly in the arable sector. Agriculture hae been massively supported by subsidies since 1931. The Agricultural Marketing Acts of 1931 and 1933 and the Wheat Act of 1932 introduced the important concepts of standard guaranteed prices and deficiency payments. In the space of three years British agriculture became heavily protected and the small owner-occupier, since the early 1920s bereft of the usually beneficent support of the large landowner, found a new and more powerful champion. This protection in no way diminished the sense of grievance against rent charge. Indeed, state-supported agriculture might be expected to press still more strongly for the permanent settlement of the tithe question on favourable terms.

So it proved. The last Tithe Act was passed in 1936 (23) when the worst days of depression for the farmer were over. Yet its terms reflect the philosophy of deep depression which worked to the disadvantage of tithe owners. Tithe rent charge payments were extinguished immediately. In their place tithe owners were to receive the gilt-edged security of 3 per cent government stock redeemable at par after 60 years. Landowners were to pay an annuity over these 60 years, so that their payments in lieu of tithe would cease in 1996. There were opportunities for speedier redemption by payment of a single lump sum at the request of the landowner. Such redemptions were compulsory if the annuity amount was £1 or under. This compulsory clause was made applicable to annuities of £3 or under in 1958, and from 1962 compulsory redemption of rent charge annuities was extended to most sales of land. As agricultural fortunes picked up, more landowners chose to redeem. By 1943, 160,000 landowners had taken advantage of the voluntary clauses. (24) This process has continued apace since the Second World War. Whereas the annual calculation of annuities was running at about £2.7m during the War, the sum had declined to £1.5m in 1972/3. The original issue of 3 per cent Redemption Stock (1986/96) amounted to £70m, the balance outstanding in 1973 being £40.6m. (25)

The royal commission of 1934 had recommended a maximum redemption period of forty years. The government, however, argued that this would prove too great a burden for the agricultural interest and extended it to sixty. The low level of annuities was also deliberately set to placate the farmers. Annuities were payable at 91.56 for every £100 of rent charge to be extinguished. Many farmers, remembering their plight before heavy protection had been introduced, argued that even this level gave too much to the church, and pressed for a redemption annuity rate somewhere in the low 80s. The government were not to be pushed this far, however, despite demonstrations in Hyde Park and other vociferous expressions of feeling.

Looked at from a distance of forty inflationary years, the 1936 Tithe Act seems crippling to the tithe owning interest. Tithe was extinguished at a very low rate reflecting recent disastrous years for farmers. Lord Hugh Cecil was stating the case mildly when he pointed out that 'It is hasty to assume that agricultural prices are always going to be as low as they are now.... As time goes on more normal influences are likely to drive agricultural values up rather than down.' (26) Under considerable pressure, the church in the end virtually gave away tithe rights she had struggled so tenaciously to maintain in the late eighteenth and early nineteenth centuries. The government's promise to lay aside £2,000,000 to compensate clergy whose incomes fell below £500 a year as a result of this legislation barely coated the pill. It has been estimated that 6,900 benefices lost £475,000 between them on the pre-1936 payments which represented a loss of some 18 per cent overall. (27) The Act soon caused the ecclesiastical commissioners to dip into capital to pay stipends. It was a settlement which would have been deeply satisfying to William Cobbett or Joseph Hume. In the light of subsequent events it may be suggested that whatever the farming interest had lost to grasping clerics or greedy impropriators over the previous two centuries it won back by the terms of the 1936 settlement and the subsequent inflation which ate away at its value.

The terms of the settlement apart, a student of earlier tithe struggles may be forgiven a feeling of 'déjà vu' when reading the debates on the 1936 Bill. The protagonists readily assume the old stereotypes. Herwald Ramsbotham, parliamentary secretary to the Minister of Agriculture, talked of 'the tithe owner being separated for all time from the tithe payer to the lasting benefit of both.... Thus will greater peace be brought to the countryside and greater harmony be restored between the Church and rural society.' (28) The words, save for a slight stylistic anachronism, might have been Lord John Russell's. Once again the opponents of the measure were led by the MP for Oxford University, which as a leading impropriator had much to lose from the proposed legislation. Lord Hugh Cecil donned the mantle of Sir Robert Inglis over a century before to defend the sanctity of property against legislative spoliation: 'By what conceivable title of equity has Parliament the right to invade the Life interest of anybody, whatever their income? It is their property just as the private investments of a person are, and to take it away is an act of confiscation which has both the dishonesty and the cruelty of an act of theft. (29)

It was fitting that the arguments deployed in the last great tithe debate should be so familiar. Tithe of its nature was at the very least an irritating burden, difficult to reconcile to a cash economy and impossible to defend rationally in an industrial society when it was due from only one sector. Though it ceased to be a tax on yield after 1836, it continued to be seen as the most vexatious of local rates, and liable to come under heavy fire in bad times for the farming interest. Tithe owners would always defend the payment as a legitimate species of property, and farmers attack it as an illogical and vexatious charge seemingly designed to set rural society at odds with itself, while the towns escaped scot free. The rationalizations of 1836 had given the payment a new lease of life by imposing some central direction and order to it, but they had not succeeded in reconciling the farming interest to tithe. Finally, the reformed system could not withstand the effects of prolonged depression and effectively militant behaviour by the new smallholding interests. One can only wonder at the tenacity and resourcefulness of those who had kept the ailing patient alive for so long.

NOTES

1 G.F.A. Best, 'Temporal Pillars' (Cambridge, 1964), p.470.
2 Nevertheless, the value thus lost to the Church was considerable. James Caird calculated in 1878 that tithe owners had lost £2m as rents increased, from its abdication of the right to a share in the increase of the soil, 'The Landed Interest and the Supply of Food', 5th ed. (1967), p.133. See also George C. Broderick, 'English Land and English Landlords' (1881), pp.244-5.
3 PP(HC) 1844, v, cl.253.
4 Ibid. cl.4093.
5 D. Spring, 'The English Landed Estate in the Nineteenth Century' (Baltimore, 1963), p.48.
6 F.M.L. Thompson, 'English Landed Society in the Nineteenth Century' (1963), pp.247-9.
7 For assessments of the Golden Age in addition to the works by Spring and Thompson cited above, see C.S. Orwin and E.H. Whetham, 'History of British Agriculture, 1846-1914' (1964), J.D. Chambers and G.E. Mingay, 'The Agricultural Revolution, 1750-1880' (1966), pp.170-86, and E.L. Jones, 'The Development of English Agriculture 1815-1873' (1968). These all modify in many important respects the classic but one-dimensional account of Lord Ernle, 'English Farming Past and Present', 6th ed. (1961), pp.349-76.
8 Spring, op. cit. pp.135-77.
9 E.L. Jones, The changing basis of English agricultural prosperity, 1853-73, 'Agric. Hist. Rev.', x (1962), pp.102-19.
10 Best, op. cit. p.472.
11 'The Times', 6 January 1887, and J.A. Venn, 'Foundations of Agricultural Economics', 2nd ed. (1933), p.173.

Chapter 8

12 J.P.D. Dunbabin, 'Rural Discontent in Nineteenth Century Britain' (1974), pp.211 and 282-96 examines the Welsh tithe war in detail. See also K.O. Morgan, 'Wales in British Politics, 1868-1922' (Cardiff, 1970), pp.84-90.
13 PP(HC) 1887, xxxviii.
14 Venn, op. cit. p.176.
15 54 & 55 Vic. c.8.
16 8 & 9 Geo. V c.54.
17 Venn, op. cit. p.176.
18 Thompson, op. cit. p.333.
19 Ibid. p.332.
20 15 & 16 Geo. V c.87.
21 It has been vividly recorded by a Suffolk novelist who was a partisan in the struggle. Doreen Wallace, 'The Tithe War' (1934).
22 Much of this footage was revealed to 1970s audiences in the BBC2 series 'Yesterday's Witness'. A programme on the tithe war was shown on 25 May 1972 and 11 August 1973.
23 26 Geo. V and I Edw. VIII c.43.
24 PP(HC) 1942-3, Report of the Tithe Redemption Commission, p.6.
25 Information supplied by the Tithe Redemption Office, Worthing, Sussex. I am most grateful for the Office's generous response to my enquiries.
26 'Hansard', 5th ser. cccxii (1935-6), p.434.
27 Best, op. cit. p.479.
28 'Hansard', 5th ser. cccxii (1935-6), p.520.
29 Ibid. p.435-6.

APPENDIX

The Progress of Tithe Commutation

	Voluntary agreements confirmed	Compulsory awards confirmed	Apportionments made
1836-8	2362	6	224
1839	1990	172	933
1840	1156	382	1475
1841	668	470	1715
1842	407	583	1347
1843	281	559	1186
1844	121	646	1034
1845	88	555	741
1846	45	502	602
1847	4	454	598
1848	14	380	525
1849	9	230	408
1850	2	218	353
1851	-	106	254
	7147	5263	11395

Source: Yearly reports of the Tithe Commissioners to Parliament, 1839-52. PP(HC).

In addition, by 1851, 619 altered apportionments correcting errors in the originals had been confirmed and a further 190 awaited confirmation. 13,160 separate mergers of land with tithe had been enrolled.

BIBLIOGRAPHY

PRIMARY SOURCES

I Manuscript sources

General note: Most of the sources, unless specifically stated to the contrary, are aristocratic or gentry estate papers. They contain material relevant both to tithe collection and payment in the form of account books and valuations, leases, demands for payment, and correspondence about collection procedures. They also contain a great deal of material relating to disputes which is usefully supplemented by the solicitors' papers which concentrate on ligitation, enclosure and tithe commutation procedures. Parish records usually include rectorial or vicarial estate books, but also contain material on enclosure and commutation.

1 Public Record Off

Chancery bills and depositions (C 11-13)
Chatham papers (30/8/310)
Depositions taken before barons of the exchequer of commission (E 133)
Exchequer bills, depositions and answers (E 112)
Exchequer decrees and orders (E 126/7)
Home Office Papers: Letters to the Duke of Portland (HO 42)
Judicial Fiats (C 234)
Tithe Files (IR 18)
Tithe Maps and Apportionments (IR 29 and 30)

2 British Museum

Auckland Papers (Add MSS 34,440)
Hardwicke Papers (Add MSS 36,138)
Leigh and Ashenhurst Papers (Add MSS 36,663)
Peel Papers (Add MSS 40,408)
Miscellaneous Papers (Add MSS 33,052)

172 Bibliography

3 County Record Offices

   (a) Bedfordshire, Bedford
Hawkins & Co. Solicitors' Papers (HA)
Garrard & Allen, Solicitors' Papers (GA)
Lucas Papers (De Grey deposit) (L)
   (b) Buckinghamshire, Aylesbury
Cavendish estate Papers (D/CH)
Chester MSS (D/C)
Lee of Hartwell Papers (D/LE)
Townsend family deposit (D/85)
   (c) Cheshire, Chester
Cheshire Society of Friends records (EFC)
Chester, Holy Trinity Parish records (P1)
Church Coppenhall Parish records (P19)
Finney of Fulshaw Collection (DFF)
   (d) Cumbria, (i) Carlisle
Benson Solicitors' Papers (D/Ben)
         (ii) Kendal
Greenwood Solicitors' Papers, uncatalogued (D/AG)
   (e) Durham, Durham
Eldon MSS (D/El)
   (f) Essex, Chelmsford
Oxley-Parker collection (D/DOP)
Sanders & Son Muniments (D/DSs)
   (g) Herefordshire and Worcestershire, Hereford
Guy's Hospital Estate Collection (C99)
Herefordshire Society of Friends records (A85)
Redcliffe Cooke MSS (RC)
   (h) Lancashire, Preston
Churchtown, Garstang Parish records (PR2448)
Dawson-Greene Collection (DDGr)
Halsall Parish records (PR284 and 282O)
Holker Muniments (DDCa)
Houghton, Maj. A.T.R., of Preston miscellaneous documents (DDH)
Hulton of Hulton documents (DDHu)
Molyneux of Sefton Collection (DDM)
Pedder of Finsthwaite Muniments (DDPd)
Queen Mary Grammar School, Clitheroe (DDX22)
Quernmore miscellaneous documents (DX1643-68)
   (i) Northamptonshire, Northampton
Ravensthorpe enclosure papers (D2778)
   (j) Northumberland, Gosforth
Blackett MSS (ZBL)
Bolam MSS (ZBM)
Dees & Thompson MSS (ZDT)
Delaval MSS (2 DE)
Middleton MSS (ZMI)
Ridley MSS (ZRI)
Society of Antiquaries of Newcastle-upon-Tyne MSS (ZAN)
   (k) Somerset, Taunton
Huntspill Parish records (D/P/Hun)

173   Bibliography

   (l)   Staffordshire, Stafford
Aquelate records (D1788)
Bagot Papers (D1721)
Bentley executorship papers (D908)
Bill Papers (D554)
Blagg & Son, Solicitors' Papers (D239)
Dyott Papers (D661)
Elde of Seighford Collection (D798)
Giffard MSS (D590)
Hatherton MSS (D260)
Hinckley Birth Solicitors' Papers (D1851)
Stafford Papers (D240)
Sutherland Collection (D593), especially the estate correspondence of George Lewis and James Loch (D593/K) and the legal papers of the Sutherland Staffordshire solicitor, Robert Fenton (D593/T)
Vernon MSS (D1790)
Yoxall Parish records (D1)
   (m)   West Sussex, Chichester
Kirdford Parish records (Par 116)
   (n)   Warwickshire, Warwick
Messrs Campbell, Brown & Ledbrooke Solicitors' Papers (CR556)
Hatton & Haseley Parish records (DR118)
   (o)   Wiltshire, Trowbridge
Savernake MSS (uncatalogued) (9)

4   Other repositories

   (a)   Birmingham Reference Library
Jewel Baillie MSS - (272 and 278 for Aston tithe disputes)
   (b)   Church Commissioners, Millbank, London SW1
File (NB) on value of livings 1832
   (c)   Friends House, Euston Road, London NW1
Book of Cases (BC)
Book of Sufferings (BS) - for testimony against tithe payment
Minutes of the Meeting for Sufferings (MMS)
Minutes of the Yearly Meeting of Friends (MYM), 2 vols
   (d)   Hull Public Library
A. Wilson Barkworth unfinished MS (L336.21) 'History of Tithes in the East Riding of Yorkshire'
   (e)   Leeds City Archives
Ingilby MSS
Mexborough MSS
Newby Hall MSS
Sutcliffe Estate Papers
   (f)   Lichfield Joint RO
Archdeacon's visitation records (A/V/1)
Diocesan Court Papers (B/C/5)
Diocesan Court Books (B/C/2)
Dean and Chapter Muniments (DC) - uncatalogued, and some remains inaccessible
Glebe Terriers (B/V/6)
Registrar's Letter Books (B/A/19) From 1828. Including much advice on tithing problems in the diocese of Lichfield and

174 Bibliography

Coventry from the relevant diocesan officer to the clergy.
  (g) University of Keele
Sneyd MSS (S.95 and 97 - uncatalogued)
  (h) William Salt Library, Stafford
Baswich vicarial account book (S.MS 429/iii)
Hand Morgan Papers (HM)
Leigh Tithe Book (93-97/31)
Parker-Jervis Papers, Solicitors (49/44)

II Printed sources

1 Parliamentary materials

Debates on tithe and related subjects for the period have been studied in the available reports which, however, become systematic and fully reliable only after 1803.
Cobbett's 'Parliamentary History of England', 1750-1803
'Parliamentary Register' (to 1803)
'Hansard's Parliamentary Debates' 1st series 1803-20
                                   2nd series 1820-30
                                   3rd series 1830-50
                                   5th series 1935-6
'Journals of the House of Commons' (1750-1850)
'Journals of the House of Lords' (1750-1850)
Parliamentary Papers (Commons and Lords) This huge series contains bills, reports, accounts and miscellaneous papers from 1713, but the most useful material relates to the early nineteenth century
Abstract of the amount paid from public taxes for the tithe commission, 1837-48 (HC), 1849, xxx
Account of expenditure by the tithe commissioners in 1841, (HC), 1842, xxvi
Account of augmented livings (HC), 1817, xv
Papers relating to the clergy and non-residence (HC), 1808, ix; 1809, ix
Papers relating to magistrates, showing clerical and non-clerical appointments, (HC), 1831-2, xxxv
Papers relating to Queen Anne's Bounty (HC), 1814-15, xii
Papers relating to tithe causes (HC), 1817, xvi
Report on the jurisdiction of consistory courts (HC), 1831-2, xxiv
Reports from the tithe commissioners, yearly from 1837 to 1852 (HC)
Return of enclosure Acts in which tithes were commuted (HC), 1836, xliv. See also viii pt ii
Return of parishes where tithe commutation was authorized by Act of Parliament (HC), 1831-2, xxx
Revenues of episcopal sees (HC), 1835, xxii
Select Committees on Agricultural Distress. Evidence and reports. 1820, ii; 1821, ix; 1822, v; 1833, v; 1836, viii
Select Committee on leasing clerical tithes, report (HC), 1816, iv
Select Committee on the Poor Laws, evidence, 1834, xxviii

2 Newspapers and periodicals

'Annals of Agriculture', 1784-1808
'Annual Register', 1758-1850
'Aris's Birmingham Gazette', 1815-32
'Black Dwarf', 1817-23
'The British Magazine & Monthly Register of Religious and Ecclesiastical Information', 1832-49
'The Church of England Bulwark and Clergyman's Protector', 1828
'The Church Examiner and Ecclesiastical Record', 1832
'Cobbett's Annual Political Register', 1802-36
'Cobbett's Genuine Two-Penny Trash', 1830-2
'Edinburgh Review', 1802-50
'Farmers Magazine' (Edinburgh), 1800-25
'General Advertiser', 1747
'Gentleman's Magazine', 1750-1850
'Hog's Wash or Politics for the People', 1794-5
'Justice of the Peace', 1837-50
'Lichfield Mercury', 1818
'Leeds Mercury', 1827-30
'The Man', 1833-4
'Monthly Chronicle and British Register', 1796-1826
'The Pamphleteer', 1813-28
'Poor Man's Guardian', 1831-5
'Quarterly Review', 1809-50
'Society established at Bath (Bath and West of England Agricultural Society) Letters and Papers on Agriculture', 1783-1816
'Staffordshire Advertiser', 1817-30
'The Times', 1816-18, 1832-6, 1838-48
'Voice of the People', 1831
'York Courant', 1747

3 Books and pamphlets (note: place of publication is London, unless otherwise stated)

Anon., 'The Claims of the Clergy to Tithes and Other Church Revenues Examined' (1830).
Anon., 'Observations on a General Commutation of Tithes for Land or a Corn Rent' (Goldsmith's Library, University of London, 1782).
Anon., 'The Sacred and Indefeasible Rights of the Clergy ... Vindicated' (1817).
'T.B.', 'A Concise Exposition of the Trades and Arts used in the Collection of Easter Dues' (Manchester, 1800, copy in Lancs. RO).
BAGOT,L., 'Charge to the Clergy of the Diocese of Norwich by the Bishop' (Norwich, 1784), (Copy in WSL).
BATEMAN,T., 'A Treatise on Agistment Tithe', 2nd ed. (1778).
BATEMAN,T., 'Appendix to the Treatise on Agistment Tithe' (1779).
BENNETT,J.B.H., 'Letters and Observations on the Subject of Tithe Apportionment' (1839).
'Bibliotheca Topographica Britannica Antiquities', iv (1790).
BILLINGSLEY,J., 'A General View of the Agriculture of ... Somerset' (1798).

'Black Book, The Extraordinary' (1831).
BLACKSTONE,W., 'Commentaries on the Laws of England', 4 vols Oxford, 1765-9).
BRODRICK,G.C., 'English Land and English Landlords' (1881).
BROWN,T., 'A General View of the Agriculture of ... Derbyshire' (1794).
BURKE,E., 'Reflections on the Revolution in France' (1790).
BURN,R., 'Ecclesiastical Law', 8th ed., 4 vols (1824).
CAIRD,J., 'English Agriculture in 1850-51', 2nd ed. (1968).
COBBETT,W., 'A History of the Protestant Reformation in England and Ireland', 2 vols (1829).
COBBETT,W., 'Rural Rides', 2 vols (Everyman ed., 1912).
COVE,M., 'An Essay on the Revenues of the Church of England', 2nd ed. (1797).
CUNNINGHAM,T., 'A New Treatise on Laws concerning Tithes' (1765).
DAVIS,R., 'A General View of the Agriculture of ... Oxford' (1794).
DYMOND,J., 'The Church and the Clergy ...' (1832).
EAGLE,F.K., and YOUNGE,E., 'A Collection of the Reports of the Cases, the Statutes and Ecclesiastical Laws relating to Tithes', 4 vols (1826).
EAGLE,W., 'The Acts for the Commutation of Tithes in England and Wales', 3rd ed. (1840).
EDEN,F.M., 'The State of the Poor', 3 vols (1966 reprint of 1797 ed.).
FRY,J.S., 'A Concise History of Tithes' (Bristol, 1819).
GOUGH,J., 'A History of the People called Quakers', 4 vols (Dublin, 1789-90).
GRANT,M., 'A Defence of Tithes' (1788).
GWILLIM,H., 'A Collection of Acts and Records ... Respecting Tithes', 4 vols (1801).
HODGSON,C., 'Some Practical Directions and Suggestions concerning the Voluntary Commutation of Tithes' (1836).
HOMER,H., 'An Essay upon the Nature and Method of Ascertaining the Specific Shares of Proprietors upon the Inclosure of Common Fields' (Oxford, 1766).
KAY,G., 'A General View of the Agriculture of North Wales' (Edinburgh, 1794).
LOWE,R., 'A General View of the Agriculture of ... Nottingham' (1794).
MARSHALL,W., 'Rural Economy of the Midland Counties', 2nd ed. (1796).
MARSHALL,W., 'On the Appropriation and Inclosure of Commonable and Intermixed Lands' (1810).
MIDDLETON,J., 'A General View of the Agriculture of ... Middlesex' (1798).
MITFORD,J., 'A Treatise on Pleadings in Suits in the Court of Chancery', 5th ed. (1847).
MITFORD,W., 'Considerations on the Opinion stated by the Lords of the Council on the Corn Laws' (1791).
OASTLER,R., 'Vicarial Tithes, Halifax' (Halifax, 1827).
PALEY,W., 'The Principles of Moral and Political Philosophy', 2nd ed. (1786).
PITT,W., 'A General View of the Agriculture of ... Stafford', 2nd ed. (1813).

177 Bibliography

PLOWDEN,F., 'The Principles and Law of Tithing' (1806).
PYNE,H., 'Commutation Tables' (1837).
RAYNER,J., 'Cases at Large concerning Tithes', 3 vols (1783).
SELDEN,J., 'The Historie of Tithes' (1618).
SHELFORD,L., 'The Act for the Commutation of Tithes in England and Wales' (1836).
SHELFORD,L., 'The Tithe Amendment Acts' (1848).
SMITH,A., 'The Wealth of Nations', 2 vols (Everyman ed., 1910).
SRAFFA,P., ed., 'Works of David Ricardo', 10 vols (1951-5).
THOMPSON,T., 'Tithes Indefensible', 3rd ed. (York, 1796).
TURNER,B.N., 'An Argumentative Appeal to the Right Reverend the Bishops and the Body of the Parochial Clergy' (1788).
WALKER,D., 'A General View of the Agriculture of ... Hertfordshire' (1795).
WATSON,R., 'Anecdotes of the Life of Richard Watson', 2 vols (1817).
WHALLEY,G.H., 'The Tithe Act and the Tithe Amendment Act' (1838).
WHALLEY,G.H., 'The Tithe Amendment Act, 2 & 3 Vic.62, with Notes and Index' (1839).
WILLIAM,J., and MALCOLM,W., 'A General View of the Agriculture of ... Buckinghamshire' (1794).
WOOD,H., 'A Collection of Decrees by the Court of the Exchequer in Tithe Causes ...' 4 vols (1798-9).
YOUNG,A., 'Political Arithmetic' (1774).
YOUNG,A., 'A General View of the Agriculture of ... Oxford', 2nd ed. (1813).
YOUNG,A., 'A General View of the Agriculture of ... Sussex', 2nd ed. (1813).
YOUNGE,E., 'A Collection of the Reports of the Cases, the Statutes and Ecclesiastical Laws relating to Tithes' (1826).
YOUNGE,E., and JERVIS,J., 'Reports of Cases argued and determined in the Court of the Exchequer', 3 vols (1828-30).

SECONDARY SOURCES

Preliminary note: no attempt has been made to list all possible sources. What follows is restricted to the most immediately useful works. Place of publication is London, unless otherwise stated.

1   Books

ABBEY,C.J., and OVERTON,J.H., 'The English Church in the Eighteenth Century', 2 vols (1878).
ARMSTRONG,A., 'The Church of England, the Methodists and Society, 1700-1850' (1973).
ATKINSON,J.C., 'Forty Years in a Moorland Parish', 2nd ed. (1891).
BARRATT,D.M., 'Ecclesiastical Terriers of Warwickshire Parishes', 2 vols, 'Dugdale Society Publications' xxii and xxvii (1955 and 1971).
BEDFORD,W.K.RILAND-, 'Three Hundred Years of a Family Living' (Birmingham, 1889).

BEST,G.F.A., 'Temporal Pillars' (Cambridge, 1964).
BROSE,O., 'Church and Parliament, 1828-1860' (Stanford, Calif., 1959).
CHADWICK,O., 'The Victorian Church', 2 vols (1966 and 1970).
CHAMBERS,J.D. and MINGAY,G.E., 'The Agricultural Revolution, 1750-1880' (1966).
CHRISTIE,O.F., ed., 'The Diary of Revd William Jones, 1777-1821' (1929).
CLARK,G.Kitson, 'Churchmen and the Condition of England, 1832-1885 (1973).
COOMBS,H. and BAX,A.N. eds., 'The Journal of a Somerset Rector' (1930).
CUTTS,E.L., 'Parish Priests and their People' (1898).
DRIVER,C., 'Tory Radical: The Life of Richard Oastler' (New York, 1946).
DUNBABIN,J.P.D., 'Rural Discontent in Nineteenth-Century Britain' (1974).
EASTERBY,W., 'The History of the Law of Tithes in England' (Cambridge, 1888).
ERNLE, Lord, 'English Farming Past and Present', 6th ed. (1961).
GASH,N., 'Sir Robert Peel' (1972).
GEORGE,M.D., 'English Political Caricature', 2 vols (Oxford, 1959).
GEORGE,M.D. ed., 'Catalogue of Political and Personal Satires in the British Museum', v-xi (1935-54).
GONNER,E.C.K., 'Common Land and Inclosure' 2nd ed. (1966).
GRIGG,D.B., 'The Agricultural Revolution in South Lincolnshire' (Cambridge, 1966).
GROVE,H., 'Alienated Tithes' (1896).
HALEVY,E., 'A History of the English People in the Nineteenth Century, 6 vols, 3rd ed. (1961).
HAMMOND,J.L. and B., 'The Village Labourer' (1911).
HART,A.Tindal, 'Country Counting House' (1962).
HART,A.Tindal, 'The Curate's Lot' (1970).
HILL,J.E.C., 'Economic Problems of the Church' (Oxford, 1956).
HOBSBAWM,E.J. and RUDÉ,G.F.E., 'Captain Swing' (1969).
HOSKINS,W.G., 'The Midland Peasant' (1957).
HUNT,N.C., 'Two Early Political Associations' (Oxford, 1961).
JONES,E.L., 'Seasons and Prices' (1964).
LANSDELL,H., 'The Sacred Tenth - Studies in Tithe Giving' (1906).
LONSDALE,H., 'The Worthies of Cumberland' (1867).
McCLATCHEY,D.M., 'Oxfordshire Clergy, 1777-1869' (Oxford, 1960).
MATHIESON,W.L., 'English Church Reform, 1815-1840' (1923).
MILLARD,P.W., 'The Law of Tithe Rentcharge', 2nd ed. (1926).
MINGAY,G.E., 'English Landed Society in the Eighteenth Century' (1963).
MINGAY,G.E., 'Enclosure and the Small Farmer in the Age of the Industrial Revolution' (1968).
PHILLIMORE,R.J., 'The Ecclesiastical Law of the Church of England', 2 vols (1873-6).
PLANT,R., 'A History of Cheadle' (Leek, 1881).
POYNTER,J.R., 'Society and Pauperism' (1969).
REDFERN,F., 'A History of Uttoxeter', 2nd ed. (Hanley, 1886).
RUSSELL,R.C., 'Parliamentary Enclosure and Land Awarded in Lieu of Tithes' (unpublished survey of specimen Lincolnshire enclosures,

Barton-upon-Humber, 1961).
SAVIDGE,A., 'The Foundation and Early Years of Queen Anne's Bounty' (1955).
SOLOWAY,R.M., 'Prelates and People: Ecclesiastical Social Thought in England, 1783-1852' (1969).
SPRING,D., 'The English Landed Estate in the Nineteenth Century' (Baltimore, 1963).
SYKES,N., 'Church and State in England in the Eighteenth Century' (Cambridge, 1934).
SYKES,N., 'From Sheldon to Secker' (Cambridge, 1959).
TATE,W.E., 'The Parish Chest' (Cambridge, 1960).
THOMPSON,F.M.L., 'English Landed Society in the Nineteenth Century' (1963).
THOMPSON,F.M.L., 'Chartered Surveyors: The Growth of a Profession' (1968).
VENN,J.A., 'Foundations of Agricultural Economics' 2nd ed. (Cambridge, 1933).
WALLACE,D., 'The Tithe War' (1934).
WARD,W.R., 'Religion and Society in England, 1790-1850' (1972).
WARNE,A., 'Church and Society in Eighteenth-Century Devon' (Newton Abbot, 1969).
WEBB, S. and B., 'English Local Government', 8 vols (1906-29).
WILLIAMS,D., 'The Rebecca Riots' (Cardiff, 1955).

2 Articles

ADAMS,N., The judicial conflict over tithes, 'English Historical Review', lii (1937), pp.1-22.
BARRATT,D.M., Short guides to historical records: 13 glebe terriers, 'History', li (1966), pp.35-8.
BRAITHWAITE,A., Early tithe prosecutions: Friends as outlaws, 'Journal of the Friends' Historical Society', xlix (1960), pp.146-55.
BRINKWORTH,E.R.C., Archdeacons' court records, 'Transactions of the Royal Historical Society', xxv (1943), pp.93-119.
COX,E.A. and DITTMER,B.R. The tithe files of the mid-nineteenth century, 'Agric. Hist. Rev.', xiii (1965), pp.1-16.
EVANS,E.J., 'Our faithful testimony': the Society of Friends and tithe payments, 1690-1730, 'Journal of the Friends' Historical Society', lii (1969), pp.106-21.
EVANS,E.J., Tithing customs and disputes: the evidence of glebe terriers, 'Agric. Hist. Rev.', xviii (1970), pp.17-35.
EVANS,E.J., A nineteenth century tithe dispute and its significance: the case of Kendal, 'Transactions of the Cumberland and Westmorland Antiquarian and Archaeological Society', lxxiv (1974), pp.159-83.
EVANS,E.J., Some reasons for the growth of English rural anti-clericalism, c.1750-c.1830, 'Past and Present', 66 (1975), pp.84-109.
HUNT,H.G., Agricultural rent in south-east England, 'Agric. Hist. Rev.', vii (1959), pp.98-108.
JAMES,M., The political importance of the tithes controversy in the English Revolution, 1640-60, 'History', xxvi (1941), pp.1-18.

JONES,E.L., The changing basis of English agricultural prosperity, 1853-73, 'Agric. Hist. Rev.', x (1962), pp.102-19.
KAIN,R.J.P., Tithe surveys and landownership, 'Journal of Historical Geography', i (1975), pp.39-48.
LAVROVSKY,V.M., Tithe commutation as a factor in the gradual decrease of landownership by the English peasantry, 'Econ. Hist. Rev.', 1st ser., iv (1933), pp.273-89.
LITTLE,A.G., Personal tithes, 'English History Review', lx (1945), pp.67-88.
MARTIN,J.M., The parliamentary enclosure movement and rural society in Warwickshire, 'Agric. Hist. Rev.', xv (1967), pp.19-39.
O'DONOGHUE,P., Causes of the opposition to tithes, 1830-38, 'Studia Hibernica', v (1965), pp.7-28.
O'DONOGHUE,P., Opposition to tithe payments in 1830-31, 'Studia Hibernica', vi (1966), pp.69-98.
O'DONOGHUE,P., Opposition to tithe payment in 1832-3, 'Studia Hibernica', xii (1972), pp.77-108.
PRINCE,H., The tithe surveys of the mid-nineteenth century, 'Agric. Hist. Rev.', vii (1959), pp.14-26.
STURGESS,R.W., The agricultural revolution on the English Clays, 'Agric. Hist. Rev.', xiv (1966), pp.104-21.
TATE,W.E., The cost of parliamentary enclosure in England, 'Econ. Hist. Rev.', v (1952-3), pp.258-65.
TURNER,M.E., The cost of parliamentary enclosure in Buckinghamshire, 'Agric. Hist. Rev.', xxi (1973), pp.35-46.
WARD,W.R., The tithe question in England in the early nineteenth century, 'Journal of Ecclesiastical History', xvi (1965), pp.67-81.
WHARAM,A., Tithes in country life, 'History Today', xxii (1972), pp.426-33.

3 Dissertations

AUSTIN,M.R., 'The Church of England in Derbyshire, 1772-1832', University of London PhD thesis, 1969.
DUTT,M., 'The Agricultural Labourers' Revolt of 1830 in Kent, Surrey and Sussex', University of London PhD thesis, 1966.
ENDACOTT,G.A., 'The Progress of Enclosures in Dorset', University of Oxford BLitt thesis, 1938.
EVANS,E.J., 'A History of the Tithe System in England, 1690-1850, with special reference to Staffordshire', University of Warwick PhD thesis, 1970.
GASH,N., 'The Rural Unrest in 1830', University of Oxford BLitt thesis, 1934.
HARRISON,W., 'The Board of Agriculture, 1793-1822', University of London MA thesis, 1955.
MARTIN,J.M., 'Warwickshire and the Parliamentary Enclosure Movement', University of Birmingham PhD thesis, 1965.
POPE,R.J., 'The Eighteenth-Century Church in Wirral', University of Wales MA thesis, 1971.

INDEX

Acts of Parliament, see Statutes
Agricultural Depression, 30, 31, 71-2, 88, 116-18, 163-4
Agricultural Improvement, 67-76, 80, 94, 120, 123-4, 161-3
Agricultural Labourers, 70-1, 81-2, 120, 121
Allotments of land (in lieu of tithe), 78-9, 94-101, 105-7, 108, 110, 116
  Situation of, 102-3
Althorp, Lord John Charles, 123
Anglican Church, see Church of England
'Annals of Agriculture', 74-5, 77
Anti-Tithe League, 164
Assizes (for determination of tithe causes), 55, 57-8
Aston (Warwickshire), 25, 35, 50, 52
Auckland, first Baron (William Eden), 80

Bagot, Lewis (Bishop of Bristol, Norwich and St Asaph), 87
Bagot, Richard (Bishop of Oxford and Bath and Wells), 5
Baldwin, Stanley, 165
Barlaston (Staffs.) tithe dispute, 56-8
Barrington, Shute (Bishop of Llandaff, Salisbury and Durham), 79
Bateman, Rev. Thomas, 46
'Bath and West of England Agricultural Society' 68,77,78,79

Bedford, Sir John, MP, 76
Bennett, Joseph, 149-50, 151
Best, G.F.A., 7, 34, 67
Bethune, E. (assistant secretary to the tithe commission), 137, 138,139
'Black Book', 5, 83, 86, 109, 110
'Black Dwarf', 109
Blamire, William, MP and tithe commissioner, 122, 125, 134n.37, 136-7, 139, 161
Blomfield, Charles James (Bishop of Chester and London), 121
Board of Agriculture, 21, 68, 71, 72-3
'British Magazine', 32
Brougham, Henry, 109, 118, 122
Buller, T. Wentworth (tithe commissioner), 136, 137
Burke, Edmund, 75
Burn, Richard, 7, 43, 48

Caird, Sir James, 144, 163, 168n.2
Cambridge University, 6, 118, 119
Campbell, Sir John, 122
Castlereagh, Robert Stewart, first Viscount, 117
Cecil, Lord Hugh, 167
Chambers, J.D., 67-8, 72, 113
Chancery court, 44, 56-7, 147
Cheadle (Staffs.) tithe dispute, 46-7, 50

Church and state, mutually
    supporting, 1-2, 4, 75, 76,
    78, 80, 86-8
Church courts, 1-2, 13n.3, 43-4,
    45, 46, 51-2, 53, 54-5, 58,
    60, 61, 62n.3 and 10
'Church Examiner', 83, 85-6
Church of England, opposition
    to, 4-6, 24-6, 29-30, 77,
    80-6, 109-10, 115-16, 118,
    120-1, 122
'Church of England Bulwark and
    Clergyman's Protector', 54-5
Cobbett, William, 17, 25, 31,
    69, 83, 109, 167
Common land, enclosure of, 94-5
Cooke, George (assistant tithe
    commissioner), 139, 146-7,
    152, 156
Corn rents, 79-80, 95, 98,
    107-10, 116, 118-19, 124-8,
    143-58, 161, 163-7
Cove, Rev. Morgan, 73, 80, 87
Coventry tithe dispute, 60-1
Croker, John Wilson, 128
Cruikshank, George, 109
Cruikshank, Isaac, 83
Curates, perpetual, 2, 4, 6, 7,
    9-10, 14n.43, 56-8, 107, 121
Curates, stipendiary, 4, 9-10,
    14n.43, 121
Curwen, John Christian, MP, 69,
    116-18, 133n.6, 136

Dilapidations, 107, 116
Disestablishment of the Church,
    115, 121
Distraint of goods, 59, 85, 130,
    166
Dodsworth, Jeremiah, 18, 85,
    93n.103

Easter offerings, 51, 52, 130,
    131
Ecclesiastical commission, 123
Ecclesiastical jurisdiction,
    see Church courts
Eden, Frederick Morton, 21-2
'Edinburgh Review', 77, 109
Enclosure, parliamentary, 8, 11,
    21, 78, 79, 94-110, 129,
    131-2, 141, 142, 146, 149,
    154, 161-2

Commissioners, 98-9, 101-4,
    137, 138, 142
    Costs of, 101, 104, 156
Episcopal visitations, 1
Equity courts, see Chancery
    court, Exchequer court
Espin, Rev. Thomas, 163-4
Evangelicals, 116, 132n.4
Exchequer court, 44, 45, 47,
    56, 58
Excommunications, 1, 17,
    58-61
'Extraordinary Black Book',
    see 'Black Book'

'Farmers Magazine', 76
Farnham (Surrey) tithe dispute,
    74-86
Fergusson, Cutlar, MP, 123

'Gentleman's Magazine', 51,
    58
Gibson, Edmund (Bishop of
    London), 2
Glebe land, 6, 8, 11-12, 106,
    108, 131
Glebe terriers, 7, 18, 39n.52,
    49, 51, 146
Gonner, E.C.K., 103
Greene, Thomas, MP, 29, 105,
    118-20

Halifax tithe dispute, 48-9
Handley, Henry, MP, 122
Hardwicke, Philip Yorke, Earl
    of, 7, 18
Hetherington, Henry, 85
Hill, J.E.C., 13n.3, 18
Homer, Rev. Henry, 102
Horsley, Samuel (Bishop of
    Rochester), 3
Hovendon, J.E. (secretary to
    the tithe commission), 137
Howard, Charles, 144, 153
Howley, William (Archbishop of
    Canterbury), 115, 123, 127,
    137
Hume, Joseph, MP, 120-1, 167

Impropriators, lay, 6-7, 9-9, 17, 33-5, 70, 102-3, 106, 122, 127, 132, 145, 148, 153, 167
  As harsh collectors of tithe, 9, 45, 72, 83, 157
Incomes, clerical, disparity in, 3-6, 8, 9-11, 12, 55-8, 83, 109, 121
  Effect of enclosure on, 105-6
  Effect of commutation or, 153-6
Inglis, Sir Robert, MP, 121, 126, 167
Ireland, 84-5, 124-5, 127, 164

Jones, Rev. Richard (tithe commissioner), 136, 137, 138, 148
Juries, 55-6, 117

Kendal tithe dispute, 50, 122, 136
King, Peter, seventh Lord, Baron of Ockham, 121

Lancaster tithe commutation Act, 1824, 118
Livings, value of, 2-4, 5, 6, 105-6, 163-4
Lords, House of, 44

McCulloch, J.R., 77-8
Magistrates, clerical, 10-11, 81, 106, 109
Marshall, William, 21, 40n.63
Matthew, John Mee (assistant tithe commissioner), 147, 155
Mingay, G.E., 67-8, 72, 113
Modus, 9, 18-20, 42, 43, 45, 47, 48, 49, 56, 69, 71, 77, 117-8, 120, 122, 130, 132, 137-8, 139, 140, 146-7, 153, 155, 163
Money compositions, 21, 26-31, 72, 115, 117, 141

National Union of the Working Class, 81
Needwood forest enclosure, 70, 104

Newcastle, Thomas Pelham-Holle, first Duke of, 2
Non-residence of clergy, 4-5, 109-10
Oastler, Richard, 49
Open field, enclosure of, 94-5
Oxford University, 6, 117, 119, 121

Paley, William, archdeacon, 12
Parliamentary reform, 121, 122
Parrott, Jasper, MP, 127
Parsonage houses, 4, 12
Patronage, ecclesiastical, 2-6, 10, 56
Peel, Sir Robert, MP, 109, 118, 119-20, 121, 123, 124-6, 128, 135n.64, 136, 141, 144, 161
Pemberton, Thomas, MP, 126
Petitions on tithe, 75, 120, 133n.7
Phillipson, R.E. (assistant tithe commissioner), 146, 147
Pitt the younger, William, MP, 1, 5, 22, 79-80, 107, 116, 119
Pitt, William (of Tettenhall Staffs., agriculturalist), 74
Plowden, F., 18, 19, 42-3
Pluralism, 3-5, 9-10, 109, 121, 122
'Political Register', 25, 31-2, 69
Poor Law and rates, 30, 31-2, 70-1, 72, 75, 81-2, 88, 120, 125, 127
'Poor Man's Guardian', 85-6
Poverty, clerical, 3-4, 10, 12
Pretyman, George (Bishop Pretyman-Tomline, Bishop of Lincoln and Worcester), 5, 107-8, 116
Prohibition, Writ of, 43, 54
Pym, Charles (assistant tithe commissioner), 139, 142, 148

Quakers, 44, 58-62
Queen Anne's Bounty, 3, 12, 87

Ramsbotham, Herwald, MP, 167
Rawlinson, John Job (assistant tithe commissioner), 139, 148, 154
Rebecca Riots, 157
Rectories, 6, 7, 8, 10, 12, 35-6, 89n.21, 105-8, 109, 145, 153-4
Redemption of tithe rent charge, 131, 164-8
Ricardo, David, 77-8, 137
Rolfe, Robert Monsey, MP, 125
Romilly, Sir Samuel, MP, 118
Russell, Lord John, 87, 91n.76, 124, 125-8, 129, 136, 137, 141, 167
Ryder, Henry (Bishop of Lichfield and Coventry and Gloucester), 115, 121

Scott, Sir John (first Earl of Eldon), 76, 120, 121
Scott, Sir William, MP, 117, 118
Sinclair, Sir James, 68, 69
Smith, Adam, 67, 68-9, 110
Society of Friends, see Quakers
Stafford, Marquis of, see Sutherland, first Duke of
Statutes concerning tithe:
   1391 (15 Ric.II c.6) 6
   1549 (2 & 3 Edw.VI c.13) 17-18, 42, 81
   1696 (7 & 8 Will.III c.6) 44, 52
   1696 (7 & 8 Will.III c.34) 44, 58
   1699 (11 & 12 Will.III c.16) 42, 75
   1757 (31 Geo.II c.12) 42, 75
   1813 (57 Geo.III c.127) 61
   1832 (2 & 3 Will.IV c.100) 122
   1834 (4 & 5 Will.IV c.83) 122
   1835 (5 & 6 Will.IV c.74) 61, 122
   1836 (6 & 7 Will.IV c.71) 125-31, 154
   1837 (1 Vic. c.69) 140
   1838 (1 & 2 Vic. c.64) 131, 142
   1839 (2 & 3 Vic. c.62) 131, 140, 158n.13
   1846 (9 & 10 Vic. c.73) 131
   1891 (54 & 55 Vic. c.8) 164
   1918 (8 & 9 Geo.V c.54) 164
   1925 (15 & 16 Geo.V c.87) 165
   1936 (26 Geo.V & 1 Edw.VIII c.43) 166-8
Stoke-on-Trent tithe disputes, 7, 32, 35
Sumner, John Bird (Bishop of Chester, later Archbishop of Canterbury), 121
Sutherland, first Duke of, 27, 28, 34, 36, 56-7, 153
Swift, Jonathan, 12
Swing Riots, 81-2, 121
Sykes, Norman, 10
Symons, Jelinger, 145

'Tenterden's Act', 122, 143
Test and Corporations Acts, 1, 121
Thompson, Thomas, MP, 76, 98
'Times, The', 115, 117, 126, 157, 158
TITHE
  Agistment, 44, 45-6, 47
  Arrears of payment, 34-5, 57, 130, 154
  Barns, 23, 38-9n.38
  Collection expenses, 23-4, 28, 125, 126, 130, 152, 165
  Commissioners, 28, 36, 79, 112n.32, 119, 124-32, 136-9, 148, 150, 153, 154-5, 161-2
    Assistant commissioners, 137-9, 142, 143-9, 150-1, 152-3, 154, 156-7
  Commutation, 23-4, 86, 87, 94, 110, 118-19, 121-32, 136-58, 161-2
    Appeals, 130, 137-8, 144-5, 147-8, 151-3
    Apportionment, 139, 140, 142-3, 144-5, 149-53, 157
    Awards, 126, 139-40, 144-9
    Compulsorily effected, 128-9, 130, 137, 140-2, 143, 146-9, 155
    Costs of, 129, 136, 140, 156-7

Maps, 139-40, 151
  Proposals for, 29, 78-80, 107, 115, 123-8
  Voluntarily effected, 128-30, 137, 138-9, 140-2, 143, 144-6, 155
Corn, 7, 9, 26-8, 31, 70, 79
Customs, 20-1, 72
Defence associations, 53-4, 56-8, 74
Disputes, 8, 17, 19, 42-62, 81, 120-2, 143, 156, 158
  Costs of, 44, 50-3
  Summary jurisdiction in, 44, 61, 122, 143
Exemptions from liability, 17, 77-8, 131
Feasts, 32-3
Fish, 42, 81, 130
Flax, 62n.2
Garden produce, 19, 46-7, 126, 130, 147
'Great', 6-7, 148
Hay, 7, 45, 56-7, 69, 155
Hemp, 62n.2
Hops, 7, 74-5, 126, 130
Honey, 43
In kind, 16, 21-6, 39n.52 and 53, 47, 59, 60, 67, 68, 70, 71, 72-5, 83, 100, 120, 123, 130, 141, 162, 163
Leases, 31, 34, 45, 48, 71, 74-5, 78, 105, 117, 120, 145
Madder, 62n.2
Mergers of land with, 36, 131, 142
Milk, 18-19, 25, 46, 56-7, 120, 147, 155
'Mixed', 17-18
Payers' Associations (1920s and 1930s), 165
Personal, 17-18, 42, 130, 144-5

Potatoes, 7, 25, 46-7, 53, 120, 155
Predial, 17
Proposals for abolition, 82-6
Purchase of, 35-6
Rent charge, see Corn rents
Riots, 80-2, 157
'Small', 6-8, 44, 56-7, 155
Taxes on, 31-4
Tax on yield, 16, 76, 97-8, 131
Valuations, 26-8, 30-1, 40n.63, 48, 119, 123-4, 140, 156, 162-3
'War', 166
Wheat, 27, 162
Wood, 47-8, 130
Wool, 54, 56
Townsend, Joseph (assistant tithe commissioner), 138

Venn, J.A., 44
Vicarages, 6, 7, 8, 10, 12, 105-6, 155

Wade, John, 5, 6, 109, 110
Wales, 157, 164
Walpole, Sir Robert, 2, 11
Ward, W.R., 95, 111n.10
Waste land, enclosure of, 94-5
Watson, Richard (Bishop of Llandaff), 2, 80
Willis, Rev. James, 68
Woodforde, Rev. James, 33
Wooley, Thomas S. (assistant tithe commissioner), 145, 151, 161-2

Young, Arthur, 40n.63, 67-8, 74, 76, 86, 98, 163

For Product Safety Concerns and Information please contact our EU
representative GPSR@taylorandfrancis.com
Taylor & Francis Verlag GmbH, Kaufingerstraße 24, 80331 München, Germany

www.ingramcontent.com/pod-product-compliance
Lightning Source LLC
Chambersburg PA
CBHW052120300426
44116CB00010B/1737